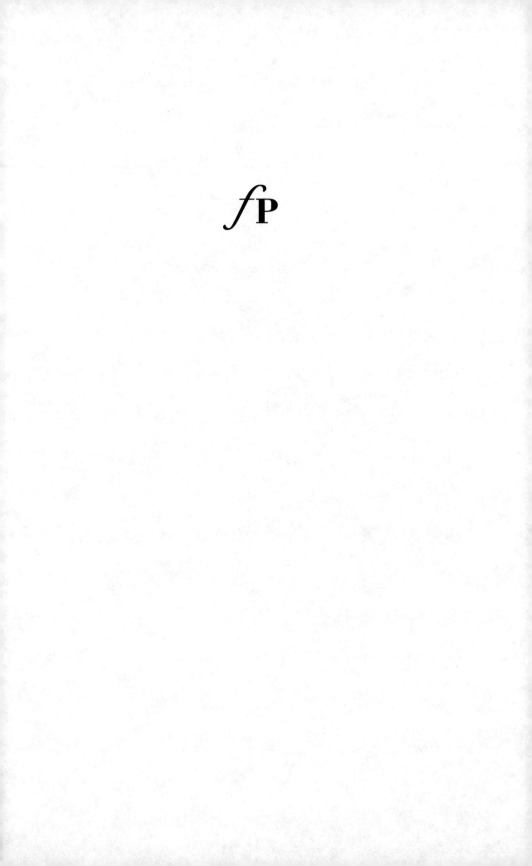

ALSO BY JOHN NATHAN

Japan Unbound

Sony: The Private Life

Mishima: A Biography

TRANSLATIONS

Rouse Up O Young Men of the New Age by Kenzaburō Ōe

Teach Us to Outgrow Our Madness by Kenzaburō Ōe

A Personal Matter by Kenzaburō Ōe

The Sailor Who Fell from Grace with the Sea
by Yukio Mishima

Living
Carelessly
in Tokyo
and Elsewhere

A MEMOIR

JOHN NATHAN

FREE PRESS

New York London Toronto Sydney

$\int$P

FREE PRESS
A Division of Simon & Schuster, Inc.
1230 Avenue of the Americas
New York, NY 10020

This work is a memoir. It reflects the author's present recollec-
tions of his experiences over a period of years. Certain names
and identifying characteristics have been changed.

First Free Press hardcover edition March 2008

FREE PRESS and colophon are trademarks of
Simon & Schuster, Inc.

For information about special discounts for bulk
purchases, please contact Simon & Schuster
Special Sales at 1-800-456-6798 or
business@simonandschuster.com

Book design by Ellen R. Sasahara

Manufactured in the United States of America

10   9   8   7   6   5   4   3   2   1

Library of Congress Cataloging-in-Publication Data

Nathan, John.
   Living carelessly in Tokyo and elsewhere : a memoir / John
Nathan.
       p.   cm.
   1. Nathan, John. 2. Japanologists—United States—Biography.
   3. Americans—Japan—Biography. I. Title.
DS834.9.N36A3 2008
952.04092—dc22
[B]   2007045502

ISBN   978-1-4165-5346-5

For my children,
Zachary, Jeremiah, Emily, and Tobias

Contents

An aged man is but a paltry thing . . .
unless Soul clap its hands and sing

    —W. B. YEATS

PART 1

If Music Be the Food of Love,
Pray (*sic*) On

I am asked "Why Japan?" with a bemusement that conveys an unspoken "of all places!" Perhaps my appearance and manner prompt the question. I am a hulking man with a hairy chest, parboiled hands, and a basso profundo voice in which I have a predilection for sounding my own horn. In short, there is nothing delicate about me—allow me to say, nothing apparent—yet delicacy is thought to be definitive of the Japanese sensibility. The truth is, my cultural wiring disposes me to appreciate Japan even less than people imagine. My roots are in New York's Lower East Side. My father's father, Nathan Stupniker, was a reporter at *The Jewish Daily Forward* and a member of the Socialist coterie led by *Forward* editor Abraham Cahan that convened on Yom Kippur Eve to feed on pork in defiance of Adonai. You'll have to look around to find someone less likely to resonate with Japan's grim earnestness than a disaffected Jew.

I was helped toward my career choice by uncertainty about my ability to vie on home ground. I arrived at Harvard from a frontier high school in the creosote desert surrounding Tucson,

Living Carelessly in Tokyo and Elsewhere

Arid-zone. We—my younger sister, Nancy, and I—had no business being there: our hypochondriac father contracted a chronic cold every New York City winter and decided, though he had never been west of the Hudson, to become a Sunbird. When I arrived at Harvard and walked into my suite in Matthews Hall South for the first time, I found on a round table a Fleet Street umbrella and a bottle of Danish mead. I considered uneasily that someone had left them there to remind me that I would have to do a lot of pretending to appear at home in Harvard's slick halls. I followed the sound of laughter down the hall to an open door and walked in on a group of freshmen dressed in khaki pants and dress shirts with school ties loosely knotted around their necks. Andover boys, it turned out, who had read the Greek classics under the stern eye of Dudley Fitts; collectively they reminded me of the young T. S. Eliot as I imagined him at Harvard, polished and superior, remorseless in the presence of mediocrity. Two had entered Harvard with sophomore standing; another was among the handful of students chosen by Robert Lowell to take his poetry course. These classmates would be my closest friends throughout college, and though I was perhaps the most entertaining raconteur among them, I wasn't about to compete in English or philosophy.

When I was eleven, the first year of our rude transplanting from the Jewish comfort of New York to Tucson, I felt invisible to my schoolmates except as a butt of ridicule for being a know-it-all, and decided a pet monkey was what I needed to distinguish myself. I begged my parents to buy me one, but they declined to indulge me. Japanese was my pet monkey.

Not to say that anything exotic would have sufficed. There were many possibilities: Old Norse, Gaelic, Sanskrit studies. But I was genuinely intrigued by the Japanese language. At lunch in the Freshman Union, a student from Japan drew for me on a napkin a two-character compound and explained that it meant an infection that occurs beneath the nails of the toes or fingers (later I learned that the English word is "whitlow"). I stared at the abstract characters, astonished that they could signify so precisely. That week, I sat in on a class in modern Japanese literature taught by a voluble Italian American named Val Viglielmo. Viglielmo was a virtuoso: he claimed to be the only foreigner to have been psychoanalyzed in Japanese. He was lecturing on Ichiyō Higuchi, a novelist who had written poignantly as a very young woman about life in the pleasure quarter in the late nineteenth century. As he introduced her he chalked on the board the characters for her name and the titles of her work with a swift, showy unerringness that inspired me with admiration and envy.

First-year Japanese language at Harvard in those days was taught by the renowned professor of Japanese history, Edwin Oldfather Reischauer. Born in Japan in 1910 and raised there by his missionary parents, Reischauer, a disciple of Serge Elisseef, the Russian émigré who had brought Japanese studies from France to the United States, was a revered figure in Japan. In Washington at the end of the war as the Japan expert in the Army Intelligence Service, he was prominent among the influential voices persuading the Pentagon to remove the ancient capital of Kyoto from the short list of A-bomb targets. When I encountered him he was in his late forties, a tall, handsome man who somehow looked Japanese, particularly about the eyes, cool and assured, intimidating in his gracious way.

Reischauer taught us grammar from a book that had been designed to train interrogators in the Occupation: we learned how to count battalions and heavy artillery and how to say "sweeping for land mines." Our drill instructor was a mysterious young woman named Rei Sasaguchi who was working on her dissertation in art history. I was in love with her; when she pointed to me to parrot a sentence my tongue tied. One day we

3

were practicing gerundial verbs: "Boarding the _____, I rode to town." When it was my turn I used what I believed to be the English loanword for bus, *busu*. Miss Sasaguchi laughed prettily and said the word I had chosen meant "an ugly hag": "Boarding an ugly hag, I rode to town." My mistake, and my scarlet face, became a standing joke in the class.

My classmates were all graduate students. A number of them had lived in Asia and had Chinese or Japanese wives. They ate lunch with chopsticks from lacquer boxes they brought from home, kept their pens and pencils in brocade bags, and carried their books in silk *furoshiki*. In their presence I, too, was able to feel identified with the society I was studying but had never experienced. I shared little of my life at the Yen-ching with my friends in artsy Adams House, who were reading Kant or Camus or Chaucer. I did take them to see Marlon Brando in *Sayonara* when it opened in Harvard Square; I felt proprietary about the film, and proud, sitting in the dark, to be offering a tour of "my" Japan. The film was a hit among us; for years afterward Brando's drawled assurance to the Takarazuka dancer Hana-ogi at Red Buttons's pied-à-terre in Kyoto became part of our standard repartee: "But, Lloyd-san, what will our children be?" "They'll be half you and half me, darlin'—half yaller and half white!"

By the end of my senior year I had acquired enough Japanese to attempt a translation for my graduation thesis. I chose Ryūnosuke Akutagawa's sardonic self-portrait, *The Life of a Fool*. Translating allowed me to feel that I was a writer; my mentor, Howard Hibbett, who was translating Tanizaki's *The Key*, praised my work and assured me I had a gift.

That spring I decided to go to Japan. I wasn't sure of a goal, but it had something to do with living a literary life. I had considered applying to the Old Vic School in London—I had played King Henry IV and Achilles and Othello in college productions—but Japan tugged at me. JFK had just appointed Professor Reischauer U.S. ambassador to Japan; he encouraged me to go and offered to help me settle in. In May I went to New York to interview for a teaching job at a newly opened English conversation school in Tokyo that had been funded by the Ford Foundation. The school was to be a laboratory for a new approach, Pedagogically Correct, designed specifically for teaching English as a second language to native Japanese speakers; it was called ELEC (the English-Language Exploratory Council), and it paid well, $300 a month for five evenings a week. To prepare for the interview I disguised myself as a clean-cut college boy, shaving my full beard, pruning the thicket of my hair, and buying a preppy sport jacket at J. Press. Afterward, the project director, a man named Douglas Overton, who had been an intelligence operative after the war, walked me to the elevator and confided, taking my arm, "You can assume you've been accepted. I like Ivy Leaguers." With an introduction from Reischauer, I was also hired to teach English literature at Tsuda College, a school for young women with a reputation for incubating ideal wives for diplomats whose careers would take them abroad.

I spent the summer after graduation in New York, working at Nomura Securities on Wall Street to earn the price of a ticket to Japan and breaking up with my Radcliffe fiancée (such an antique word, like antimacassar). We had met in the spring of 1961, during my last semester at Harvard, and I had proposed—it was very much the thing to do in those days—on Graduation Day in early June. When she phoned her parents from my room in Adams House to announce our engagement, her father ordered her to return to her dormitory at once and to wait there until he arrived from Scarsdale. She returned to school a week later hoping to clear up one or two questions. Why, she now found herself wondering, did I never suggest that we cross the river into Boston for a play, or a museum, or an open rehearsal of the symphony? Why was I content to sit on the steps of Adams House A-entry noodling on my alto recorder to the guitar accompaniment provided by my friend Kurt Fiedler, back from the Marines, or worse, to sit *passively*—she emphasized the word—in the darkness of a movie theater?

I tried to redeem myself. We attended a play by Tagore and went to see Sir John Gielgud perform *The Ages of Man*, and when we emerged from a movie we discussed it. For a time things seemed better again. Then the parents delivered a clever ultimatum: they would sanction our marriage only if their daughter agreed to see a psychiatrist first. I was waiting for her when she emerged from her first session; it was 4:30 on a baking summer afternoon on the Upper West Side. Her eyes were puffy from crying; I took her hand—it was lifeless—and we walked in silence. At the corner she stopped and turned to me. "I guess I never had an orgasm."

"Not even in the bathtub?"

She shook her head, her eyes filling with tears.

"You could have fooled me."

"I was fooling myself."

Through the summer we held on to each other, but I knew, and I'm sure she suspected, though I could never bring myself to be honest with her about it, that when I left for Japan in the fall I would leave alone. Early in September, she saw me off the day I drove out of the city in a car I was delivering to San Francisco. The last time I heard from her was about a month after I arrived in Tokyo, when I received a short letter and a lock of her hair.

I had lied—exaggerated—my way into my summer job, claiming to read Japanese fluently. I spent most of my time translating pamphlets touting Nomura's financial services. This I could do; the problem was the cable that arrived each morning from the head office in Tokyo (the end of the day in Japan). It was my responsibility to translate these daily updates of market conditions and to phone the information to banks that Nomura serviced. But the combination of financial terminology and cable-ese written in Japanese phonetic syllabary stymied me. I wouldn't have lasted a week if it hadn't been for Kenji Naitō, who was studying Shakespeare at Brooklyn College and working in the mailroom part time. When the cable landed on my desk I would scan it as though assuredly for the benefit of my colleagues in the room, then amble into the mailroom to ask Kenji to decipher it. He was a wisp of a man, tight-lipped and deliberate but full of mischief. On our way home to the Upper West Side we often stopped for dinner at the Times Square White Castle, whose bite-sized burgers were an ample meal for him. His knowledge of English literature, about which he was never anything but modest, was prodigious; later he became a professor at Meiji University and was a kind and generous friend to me throughout my years in Japan. The last time I saw him, many years ago, he was living in a small house on the outskirts of Tokyo with his wife, a Parisian with whom he had corresponded amorously for years before they married, and their two daughters. I remember feeling that he was resigned rather than content about his life as a college professor and a family man; he told me quietly, with a smile that struck me as forlorn, that he was happiest when he was alone in his study with his books. Perhaps my perception was colored by my arrogance about what lay in store for me.

After a brief visit with my family in Tucson, I drove to San Francisco to take a JAL flight to Tokyo. No one saw me off; I must have been excited, but what I remember is feeling lonely. The plane stopped in Honolulu, where we were served complimentary plates of pineapple, and again in Guam to refuel. When I emerged from customs at Haneda Airport I was startled to encounter a wall of Japanese faces.

Living Carelessly in Tokyo and Elsewhere

I had reserved a room at the YMCA Hostel in Kanda, near the Awajichō subway station and a ten-minute walk to the secondhand booksellers that lined the streets of Jinbōchō. The Y was a dreary place, a cavernous old building with polished concrete floors and a flight of worn concrete steps that led upstairs to sparsely furnished bedrooms. In the dining room on the ground floor you paid for meals with coupons; a breakfast ticket bought miso soup and rice, two gelid fried eggs that had been cooked the night before, and either coffee, green tea, or, my choice, Coca-Cola served in the original glass bottles.

I was timid about going out. Looking for the right limousine bus at the airport, I had assembled questions in Japanese, but the answers had come back at a speed I couldn't comprehend. I chose a bad day to explore: September 15, 1961. As I was walking on the Ginza a typhoon slammed into the city, ripping billboards off buildings and whirling them into the street like helicopter blades. Pedestrians ran for shelter; I lost my way, panicked, and tried asking directions of people running for the subway, but no one stopped. Eventually a businessman with some English helped me find the way back to Awajichō. For two days I stayed indoors, practicing counting in Japanese.

I braved the telephone for the first time to call the International House of Japan to request a meeting with the executive director, Yasaka Takagi, a professor emeritus of the University of Tokyo who is known as the father of American studies in Japan. Then as now, foreigners other than businessmen or diplomats who planned to remain in the country for an extended period were required to have a Japanese sponsor who agreed to serve as a personal guarantor. Formal responsibility in Japan is not undertaken lightly; Professor Takagi had agreed to look after me as a personal favor to Reischauer, his colleague and old friend.

He was waiting for me when I arrived at 10 a.m., sitting erect on a bench just inside the lobby, and he greeted me in faultless English. Takagi was a gentleman from Japan's past, impeccably dressed in English tweed; the glabrous skin stretched across his brow, and the bones of his face and neck put me in mind of an ancient turtle. He walked me around the premises, introducing me as a protégé of Professor Reischauer to the director of cultural programs, the hotel manager at the front desk, the maître d', and, a final stop, the cashier's office, where he informed a man with an abacus and black sleeve guards over his white shirt that I would be dropping in from time to time to cash an American check and convert dollars to yen.

Japan's institutional memory, for better or for worse, is long: Takagi's brief introductions installed me permanently at I-House as someone to be trusted. Long after he was gone, I could write a check on an American bank and it would be cashed for me with no questions asked, a service that wasn't normally provided. Even when I violated house rules, which I did more than once over the years, my conduct was overlooked, as if I had diplomatic immunity.

Takagi said he wanted to show me a special place nearby, and we walked up Toriizaka to the Roppongi thoroughfare and took a ten-minute ride on a trolley car to the end of the line at the moat around the Imperial Palace. The stop was Sakurada-mon (Cherry-fields Gate). He said this was his favorite spot for a walk when he wanted to reflect calmly on his life, and he suggested I should come here when I was feeling agitated. It was particularly beautiful at cherry blossom time. I never returned to Sakuradamon to walk along the moat, but I have often recalled what my sponsor told me about the tranquility that has continued to elude me. I don't know if I realized he was offering me a lesson about how to lead my life.

■　■　■

Living Carelessly in Tokyo and Elsewhere

Tsuda College is in the countryside west of the City of Tokyo, past suburban Ogikubo and Kichijōji and beyond the Koganei flatlands all the way to Kokubunji. My first train ride from Shinjuku seemed endless, and I was nervous about missing my stop because station names in those days were written only in Japanese. The campus was a fifteen-minute bus ride from the station down unpaved country roads. At the entrance to the main building I changed to a pair of green guest slippers and flopped along the shiny main hall to the office. The president, Miss Kasuya, who had studied at Bryn Mawr as a Fulbright exchange student in 1909, congratulated me for finding my way to Tsuda. "And where is Mrs. Nathan?" she then inquired. "There is no Mrs. Nathan," I replied. She blanched. I learned later that I was the first single male to teach at Tsuda since it was founded in 1900.

"I see—well, it is nice to have you here with us. The Shakespeare Club in particular has been anxiously awaiting your arrival." The old woman gestured toward a closed door that now, as if by magic, opened to admit into the room a dozen young women who surrounded me, bowing and giggling in their excitement, cheeks on fire, each clasping an identical red-bound volume that turned out to be the Arden edition of *Twelfth Night*. The annual Shakespeare play, with all the parts performed by the girls in English, had been a tradition at the school for as long as anyone could remember; part of my job that year was to direct the performance. Roles had been assigned before my arrival, and I was introduced to my bashful, enchanting cast. Viola was a gentle, open-hearted girl who wheezed with chronic asthma. Olivia was a fluttery beauty who seemed very taken with herself; I never got to know her well. Sebastian was a solemn senior who would later identify me as a bounder inclined to spend more time coaching the attractive girls. Sir Toby Belch was a junior named Ikeda with fluent English.

10

If Music Be the Food of Love, Pray (sic) On

She was dressed like the others, in a flared navy-blue skirt and white blouse buttoned to the collar, tennis shoes she kept in her locker at school, and sheer white socks which she wore, as did they all, rolled down below her ankle bones on even the rawest days, a fad I imagined had originated in the need to add a touch of sauciness to the drabness of their uniforms. But though she dressed like the others, something about Miss Ikeda was different, more familiar to me. Later I learned that she had spent a year as an exchange student in an American high school in Cleveland. That accounted for the difference: doubtless she had already received a first kiss at least in the back of a car. Malvolio was a short, corpulent young woman named Muragi with ankles as thick as her knees, probably the sweetest and kindest of the girls and, unfortunately, as I felt at the time, the most attached to me.

Mornings twice a week I taught two sections of Reading 1; the texts I had chosen were *Heart of Darkness, The Dead,* and *Sons and Lovers.* When we discussed sexual imagery in D. H. Lawrence, the girls surprised me with their sophistication; they had read widely and seemed to have thought a lot about sex. I wondered if some of them might not be as innocent as they appeared.

Outside my classroom, the Shakespeare Club was waiting to escort me to lunch. The cafeteria was a ramshackle wooden building that once had served as an auditorium and was still in use as a gymnasium. During lunch hour, the girls sat on benches at long wooden tables that were pulled onto the playing floor. The food, for those of us who did not bring our lunch from home, was unappealing and, as I later learned, typical of every college cafeteria. There were two cold plates, A and B, identical portions of cabbage doused in soy sauce, a few chewy pickles, and a slice of pressed ham; the B, deluxe, version included a piece of fish that had been deep-fried earlier in the day. For

11

those who wanted something warm there was a bowl of flat noodles in broth with a raw egg yolk representing the moon. And finally, the "sandwiches" still to be found in every bakery in Japan. "Salad bread" was a hotdog bun stuffed with potato salad and sharpened with Japanese horseradish. "Cutlet bread" was the same bun loaded with chopped cabbage and baited with a thin strip of pork poised on the outer edge of the bread. The trick was to buy several and to consolidate the strips of pork in one roll—one of these and a salad roll became my invariable lunch.

At the Shakespeare Club table, a place was always reserved for me by devoted Malvolio. Apparently she arrived early, staked out a place for herself at an empty table, and then sat there immovably, saving the seat next to hers. As she was a Tokyo girl and not a boarder, she brought a box lunch lovingly assembled at home, always the most elaborate at the table. Throughout the meal she sat attentively at my side, watching me owlishly through her heavy glasses, rarely joining the conversation but always quickest with an explanation when something said in Japanese confused me. Her chief pleasure at lunch, once she had overcome her shyness, was modestly to offer me choice morsels of fish or shrimp or meat from her own bountiful lunch.

The seat to my left or directly across from me was usually reserved for solicitous Viola; next to her, or somewhere near, sat the senior girl elected by the club to serve as temporary director until I arrived to take over. And so on hierarchically down the table, players with smaller parts sitting at correspondingly greater distances away from me. Sometimes the girls brought friends from outside the club, who were required to sit quietly at the far end of the long table, straining to catch the thread of mostly English conversation with the school's new curiosity. At one time or another almost everyone I knew in or out of class sat at our table for lunch. Except the one I most longed to see,

12

who was never there, not at first and certainly not later, when we had begun to meet off campus: the Duke Orsino.

When we finished eating, we went to the new auditorium for our afternoon rehearsal of *Twelfth Night*. The girls had studied the play in class the previous year and knew it literally, word for word. To be sure, I had to spend considerable time reversing *r*s and *l*s and adjusting intonations so the lines might fall comprehensibly on native English ears. But once the players could pronounce the lines, they performed them credibly—those who could act. Those who could not act were awful, but no worse than American students similarly ungifted. Unlikely as it seems, *Twelfth Night* at Tsuda College was no more or less ridiculous than it would have been at an all-girls school in Poughkeepsie, New York.

I devoted myself to this part of my day at the college with close to complete seriousness. I mean I worked hard as a director on those autumn afternoons and flirted only a little. The cast responded by mostly forgetting during those hours that I was the first young American man they had known, and by trying their best to follow my direction. It was good for a while to be away from the giggling and the sidelong glances that followed me wherever else I went on campus: it was gratifying for those few hours to have a project more substantial than romance. In the auditorium, time flew, and 4:30 always arrived as a surprise.

From the first day I was reluctant to leave Tsuda in the failing light for the long bus and train trip back to Tokyo; it felt like being expelled into bleakness from a fragrant garden. I was lonely, but I couldn't bring myself to invite the dormitory girls to accompany me to Shinjuku for coffee or dinner. I was shy in my way and, though they were roughly my own age, I was aware of the boundaries my status as *sensei* required. As luck would have it, only Viola, boyish, hostile Sebastian, and

13

Living Carelessly in Tokyo and Elsewhere

stalwart Malvolio lived in Tokyo and rode the afternoon train. Viola and Sebastian alighted after just a few stops. Malvolio, who lived only three stations away from me, remained at my side for most of the trip, changing trains with me at Shinjuku and again at Shibuya, trotting along at my side as I hurried up and down station stairs, tirelessly explaining the meanings of billboard advertisements and, since I was considered the property of the Shakespeare Club, keeping other girls on the train at a distance. I resented being chained by circumstance to Malvolio. But I couldn't bring myself to tell her that I preferred to ride home alone.

Week by week the 4:30 end of rehearsal lowered me deeper into gloom. Finally I rebelled. I delayed my arrival at the front gate so that the others were ahead of me in line for the bus. They waved to me to join them, but I smiled and indicated that I would see them on the bus. They boarded, Malvolio last. I made as if to board and then hung back; the door closed and the bus drove off down the country lane. I watched it go happily. Now I was free to tarry, possibly to meet someone new; maybe I would even find the courage to wander over toward the dormitories in hopes of running into the Duke Orsino. And then I saw the bus slow down and stop eighty yards down the road, where I knew there was no bus stop. I watched in disbelief as the door opened and Malvolio stepped down and jogged pudgily toward me in the thin light. I understood: she had made the driver let her out, and now she had come to fetch me and there was nothing I could do. I stood there helplessly as she ran up panting and said, squinting up at me with no reproach in her voice, "You didn't get on the bus!" I smiled and was silent; we waited together at the gates to paradise another twenty minutes for the next bus, and this time I boarded obediently and we rode home.

If Music Be the Food of Love, Pray (sic) On

■ ■ ■

A month at the Y and I was ready for an apartment. I found one in Denenchōfu, an upper-middle-class residential district south of Shibuya. The rent was 25,000 yen a month ($70), but I was also required to pay two months' deposit and a third month called "key money" that went into the owner's pocket. Kenji Naitō, returned from New York, had to come up from Kamakura to sign for me; in those post-Occupation days, no one would do business with foreigners without a Japanese guarantor, and I was reluctant to trouble Professor Takagi. My landlords were the Sano sisters, who lived alone behind the rental unit in a large house, spanking new, with a showy blue-tile roof that advertised affluence. I dealt with the younger sister, but it was the elder who intrigued, I should say excited, me. She was a pale woman in her early forties, beyond marriageable age by Japanese standards, but she was no spinster. Though she comported herself around me as demurely as she dressed, there was something hidden about her, a hint of compliant sensuality that lighted fantasies in me. One night, the only time I was ever in their house, the sisters invited me to dinner. There was another guest, a well-dressed man in his sixties perhaps who was introduced to me with no word of explanation except that he was the owner of the Imamura Rose Gardens. He seemed at home in the sisters' house, and though the elder sister treated him with the same muted cordiality she offered me, I sensed intimacy between them and came away wondering if she were not his mistress. A kept woman—it was an exciting idea—living in the house he had built for her and supporting herself on the revenues from the apartments he had built at the front of the property. I never saw him again and was unable to confirm the truth of what I imagined. The Sano sisters remained a mystery, and like so many of the mysteries life in Japan revealed to me, I

15

was aware of something erotic beneath the baffling surface of appearances.

My train stop was Tamagawaen mae (Tama River Amusement Park), a twenty-minute ride on the Toyoko Line south from Shibuya toward Yokohama. The apartment was a short walk past the entrance to the park and down the High Street of shops and eateries. Like the sisters' residence it was brand new. It was a kind of townhouse, three two-story units with adjoining walls and their own front doors. There was one room downstairs, with a linoleum floor, about 12 feet by 15 feet; a "kitchen" with a single gas burner, a wooden tub just large enough to accommodate me to the shoulders if I hugged my knees—the tap was cold water which was heated by a blast furnace installed beneath the tub; and, the feature I was most grateful for, a Western-style toilet with a civilized seat, not easy to find in those days. I furnished the room with a small table and two chairs only and spent little time there. Up a flight of stairs was an eight-mat tatami room (11 feet by 11 feet), where I lived. A large window looked out on a small garden below. I slept on a quilted futon on the new tatami mats, which made it smell as though I were sleeping in a hayloft; the bedding was meant to be neatly rolled each morning and stowed in the cupboard-closet behind a sliding door called a *fusuma*, but I'm sure I left mine on the floor. I bought a record player and a low Japanese table at which I intended to study, and I lugged home from a secondhand bookseller in Jinbōchō a forty-volume set of modern Japanese fiction, three columns to the page in a very small font. I lined these volumes up against the wall—they were bound in yellow covers—and contemplated them with satisfaction and resolve. On the road to becoming the F. R. Leavis of Japanese fiction, I would read these voluminous pages from beginning to end. In fact, I spent little time at my books. I could see my breath in the apartment at night, and the portable gas heater I bought for the upstairs was inadequate to the cold. Besides, I was usually feeling too lonely or, later, too distracted to sit indoors by myself for long.

I lived in the apartment for eight months but never got around to equipping my kitchen; when I was home I ate the same meal every night at a cheap restaurant near the station, a "hamburg-steak" with a fried egg on top served on a sizzling platter and garnished with half a dozen "fry-potatoes." Two days a week I made the long trip to Tsuda to teach in the morning and rehearse my cast in the afternoon. Weekday evenings from 5:30 to 8:30 I was an English language drill instructor at ELEC, which was renting classrooms at Tōyō Eiwa, a parochial school for girls across the street from International House. Saturdays I spent in the darkness of movie theaters watching Japanese movies until my eyes ached to sharpen my hearing of the language. Sunday, family excursion day in Tokyo—the company man still worked a six-day week—was the loneliest day. I wandered the Ginza observing the crowds of shoppers or stayed in the neighborhood to take pictures of families coming in and out of the amusement park on the banks of the Tama River. Often I felt forlorn, like an eavesdropper on life. What I longed for was romance, the feeling of being preferred that I have always required to shore up my wavering self.

As I learned much later, the dean of students at Tsuda, Professor Fumi Takano, had summoned the junior and senior girls to the auditorium the week after I arrived and informed them that no one was to accompany me off the Tsuda campus under any circumstances. I don't think Fumi was a prude, but as the translator of *The Golden Bowl* she had no trouble reading me and wanted to ensure the safety of the girls in her charge.

Not all the girls complied with the dean's order. By the end of October I was receiving return postcards; on the stamped and addressed portion of the card was an invitation neatly inked in English: "Would you like to join for a walk next Sunday?" Beneath were two squares with the words "Yes" and "No" beside them. I checked exuberantly the "Yes" box and mailed back the cards.

How I loved those bashful walks around the pond in Kichijōji Park! The faces are a blur, but I remember the thrill of feeling the sweet, unimaginable innocence of these girls. Often we stopped at the stands at the entrance for a bowl of noodles or thick pancakes filled with seaweed and little shrimp or salted fish or octopus. Occasionally I persuaded my companion to go with me to Shinjuku for coffee at a café, but the girls had to be back on campus by 4 p.m. on Sunday afternoons.

When I received an invitation from the Duke Orsino my heart leaped. Her name was Kiyoko—"pure child"—and I had longed for a chance to be alone with her. She was tall and slender with long black hair and the aquiline face of a classic Japanese beauty. I had observed that she kept apart from her schoolmates and carried herself with haughtiness, but as we walked through the autumn park she confessed to me with passion that colored her cheeks that she lived for literature and dreamed of being a writer whose theme was love. If she was a sentimental romantic she had met her match in me—before we parted she had promised to cook a meal for me at my apartment the following week.

When my phone rang on Sunday morning I picked it up and heard her say only, "*Tsuita wa yo.*" I deciphered the words in my mind: *tsuita,* the informal past tense of the verb *tsuku,* to arrive. *Wa yo,* particles used in feminine speech to convey emphasis, a spoken exclamation point. Translation: "I'm here!" I ran to the station to meet her and led her back to my apartment.

At the table downstairs she wrote out a shopping list in Japanese of items she would need. I had learned the words at school, looking them up and writing them out in my character notebook, and now they assumed a reality connected to my own. I was to shop at the market while she prepared rice in the electric cooker

18

she had brought with her. I grabbed the list and raced back to the shops near the station. I felt for the first time that I was living life in Japan instead of observing it. Spring onions, one bunch; a small carton of mushrooms; rice noodles, two portions; bamboo sprouts, a lotus root, soy sauce, and sugar and, finally, at the butcher shop, 500 grams of beef sliced wafer-thin—I wonder if I have ever again shopped with such excitement.

I ran back to the apartment, placed my shopping bags on the table, and, carried on the wave of my exhilaration, took the Duke in my arms and kissed her. She was startled but not repelled. She returned my kiss, and as it deepened someone knocked at my front door. I opened it and encountered two uniformed policemen who began speaking in Japanese I was too rattled to comprehend. The Duke emerged from the shadows at the back of the room to which she had retreated and explained in her halting English that someone had found the wallet I had left at the market and was waiting for me at the police station. In those days if you found a wallet and turned it in you were entitled by law to 10 percent of whatever money it contained. I was required to go to the station to complete the paperwork, and the Duke interpreted for me. As I had just cashed my ELEC check, the butcher's boy who found the wallet was well rewarded for his honesty. We returned to the apartment in silence; perhaps exposure to the eyes of the law had embarrassed Kiyoko. I watched blissfully as she turned the ingredients I had bought into sukiyaki, but she seemed withdrawn, and I didn't try to lead her back to amorousness.

Twelfth Night played for three nights in early December. The wooden auditorium was packed with students and their friends and families. Kenji brought his doctor brother and his family with him from Zushi, and my friends Ernie Young, Reischauer's political aide, and his wife, Marilyn, came too. The play was well received; there was a lot of clapping. It was amazing to me

19

that the young Japanese audience seemed to have learned the play in English well enough to laugh at appropriate moments.

I had eyes only for the Duke, gorgeous in a tangerine frock coat over a white blouse with a high, ruffled collar. I had been coaching her privately at my apartment and I waited at the back of the auditorium for the lines that had continued to challenge her. She had never mastered the first line in the play; there was no telling whether she would get it right. Opening night she lowered herself regally onto the high-backed wooden chair that was her throne and declaimed: "If music be the food of love, PRAY on."

By that time she was sending me long letters which she signed "Aya of the dark eyes" and visiting me every Sunday. She was a proud beauty and had her moods, peevish or brooding. She was religious and prayed to her private God and whispered to me that I was God's first angel and that our love was pure and everlasting. Our physical intimacy had progressed; we kissed hotly and embraced in a tentative way, but I never pressed her to go further. She had told me that she was engaged to a boy she had met the previous spring at a *miai,* a formal marriage interview that had been arranged by her family and his, and I knew this troubled her. Besides, I wasn't hungry for sex; what I wanted was enchantment.

Japan closes for a week to celebrate the New Year. I spent two days in Zushi with Kenji's family, visiting temples in the hills of Kamakura, and was invited for dinner at Viola's home in Ogikubo. On the way I stopped at the Toyoko Department Store in Shibuya to buy a New Year's gift for the family. The food hall in the basement was dressed like a Christmas tree with the New Year's gift baskets the Japanese call *o-seibō.* The most extravagant assortments combined Japanese delicacies, fine rice crackers, teacakes, slices of Kobe beef marinated in miso, and Western luxury items: cans of Libby's fruit cocktail and bottles of Johnny Walker Black. I chose a whole smoked salmon with the head attached, and when I presented it to Viola's mother she seemed pleased. While she worked in the kitchen Viola and I and her teenage sister and brother and Sir Toby, who had also been invited, played *baba-nuki*, Old Maid. Dinner was broiled fish and steamed vegetables and rice. (With my inherited love of lox I had been hoping for some salmon but later learned it was impolite to serve a visitor his own gift.) Viola's father staggered in after nine, home from an end-of-the-year party with his colleagues at the office. I wondered if this was awkward, but no one seemed uncomfortable: the man of the house in a Japanese family has rights. He greeted me in English—"I'm in the neck of time"—paused to tug at the zipper of his fly, which he had noticed was unzipped, and switched into formal Japanese too slurred for me to fully understand. I heard "Have you ever seen such a home as this?" and replied, thinking a compliment was in order, "No, Sir, this is my first time!" Stunned silence, followed by hilarity. Viola explained when she could catch her breath that her father had offered a modest self-disparagement—"Have you ever seen such a cramped and squalid home as this?"—to which the proscribed response was "On the contrary . . ."

I was invited back the next day for a formal midday New Year's meal. This time the extended family was there: grandparents, aunts and uncles, and cousins. Bowls and nested lacquer trays of traditional New Year's food were arrayed on low tables installed end to end on the tatami mat floor in the main room. As I took my place near the center of the table, accepting an invitation to sit with my legs in front instead of under me, I felt a familiar quiver in my bowels. My father's legacy to me was a spastic colon; in the house of my childhood, bottles of Kaopectate were concealed in every drawer like an alcoholic's gin. Feeling trapped at that formal New Year's table triggered my affliction. I had to ask for the nearest bathroom. Viola's brother

21

pointed at a paper door at the rear of the room, and when I had clambered up from the table and crossed the room to slide it open, I saw that the toilet, though plumbed and porcelain, was nonetheless a squatter. I have memories of squat toilets across Japan, nightmarish in winter particularly, when I was obliged to remove and place out of harm's way in the confines of a cabinet not only my trousers but a bulky overcoat. I say "obliged" because I was never limber enough, even as a young man, to assume with any poise the position Asians—and, I suppose, sharecroppers—master in their infancy. I slid the door closed and confirmed that the chatter at the festive table just feet away was clearly audible. I undressed and straddled the bowl. A metal bracket like a towel rack was screwed to the wall in front of me near the floor. As I hunkered down I grasped the bracket with both hands to steady myself and, losing my balance and sitting heavily back, yanked the fixture from the wall with a splintering crack. The table next door went silent. I sat on the toilet bowl, the bracket in my hands, and watched the plaster spill from the two holes I had opened in the wall. I prayed for transport back to my home in Tucson or, if that was unreasonable, to be flushed down the toilet. Aware that the family was still sitting in silence, I stuck the bracket into the wall, sagging on its bent screws, and returned to the table. I have never felt so embarrassed before or since. The party resumed as if nothing had happened.

Winter break, in mid-March, I traveled west across Honshu for the first time. My first stop was the Duke's home in the commercial city of Nagoya. She met me at the train station, and when we arrived at her house in what appeared to be an expensive residential quarter her parents were waiting to welcome me on their knees in the vestibule and thanked me, bowing deeply, for mentoring their daughter. Under the circumstances, their deference made me uncomfortable. My second night at the house, Kiyoko's husband-to-be joined us for dinner. He was a pleasant fellow in his mid-twenties who worked for his father in the family appliance store that he would inherit. Kiyoko was on her best behavior, attentive to him and appropriately diffident in the presence of her *sensei*. That was fine with me: I had heard her breath quicken in my ear, and as I entertained the table with tales of Tsuda I swam in the pleasure it gave me to suppose it was me she preferred.

After dinner, Kiyoko and her beau left on a date. When she returned she knocked on the door of the guest room where I was staying to ask if I needed anything before I went to bed. I joined her in the empty living room and she poured me some green tea. "He was in a bad mood," she offered abruptly. "What did he say?" "*Anna da to omowanakatta*," she replied with a troubled smile on her beautiful face. All these years later what I remember of this moment is hearing her words, a Japanese construction that was unfamiliar to me, and the process, as a feeling, of deciphering them. If I speak Japanese with fluency that is unusual in foreigners who acquired the language as adults, it is because I encountered and absorbed it bits and pieces, much as a child learns its native language, tied to distinct experiences in my life: "He didn't think (was surprised) that it was as much as that (between us!)." In other words, the man Kiyoko would marry shortly after she graduated had detected intimacy between us that bothered him. I don't think we said much more that evening; Kiyoko was distant with me, perhaps regretful. Not long after I returned to Tokyo she stopped visiting me at my apartment.

The next morning I rode the train further west, through Kyoto and Osaka and Kobe and past Kurashiki all the way to Hiroshima. As the conductor announced the station over the loudspeaker in the nasal twang affected by every Japanese train man, "*Hirooo-shima, Hirooo-shima de gozaimasu,*" I felt my cheeks burn. I looked around to see if other passengers were observing me; I seemed to be the only foreigner on the train. In the city we had melted with a single bomb, I felt ashamed.

My destination was the provincial town of Yanai, two hours southwest of Hiroshima above the Inland Sea. The youngest player in the cast, a first-year student who had been assigned a bit part as the Sea Captain, had invited me home to visit her family. At nineteen, Kazuko Denda was unabashed, an exuberant child who hid nothing she was feeling and reached eagerly for what she wanted. She met me at the station with three of her friends from high school and took me home to her mother's house. Her parents were separated. Her mother ran a milk-delivery business; her father was mayor of Yanai. He picked me up that evening and took me out on the town. We were the focus of attention everywhere we went; when he indicated with a wave of his hand which girls were to sit on either side of me— he designated the prettiest—he introduced me proudly as his daughter's *sensei* from America. The girls kept our glasses filled from his personal store of Scotch whiskey, and inevitably the banter edged into lewdness. The girls had heard that foreigners were huge and covered in hair; I wasn't asked to confirm the rumors about size, but more than once that night I complied with requests to unbutton my shirt to allow inquisitive hands to play with the hair on my chest. I was at first uncomfortable to be carousing with Kazuko's father. But he appeared to be having a grand time showing me off, and as the evening got drunker and he began disporting himself as if I weren't there, I relaxed and indulged in some carrying on of my own.

Mid-morning the next day Kazuko woke me and announced that she and I were taking a bus into the mountains at noon to visit her grandmother. I had no memory of coming back the night before, but I supposed from my headache that my return had been late and drunken and probably noisy. Kazuko didn't say a word; whatever her father had chosen to do with me was not something to be questioned.

The bus wound its way past terraced slopes planted with tea into the mountains that rose steeply to the north of Yanai; the Inland Sea below us was a sparkling turquoise inlaid with clusters of small islands. The trip took hours: the light was failing when we arrived at the village of Hizumi, a bus stop in the middle of rice paddies on a plateau. We walked for half an hour on dirt paths that zigzagged across a checkerboard of flooded paddies to a small house with a thatched roof surrounded by a bamboo grove in the middle of nowhere.

The door was opened by an old woman bent almost double, Kazuko's grandmother, who lived alone in the house where Kazuko's father had been born. She smiled at us but didn't speak; Kazuko explained that she was deaf. A low table in the central room was already laid with a simple meal. As we ate, Grandmother shuffled off to the kitchen and returned with two bowls of *tamago-zake,* a toddy of raw eggs folded into clouded sake brewed from rice dregs. The drink brought an instant flush to Kazuko's cheeks. I wondered if the old woman was a witch who was casting a spell on us. She watched us drink, nodding with pleasure, and when our bowls were empty she disappeared into the back of the house. Grandma had already started a fire beneath the tub, and Kazuko insisted I bathe first. I put my clothes in a basket and lowered myself gingerly into the steaming water. When I stepped out, my clothes had been replaced with a *yukata* that barely reached to my knees and a cotton sash. In the main room, Kazuko had unrolled two sleeping mattresses side by side on the tatami-mat floor and was covering them with quilted bedding. I hadn't thought about sleeping arrangements, but I hadn't expected this; I don't think I knew at the time that

25

sleeping in the same room, *zakone* in Japanese, was a common occurrence, especially when on a trip. Kazuko left the room to take her bath; I lay down on the futon and stared up at the rafters in the ceiling with my head on the uncomfortable sandbag that is the Japanese version of a pillow. Kazuko emerged from the bathroom in a cotton *yukata* of her own, her bare arms and face flushed from the hot water. She lay down on the mattress a foot away from mine and wished me good night; in the morning she would take me on a walk to see the first wildflowers of spring. The only light in the shadowed room came from a single lantern in the corner. A wind had risen and was whistling through the bamboo outside. Her deaf grandmother was sleeping at the back of the house. The sake was buzzing in my brain. I closed my eyes and willed myself to sleep.

2

Mayumi

In June of my first year in Japan, a Tsuda student asked me if I would like to meet a friend of hers from high school, a "beautiful Bohemian girl." The occasion was a party to welcome young foreigners in Japan for the summer. We gathered at the Kōrakuen gardens on a Sunday afternoon, twenty or so young men from England and Australia and a group of Japanese students who had volunteered to join them in fellowship. My memory of the refreshments, barley tea and rice crackers, reinforces my impression that missionaries were involved. The Tsuda girl introduced me to her friend; she was a student at the National University of Fine Arts and Music (Geidai), Japan's premier art school, and her name was Mayumi Oda. I found her beautiful as promised, with deep eyes that seemed to be looking inside me and lustrous black hair down her back. But it was her presence that captivated me: she was charming and intense at the same time; moving around the room greeting the visitors in her limited English, she seemed luminously alive. As we began to tour the garden a summer rain was falling; in my affected way I was carrying a large Japanese umbrella, oiled rice paper with a long bamboo handle, and I invited Mayumi to join me beneath it with a line from a popular song: "Let us share this umbrella, each offering one shoulder to the misting rain." Foreigners were unlikely to know this variety of Japanese, but Mayumi merely rolled her eyes as though making fun of me. We walked side by side for a few minutes and then she moved away to join others in the party and ignored me for the rest of the afternoon. She and her friend rode the train with me back to Shinjuku Station, where we parted. I suggested another meeting would be a pleasure if convenient; she smiled, brushing her hair away from her brow.

We began to meet at a coffee shop in Shinjuku that was popular among students in those days, the Fūgetsudō. As there was no telephone in her house—her father, a Buddhist scholar who was deputy chief librarian of the National Diet Library, was an old-fashioned man—I had to convey my invitations by mail. I have a few of the stilted letters I wrote her that summer in my misshapen foreigner's hand:

> Thank you so very much for the other day of walking and talking as the rainy season approached a finale. Foreigners living in Japan frequently encounter a human wall, and feel that they are "No Longer Human" [always at pains to impress her, I used the title of Osamu Dazai's novel]. The response I evoked from you, *warm, friendly, and interested* [in English] was particularly gratifying to me. Now then, if you have time and inclination, might we meet again? You can reach me every evening between six and eight at Tōyō Eiwa College where I am teaching English conversation. The number there is . . .

Our talk was intense in the manner of young people, especially when one of them is in love with the other. Mayumi was already fervently committed to being an artist, and we agreed that creating beautiful paintings or writing great books was the noblest aspiration in life. I searched my book of Yeats and found "Adam's Curse," which seemed perfect for us, as though I had commissioned the poet, and taught her to read it:

> *I said: "A line will take us hours maybe;*
> *Yet if it does not seem a moment's thought,*
> *Our stitching and unstitching has been naught. . . ."*

Mayumi always seemed pleased to see me, but I was never able to feel that she was love-struck as I longed for her to be. She invited me home for dinner and I spent the evening discussing history with her father. I bought a motorcycle to impress her, a Honda 250 cc, and began dropping in at the house after eight when I finished at ELEC. (Later, her mother would confess that she would hear the chugging engine approach with a sinking heart.) Gradually, I became an accepted fixture in the house, on familiar terms with her younger sister, Hiromi, and her two younger brothers, Masando and Masayuki, and increasingly at ease with her father. Sometimes Mayumi would join us for a cup of tea at the table in the living room next to the kitchen, but never for long; sometimes she wouldn't appear at all, and I would have to content myself with reading texts with her father.

One Saturday we rode the motorcycle to Kamakura. We were standing at the foot of the Engakuji temple at dusk when the temple bell began to toll. I wanted to watch the monks swinging the heavy log clapper into the bell and we began running up the long flight of stone steps to the temple ground. Suddenly our hands were clasped; I nearly swooned with the pleasure of feeling her hand in mine. I dropped her at home that night resolved that I would kiss her the next day. When I arrived at the house the following evening she was as friendly as ever, but nothing more. I invited her to take a walk and she agreed and asked her little brother, Masayuki, to come along. Later, as she was showing me her work in the room she shared with her sister upstairs in the annex at the far end of the house, I did kiss her, perhaps her first kiss, and told her I loved her. She began to cry. As her sister walked into the room, she exclaimed, through her tears, "Hiromi, you're lucky, life is so simple for you!"

A few days later I received a letter on three pages of rice paper. It began, "*Shin-ai naru* John." The two characters in *shin-ai* mean "intimate" and "love," and my heart leaped. I don't think I realized that this was the standard Japanese translation of the epistolary English "dear." I have the letter in hand and will translate it because it conveys so clearly Mayumi's innocence and passion and forthrightness:

> I've wanted to speak out to you but I can't when we're together. I am grateful to you because you give me strength; when I'm looking into your eyes I feel that I can take strength from you. My friend Misa and I have been longing to meet a real human being, a *human* human being, and that's what you are. I felt it the moment we met. I want to become a real human being too: small joys and mild sadness—I don't want to live that kind of poverty. I want a life with challenge in it. Until now I have been wretched: there was no one to understand the truth of who I am. I have felt hopeless and sad. Now there is someone who will turn toward me no matter how sad and lonely I am feeling. John, please be my real friend! I will try hard to understand you, too; together, taking from each other, we can grow.
>
> I wonder if you've finished Arishima [Takeo]'s "Love Takes without Regret"? I feel I understand it

now better than before. But there is one thing I don't understand.

"Do I love you?" That's the most important question yet I haven't the vaguest idea. I like you so very much; but I felt the same way about my dear friend Kuro. I still feel that way about her. When I realized how confused I was, I cried. You seemed puzzled, but I was miserable. What is love between a man and a woman?—I have no idea.

John, I get so lost. Even when we're having a wonderful time together I feel lost. Forgive me. I get so sad wondering if I have no real feelings. I feel I am treating you badly—next time we meet please help me understand.

Your friend, Mayumi

(Alongside her signature she had inked a cartoon of a young woman's face, her parted hair framing her cheeks and her brows knit in consternation.)

Have I ever again scrutinized a text as closely as this? I wasn't able to feel certain it was a love letter, there was so much talk about "friends." It left me feeling exhilarated and disappointed.

A few nights later we took a long ride on my motorcycle and stopped along the way to kiss some more. The following week she rode with me across the city to her school in Ueno, and at a stoplight at the top of the hill that descends to Ochanomizu I turned in my seat and asked her to marry me. She said yes. We drove down the hill to a coffee shop and telephoned her father at work. He scolded Mayumi for not being at school but agreed to see us at once; we drove straight to the Diet Library. Facing him in his office I blurted nervously, "We love each other and we want to get married!" I wondered if he had been expecting this: he didn't seem dismayed or even surprised. "This is a decision that must be made between the two people involved," he said with the generosity I always admired in him. He added that there would surely be "many problems in a marriage of this kind," and asked me to come to the house for a formal discussion with the whole family.

I went to Mayumi's home that weekend for dinner and brought a gift for her grandparents, a tin of fine green tea. I had prepared for opposition by practicing in front of the mirror an elaborate Japanese sentence: *Ippō mo shirizokanai kesshin de gozaimasu!*—"I am determined not to yield a single step in this!" Mayumi's father began by letting me know that "some members of the family" were experiencing a vague but persistent anxiety, not about me as an individual but because I was a foreigner. Mayumi's mother began to cry. "I like you, it's just that foreigners," she paused, searching for the word, "make my skin crawl." I did not yield a single step; I said I understood her feelings and hoped she would learn to trust me. Mr. Oda said the family could not afford an elaborate wedding at this time, and I assured him that was fine with us; we were determined to be married before the year was out. Mrs. Oda was concerned that Mayumi would not be able to finish school; I promised that we would not leave Japan until she graduated and that she would have the freedom to pursue her art. Before I left that night I had the family's formal consent.

I took Mayumi to meet the Reischauers at the embassy. Professor Reischauer suggested a game of croquet; he was an enthusiastic player and had installed a set on the lawn behind the residence. I am not sure Mayumi had ever seen a lawn except in a park, and I know this was her first experience of croquet, but she managed to follow Reischauer's instructions to the letter, knocking balls through wickets unerringly, and charmed him. Haru Reischauer asked how Mayumi's parents were feeling about our engagement and volunteered to invite them to the embassy residence for afternoon tea. On that Sunday, Haru greeted us and took us on a tour of rooms that were familiar to me but may have overwhelmed Mayumi's parents. I remember her father pausing in front of a calligraphy scroll on loan from the National Art Museum in Ueno, and I remember that the ambassador joined us late, moving into the sitting room with the quiet, dignified assurance that was his style, and that he spoke to Mayumi's parents in Japanese, vouching warmly for me as a dependable young man with an important role to play as "a bridge of understanding between Japan and the United States." I sensed that this generous assurance from the most famous American in Japan and his *Japanese* wife went a long way toward mollifying Mayumi's mother, giving her something to boast about to her anxious relatives.

In those days, many Japanese had judgments about international marriages, which still invoked the image of a compromised Japanese girl and a GI who wore his shoes into a tatami-mat room and soaped himself in the tub in the public bath. I ran into this bias when I paid a courtesy call on Professor Takagi at the International House to inform him of my engagement. He made no attempt to mask his disapproval, his jaw tight as he told me that my distinguished sponsors had not anticipated that my purpose in Japan would be hitching up with a Japanese girl. I fear I responded disrespectfully with something about living my life as I saw fit. Takagi knew Mayumi's father and for years afterward went out of his way to snub him when they met in scholarly circles. This must have been awkward for my father-in-law, but he never complained to me.

I told Dean Takano that I was engaged to be married, and she paled. When I assured her it was not a Tsuda girl, she brightened and wished me heartfelt congratulations. The next day I walked into my classroom to find "Nathan-*sensei* is a big dope!" scrawled across the blackboard. When I called the roll as always, my enchanting class stared at their desks and declined to answer. I received a postcard with an inked picture of a young woman with a string of tears beading her cheeks; I believe it came from the Sea Captain. I explained to her and one or two others that my American girlfriend and I had decided to marry after all—I have never been good at honesty under difficult circumstances.

After some uncomfortable interviews with a Presbyterian minister and then a rabbi who told us Mayumi would have to convert to Judaism for him to marry us, we decided on a Shintō wedding. The ceremony required the presence of a go-between, a *nakōdo*, and I asked my friend from Harvard, Tatsuo Arima, just embarking on his career as a diplomat, to serve as ours. As our marriage had not been arranged his role was symbolic, but he performed it with his customary gravity. With his wife, Fumiko, he paid a formal visit to Mayumi's family to vouch for me and promised to guide us through difficulty throughout our married life. I think I was amused by the solemnity of his assurances, since he himself was a newlywed. (I had attended his Protestant wedding just three weeks before.) But he was accepting his role with a seriousness that I was unable to fathom. Seventeen years later, when Mayumi and I separated, he was upset with me for violating a pledge he felt was also his responsibility.

We were married at the Prince Hotel in Akasaka on October 29, 1962. On the twenty-eighth, we took a walk in the Shinjuku Gyōen, an imperial garden that had been opened as a public park. It was chilly, and the autumn leaves had mostly fallen. Our mood was solemn: it was the last day of the Cuban Missile Crisis and it felt like Judgment Day. I remember declaring to Mayumi that I didn't care if life was coming to an end so long as we could die together.

The morning of the wedding I felt lonely and at a loss for

how to pass the time until the ceremony began. I went shopping on the Ginza and bought a ring for Mayumi (I can't think why we didn't purchase it together) and arrived at the Akasaka Prince Hotel alone and hours early. There were ten guests in addition to Mayumi's family: Tatsuo and Fumiko; Dean Takano; my good friends Ernie Young and Kenji Naitō; Reischauer's daughter, Joan; Mayumi's best friend, Kazuko Kuroda, and her boyfriend, Kazufumi Watanabe, who was our photographer. Mayumi wore a simple white dress and a Hopi Indian squash blossom necklace of silver my parents had sent her as a gift. I was dressed outlandishly in formal pinstripe mourning, which I had rented from a shop in Ryōgoku that catered to sumo wrestlers. The jacket fit—it was the only one large enough I could find—but the trousers were so large I had to secure them with a length of rope.

At 5:30, we filed into the Shintō shrine. Mayumi and I faced the altar and I read aloud the marriage oath, a difficult text I had received less than an hour before the ceremony. I remember the opening lines: "On this auspicious day of the thirty-seventh year of Shōwa, in the presence of the sun goddess Amaterasu Ōmikami, I solemnly swear never to stumble along the road of marriage." Finishing, I bowed twice, clapped my hands together twice, and bowed twice again, as I had been taught to do. Tatsuo and Fumiko paid their respects in a similar fashion as our go-betweens, and the ceremony ended with a toast in which everyone joined. I don't think I was aware at the time how far I had traveled to this moment from my life as a Jewish boy in New York. Nor did I realize how hard it would be for me not to stumble along the road of marriage.

Our party moved to an adjacent banquet room for an informal wedding dinner; Dean Takano, Ernie, Kenji, and Tatsuo flattered me with little speeches that made us all happy. Before we sat down, Tatsuo drew me aside and, in his role as

Living Carelessly in Tokyo and Elsewhere

go-between, cautioned me to keep my conjugal duty in mind and to moderate my drinking accordingly. Midway through the meal, Mayumi's mother had an attack of high blood pressure and had to lie down on a couch. After dinner, Kenji and the Arimas came up to our room for a beer and then left us alone.

Recently, I revisited the Akasaka Prince for the first time in over forty years, though I have often stayed across the street at the Hotel New Ōtani. The original three-story building where we stayed that night still stands in the courtyard of the modern hotel that now rises forty floors above it. An ornate brick and wooden building with the antique feel of the nineteenth century, it has been preserved as a museum. I stepped inside and walked down the worn vermillion carpet of the hall, opening doors to banquet rooms that were empty and long unused. I was hoping to recognize the room where we had dined on our wedding night, but I found nothing that looked familiar. I listened for the plaintive whine of the *shō*, the mouth organ that had played throughout the ceremony. I was aware in the silence, saddened, that I could not reclaim my past.

Next morning we took an express train to Goshiki Numa (Five-Color Pond) at the foot of Mount Bandai for a three-day honeymoon (three days was all I could take off from my nightly English teaching at ELEC). Mayumi's schoolmates saw us off at Ueno Station; the girls were giggly with excitement, while the boys seemed sullen, as if they resented losing Mayumi to a foreigner. On the long train ride north to Fukushima Prefecture, Mayumi taught me the words to a wartime ballad in a minor key:

A shrike is crying on a withered branch
We are pounding the straw as the waterwheel turns
All is the same as last year
But something is missing:
The sound of my brother splitting firewood;

36

Mayumi

> *My brother has gone to Manchuria*
> *Tears gleaming on his rifle barrel;*
> *Cry away in the cold, little shrike:*
> *But my brother is colder.*

We set up house in the apartment I had been renting on Miya-zono-dōri in Higashi-Nakano, a few stops west of Shinjuku toward Tsuda. On the ground floor, with its own small garden, there were two adjoining tatami-mat rooms, fourteen mats in all, a large kitchen and bathroom, and a smaller room with a wooden floor. We turned this Western room into a study for both of us, fashioning a desk for two out of cinder blocks and a long door of Luann wood. The Odas gave us a *tansu*, the traditional Japanese chest of drawers, and Mayumi's mother sewed our bedding, the largest she had ever made, and a woolen kimono for me, laughing at how many bolts of cloth she needed, and a pair of warm cotton pajamas. Somehow she had managed in the space of a few weeks to overcome her dread at having a foreigner as a son-in-law; from the moment we were married until she died in 1996, she made me feel in her uncomplicated way that I was a member of her family.

Weekdays, I would often arrive home from ELEC around nine to find Mayumi studying with a group of her friends from school. I was earning decent money for those days, and I think she enjoyed the freedom to treat them to sushi or noodles from a local shop while they studied, and perhaps to show them that we were prospering. Once a week I was awaited with particular eagerness. One of their teachers in a required class had assigned an essay in English by the Scottish philosopher Thomas Reid, "Inquiry into the Human Mind on the Principles of Common Sense." Mayumi and her friends were unable to extract from Reid's opaque English anything resembling common sense, and it was my job to help them decipher the weekly assignment. I

37

took pleasure in this, chiefly because I knew it made Mayumi proud, and went so far as to offer my own attempts at translation into Japanese as we sat around our living room drinking beer and eating sushi. I felt completely at ease in the company of these aspiring painters (a number of whom went on to establish themselves as important artists) and felt increasingly that they accepted me as an insider in their group.

We worked hard that winter. Mayumi was majoring in fabric dyeing; in her studio at the university she was creating batik landscapes of dwarfed trees and ghostly figures overhung by an infinitude of stars; at home she was painting in oil on canvas. I was holding down three jobs, two days a week at Tsuda, one morning at Hōsei University, and, every night from five to eight, my hard labor as an English drill instructor at ELEC.

I was also working on my first translation job for money. My employer, Charles Terry, had arrived in Japan late in 1945 with the Occupation Forces; like a number of other talented young Americans who had been trained as interrogators at the army and navy Japanese-language schools, Terry had tumbled into love with Japanese aesthetics and with the alluring innocence of Japanese men, and had remained in the country as an expatriate. At the center of his circle was Meredith Weatherby, an affable epicurean from Texas who produced elegant coffee-table books on Japanese art at the publishing house he had founded for that purpose, Wetherhill. Donald Richie was another regular member of this circle, which included an occasional visitor, the novelist Yukio Mishima, who was just awakening to his own homosexuality.

I don't remember who sent me to Terry; it may have been Richie, who was all over town in those days shooting the noir 16 mm films he wrote and directed. Terry received me in his apartment in a David Niven sort of dressing gown—I remember thinking he was very fey with his long cigarette holder and bejeweled hands—and handed me an illustrated booklet on *ike-bana* he wanted translated into English in three weeks. I was to be paid by the page, I don't remember how much, but I realized as I worked in our study at home that I could earn good money at this if I increased my speed. Eventually I did get very fast. Before long I was translating entire issues of the *Japan Quarterly*, rendering into English stacks of handwritten Japanese manuscript as fast as I could type on my portable Olivetti.

Whatever time I could spare I devoted to preparing for the entrance examination to the University of Tokyo, abbreviated in Japanese as Tōdai, which I was planning to take in March. Formerly the Imperial University, Tōdai was Japan's most powerful and elite school, the sole gateway to careers in the Finance Ministry and the Foreign Service. When I heard that no foreigner had been admitted as a regular student since the Russo-Japanese War in 1905, I resolved to get in. If I had any chance at all, it was because of a special program that offered students who had already graduated from any college a second BA; if you were accepted you entered as a junior and had up to four years to obtain a new degree. The entrance exam for this program was less comprehensive than the hellish tests that darkened the lives of high school graduates for years.

I was required to prepare two foreign languages, English and French; classical literature (Japanese, of course); and an essay on a topic that would be provided. The essay was the problem: I had to learn to express myself adequately in the diabolical Japanese language, and that meant sufficient numbers of Chinese characters in hand, since dictionaries would not be allowed, and a better command of syntax than I had managed to achieve so far.

All that winter I studied Chinese characters and wrote, filling manuscript pages with my poor imitation of Japanese handwriting. Weekends I would bring the week's stack of pages with

Living Carelessly in Tokyo and Elsewhere

me to Setagaya and submit them to Mayumi's father for correction. As we sat together with our legs in the heated pit beneath the table in the eight-tatami room where the family ate, I would watch him circle my mistakes in red ink. He marked miswritten characters, awkward phrasing, and sentences that made no sense. The failure to convey meaning was often due to my misuse of the infernal postpositions, *wa* and *ga*. Correct placement of these tiny particles inside the Japanese sentence is critical to making sense; alas, learning to use them properly turns out to be a metalogical task. In the final stage of my preparation for the exam, I watched Yasumasa (I called him *Otōsan*, Father, but I shall use his first name in these pages) ink one of his unhesitating circles around almost every *wa* and *ga* I used; in other words, the choices I was making after deliberate consideration were almost always wrong. Did that mean I should think hard about which particle was required and then choose the other? I tried that approach, with the same disheartening results. It was like dealing with subatomic particles that declined to behave according to principles that should have governed them. Slowly, over time, I began to get the feel of it, and my accuracy climbed through 50 to possibly 70 percent. I am not certain I ever got much better than that, not in written Japanese. Native perfection here may be unattainable.

The exam was administered in February in a large, dimly lit room in an ancient building on the Hongo campus. The English and French were not difficult for me, and I had carefully studied most of the passages from the classical literature that I was asked to explicate. As for the dreaded essay, I remember only switching to automatic pilot and writing furiously, filling more than ten pages of manuscript paper provided for the purpose.

The following week I was called back to the campus for the oral exam. When I got to the Department of National Language and Literature, a graduate student ushered me to a

40

cramped office at the rear of the stacks where four professors awaited me. I had met only one of them, Professor Shimamura, to whom I had spoken originally about becoming a regular student at the university. He welcomed me and introduced me to his colleagues, Gomi-*sensei*, ancient poetry and prose; Maruyama-*sensei*, Heian literature; and Matsumura-*sensei*, Japanese linguistics.

We chatted briefly about the difficulty of the Japanese language, how hard it was even for Japanese students to comprehend the national literature, the goal I had chosen for myself. I was nervous, but things were going along smoothly enough until, suddenly, Professor Maruyama looked me in the eye and asked what I thought of Impressionist painting. I liked it, I replied, a little put off by the abruptness of the question. In that case, he said, why not name a few of the French Impressionists? I had no idea where this was heading, but I was very uncomfortable now and beginning to panic: I sat there in silence, drawing a blank. "Monet?" he suggested helpfully. I nodded, racing through my memory in search of names and coming up with none.

"Manet? Pisarro? Cézanne? Can you name any others?" he asked, watching me closely. I tried for a smile and confessed I was somewhat nervous. "Strange," he said, "because in that essay of yours," he pointed to a manuscript on the desk that I now recognized as my essay, "you refer to Impressionism and the French Impressionists eight times in eleven pages!"

I had no idea then or now what my essay was about, or why I alluded to Impressionism. The simple explanation may have been that I used the term, worked it in, because I knew how to write it in Chinese characters and thought it would impress my examiners. I was mortified; I felt my face burning as I tried hard to resign myself to having failed my oral exam. Just then, Gomi-*sensei* spoke. I can hear his words even now: *Sore ni shitemo, Reischauer Taishi yori mo Nippongo ga jōzu jya nai ka na,*

41

Living Carelessly in Tokyo and Elsewhere

Neisan kun wa—"In any event, he speaks amazing Japanese, maybe even better than Ambassador Reischauer."

"I wouldn't go that far," Shimamura demurred. "The ambassador speaks like a native." As I listened in disbelief, a debate began, and, mercifully, my presence in the room seemed to be forgotten. Presently, Shimamura turned to me and nodded, motioning toward the door. The interview was over and I was free to leave.

Admissions were announced in early March. On the appointed morning I arrived at the campus at 6:30 with a thermos of coffee from Mayumi and joined a crowd of applicants and their families in a small courtyard behind the Law Building. It was cold, drizzling, not quite light. I looked around; some people had suitcases with them—they had come straight from the train station, or were planning to return home as soon as they heard the news. They waited quietly in their rain gear, but there was terrific tension in the air: for many of these students, the announcement that morning was the culmination of years of preparation. The stakes were high: admission was tantamount to a first-class ticket to a successful career that could not be purchased elsewhere.

At precisely 7 a.m., an official appeared with a stepladder and a rolled scroll of rice paper. Without a word of welcome or explanation, he stepped to the top of the ladder and began to unroll and tape the paper scroll across the wall of the building just above his head. As the scroll slowly unfurled it revealed the examination numbers of students who had gained admission, in order, beginning with number one. As new numbers appeared shouts of joy burst from the fortunate families in the crowd. Those whose numbers had been skipped stood dejectedly in silence or turned and walked away. Because he had to pause every few feet to move his ladder down the wall, the official's progress was tortuously slow; there was plenty of time to observe the fate of others, to feel their exhilaration and their sorrow, and, as the count approached your own number, to feel your heart accelerate to pounding. I can recapture now with vividness how it felt to be waiting in the early morning light completely identified with that unfamiliar ritual; what happened there that morning was every bit as important to me as it was to the others. Those moments of belonging, the more so for how rare and far between they were, live in my memory incandescently.

My number was 107—and there it was on the scroll, in Japanese numbers, *ichi maru nana*. Tears came to my eyes. I had been admitted to the University of Tokyo.

That summer, we accepted my mother-in-law's repeated invitation and moved in with the Odas. The family lived in a typical wooden house that predated the war: Kyōdō, in Setagaya Ward to the southwest of the city, had escaped Curtis LeMay's murderous firebombing of 1944. The house was a five-minute walk from Kyōdō Station, past the merchant establishments to be found in every Tokyo neighborhood—a greengrocer, a bakery, tobacco and sake shops, a small clothing store and a sushi shop—then right at the ubiquitous beauty parlor on the corner and down an unpaved street to the end.

Mayumi and I moved into an annex at the back of the house that had its own entrance. Mayumi's sister, Hiromi, a freshman in high school when we first moved in, slept in a room above us up a second flight of steep stairs. We studied and worked and ate when we wanted to eat alone and entertained our friends in a large room with a carpeted floor and sliding glass doors that opened on the garden. Just inside our front door was our own kitchen, in which we installed an oven in time for Thanksgiving turkey that year (the Japanese neither roast nor bake). Down the hall on the left was the eight-mat tatami room where we slept and, on the right, our own unplumbed toilet. Once a month, the toilet man would pull up in his pump truck to drain the toilets in both parts of the house. In a perennial family joke, Mayumi's mother would pantomime, her face averted and her eyes shut, dropping the coins to pay for the service from the height of her shoulder so as to avoid contact with the pumper's hand and waving away his attempt to return her change.

Several mornings a week I rode my motorcycle across the city to the Tōdai campus in Hongo; sometimes I took Mayumi all the way to her school in Ueno. At night, when we weren't studying, I read her poetry in English, Frost and Yeats, and Faulkner short stories. She read *On the Road* by herself, pausing to ask me for help when she didn't understand. I believe we were happy in our lives together, loving each other in the uncomplicated way that is the privilege of young people still unencumbered by their pasts. But I think even then that I looked to her for the sense of wholeness and well-being that has always eluded me, and that she was less dependent on me. I see evidence of this in letters we exchanged in April of that year, when Mayumi and her classmates spent three weeks in Kyoto touring temples and gardens and living the student life in a dormitory owned by her university. Her postcards convey insouciance: "Life here is so different from our life together! I find it so strange that I feel comfortable being here with my friends and apart from you—as if I'm a different Mayumi—still I can't wait to come home to you. Give Mother five thousand yen or so and ask her to cook for you sometimes." Affecting the gruff tone and imperative verbs used by a husband to his wife, I sound lost and needy: "With you gone nothing seems to fit together; everyone is kind to me and I'm working hard so I don't feel especially sad or happy, but somehow I can't concentrate. In a word, I'm pining for you. Let's promise that neither of us will ever go away for so long without the other."

Mayumi

Friday and Saturday nights we joined the family for dinner in the main house. The menu was Japanese home cooking: rice and pickles, miso soup with pork, oyster or shrimp fry, salmon or mackerel grilled on the stovetop on a wire mesh, occasionally tempura or sukiyaki. Mayumi and her sister worked with their mother in the kitchen preparing the meal. We watched television while we ate: replays of the day's sumo matches during the four tournaments a year, *Kamen Raida* (Masked Rider), the earliest *shazam* superhero who rode a souped-up motorcycle, and our favorite weekly serial dramas. I remember two of these that ran for consecutive seasons on Saturday night: *Jikan desu yo!*, which means "It's time!" (as in T. S. Eliot's "Hurry up please, it's time"), was a comedy set in a public bath in downtown Tokyo; *Akai daiya* (Red Diamonds) was a rags-to-riches drama about a merchant grifter who makes his fortune in the Osaka *azuki* bean market.

We lived happily under the same roof with the Odas for nearly four years. Looking back, I can see that the harmony we maintained was often in spite of me. The Japanese are instinctively masterful at affording one another privacy in very close quarters. They are respectful of personal belongings and private space, and they are scrupulously respectful of feelings. Confrontation of any kind is taboo: injuries are healed over time by the communal salve of the family. I lacked the inherited sensitivity to meet this exacting standard of behavior; I was often intrusive or, not always unwittingly, insulting. I remember an incident with Mayumi's grandmother that mortifies me even now. Her name was Sayo. All day long, sitting in the sunniest corner of the main room with her legs beneath her on a cushion, she worked at her sewing, lifting pieces of cloth from the heaped basket at her side and holding them against her nose as she sewed until she was out of thread and then waiting with her hands folded in her lap until someone happened in to thread her needle so she could begin again. I was unable to see that this was a dignified way for an old woman who was nearly blind to spend her day, and was annoyed that I couldn't figure out to what purpose she was stitching and unstitching. One day I happened to glance across the garden from our living room and saw her lift the family cat by the scruff of its neck and toss it out the open screen to the ground just below. Though I had no particular fondness for the cat, I stormed down the hall that led to the main house and confronted her. "I don't like that cat," the old woman explained. "I'm not so very fond of you," I retorted, "but I wouldn't throw you out the window!" No one spoke of this, but I knew it had been reported to the family because there was awkwardness in the air for the next several days. I imagine that Yasumasa, who assumed the burden of discharging whatever tension existed in the family, must have mollified his mother by explaining that foreigners were capable of disrespect and that I was, after all, a foreigner.

Sometimes my crudeness amused the family in an uncomfortable way. Though he thought it was a secret, everyone knew that Goichirō, Mayumi's grandfather, wore a belt of magnets beneath the underrobe of his kimono because magnets against the skin were said to promote longevity. The family thought it unseemly for an elder to be so intent on living even longer and sometimes joked about Goichirō's vanity behind his back. One night when we were all having dinner in the main house a thunderstorm rolled in and I exclaimed, seizing the opportunity for some mischief, "It's a good thing there are no magnets around here!" "Why is that?" someone prompted me. "Because magnets attract lightning and it would be very dangerous." Without a word the old man rose and left the table and the rest of the family had a good laugh.

Perhaps my worst offense was my habitual carelessness about other people's belongings. Alone at work in the house

46

Mayumi

I would often help myself to a pack of Peace cigarettes from the carton Yasumasa kept on top of his desk upstairs, intending to replace them but never getting around to it. I don't think this bothered him much; I always told him about it when he got home from work, and he was a generous man. His shaving cream was another matter. Yasumasa is the only man I have ever known who shaved after breakfast, when he was fully dressed in his suit and tie. He kept his razor and shaving cream on a shelf above the basin next to the *o-furo* (wooden bathtub) near the front door; every morning he would stop to shave as he was leaving for work. I shaved in the late afternoon; when I had allowed myself to run out of shaving cream, I would take his can of Gillette with me to the annex and, often enough, neglect to put it back. This annoyed Yasumasa immoderately. He must have mentioned it to Mayumi more than once, for I remember her warning me that I was getting on her father's nerves and asking me to return whatever I borrowed. One day Yasumasa commanded me to enter the room where he was sitting by himself—"*John, koi!*" (John, get in here!)—and gave me a proper talking to. He was normally so mild, it was terrible to feel his anger. Afraid I might forget to put it back, I never borrowed his shaving cream again.

I was the only member of Yasumasa's family who shared his passion for study: his face always lit up when I appeared in the main house with a book in hand to ask for help with a passage that had stumped me. He would read the page I showed him, the fingers of his right hand worrying the hair above a lump at the back of his head, then he would nod sympathetically and say, "No wonder this confuses you—our language is impossible!" Sometimes, rarely, when the obscurity or opaqueness of a passage baffled even him, we would go upstairs to his study and search for an allusion in his battery of dictionaries. We spent many hours sitting on the floor at his low scholar's desk drinking green tea or brandy and smoking as we pored over texts; these were our happiest moments together. I believe Yasumasa came to think of me as his son; certainly I loved him as a father.

An unassuming man, he bore his responsibility as provider and mentor to his family uncomplainingly, with an amused resignation that had its source in his Buddhism. "I have five children to take care of," he told me more than once with a shake of his head. "My wife is ignorant as a child and needs a lot of looking after." During the war, he had taught Japanese history at the Imperial Navy Academy. On Surrender Day, the navy officers who were his colleagues committed *hara-kiri* in fealty to their defeated emperor. Yasumasa thought this a senseless sacrifice; stepping over the bodies, he gathered the books he had taught from and carried them home for safekeeping.

The early postwar years were particularly hard for families who lived in Japan's devastated cities. Yasumasa worked as a hod carrier; on days when there was no work he exchanged family kimonos for rice, carrying them in his wheelbarrow to farmers who lived nearby. Mayumi remembers living on sweet potatoes for months at a time. Yasumasa held the family together and buoyed them by teaching that the harsh reality they experienced was an evanescent moment in an unending cycle of birth and death and rebirth; the important thing, he always said, was accepting whatever life had in store with humility and gratitude.

He was a man of precepts; the family looked up to him as their life teacher, and when he spoke, though I rarely heard him raise his voice, his wisdom and authority were unquestioned. More than once during the years we lived together he tried to liberate me from my own fixation on illusion as reality. Our first summer in the Kyōdō house, there was an outbreak of Japanese Type B encephalitis. Despite the fact that all but a few of the

cases reported were in rural regions, the thought of fever consuming my brain, an image I dwelled on so obsessively I could
feel it as a sensation, drove me crazy with fear. The disease was
carried by mosquitoes. I took to wearing a raincoat and gloves
even indoors; when I discovered a mosquito bite on my body I
circled it in red ink and marked a calendar so that I could track
the ten-day incubation period.

Mayumi teased me for being a hypochondriac like my father,
but Yasumasa must have observed my madness with alarm. One
Sunday he came into our room in the annex and invited me out
for a walk. I protested that the early evening was mosquito time,
but he insisted I accompany him. We must have been a sight:
a slender Japanese gentleman in cotton *yukata* clopping down
the street on his wooden clogs alongside a giant, unshaven foreigner in overcoat and gloves. That summer evening, Yasumasa
didn't say the only thing I wanted to hear, that I would certainly
not contract encephalitis. Instead, he spoke about the "great
passing" ascribed in history books to Buddhist masters of the
past; he told me about the poet-monk Kūkai, who summoned
his disciples into his presence when he knew that he was dying,
sat before them on a cushion with his hands palm up in the
Lotus position, closed his eyes, and expelled a long, measured
breath that was his last. A man like that, he said, who knows
that death is just a moment in an ongoing journey, can be fully
and joyously present in every moment of his life. He hoped I
would not allow a misguided fear of death to turn precious life
into hell. I tried hard to calm myself sufficiently to take in what
he was saying, but I believe I was mostly impatient, anxious to
return to the relative safety of the house.

3

Yukio Mishima

I have retained only one of the notebooks I used at Tōdai. It is a small folio, nine by seven inches. The English notice on the cover feels antique, recalling an era when Japan was still proclaiming its recovery to the world: "Made of paper Specially prepared in Japan." Below I have written in my appalling Japanese hand, "Studies in Early Modern Japanese, Matsumura-*sensei*." Skimming the contents I see that our subject was orthographic changes in Japanese from the fourteenth to the midseventeenth century. Half the yellowed pages inside are filled with Mayumi's handwriting in pencil; I suppose I borrowed notes from one of my classmates and had her copy them down for me. The remaining thirty pages, highlighted in preparation for the final exam, are my own notes in ink. They reveal a command of the written language I no longer possess, characters I couldn't begin to write today, and not a few words and phrases I would have to look up.

In addition to linguistics, I enrolled in lecture courses on *The Tale of Genji*, the haiku poet Bashō, and the *Manyōshū*, the eighth-century collection of Japan's earliest poetry. Classes were formal lectures—there was never any discussion—and very dry: professors spoke from sheets of paper that were yellowed and crumbling with age. (I have often recalled this with amusement when I find myself lecturing to my own classes from typescript notes I prepared thirty years ago.)

There was one other foreigner in the department (the only foreigner I ever saw on campus), a jocund Hungarian named Zoltan Bihari who was on the Jesuit faculty of Sophia University. Bihari regularly interrupted the class to ask for explanations in his heavily accented Japanese. I envied his freedom from inhibition without understanding it was modesty. I wanted to be admired for my fluency and spent my time in class in dread of being exposed. I recall with a shudder a moment in the *Manyōshū* class, which was taught by Professor Gomi, the department's elder statesman. Gomi's erudition was overwhelming; in the course of his one hundred-minute lecture he would cover the wall of blackboard with scribbled terms that taxed the knowledge of even my bookish classmates. One morning, having chalked a two-character compound on the board, he pointed abruptly at me and asked if I could read it and explain its meaning. I don't think he meant to discountenance me but was simply curious, as were the students, as if I were an extra-terrestrial in their midst. Mercifully, I can't imagine how, I recognized the compound and, standing at my seat, pronounced and defined it: *sōkyū*, a poetic term for "azure-blue sky" used in early poetry. Gomi paused an instant, looking hard at me, and remarked how refreshing it was to receive a response "so promptly," *sōkyūni*, a pun on the word I had identified. This brought down the house.

I never got close to my classmates in the Department of National Literature. They struck me as throwbacks to a prewar era of student life and attitudes, among the only students on campus who persisted in wearing the student uniform though it was no longer required, a long navy-blue jacket with silver buttons and a high collar and a student cap with a Tōdai badge affixed to the front. Some even wore wooden clogs that were reminiscent of Ōgai Mori and Sōseki Natsume the great novelists at the turn of the century, their feet uncovered on the rawest of winter days. And they were unremittingly serious about their subject and their calling; at New Year's they exchanged cards, written in *sumi* ink with a Japanese brush, resolving to devote the coming year to a deepened understanding of the timeless classics of the literary canon. Thinking back on this I admire their purposefulness, but at the time I was not equipped to appreciate an absence of irony and felt put off.

They were cordial enough to me, but they were aware, as was I, that our lives were fundamentally different. I was married and employed; they lived on pennies in closet-size rooms in boarding houses, dined twice a day on "curry rice" (a plate of rice moistened with a thin gravy with some shreds of meat in it that was spooned from a tureen), studied all night or, on weekends, gathered at mah-jongg parlors to drink and play until dawn. But beyond the difference in our circumstances, they approached me with the certainty that I was an alien with no hope of understanding them. The discomfort this produced in them was general in Japan. I encountered it often enough among intellectuals in various corners of the society, and even in academics. A professor in my department commented in an interview in the school paper that he experienced my command of Japanese as *usankusai*. I thought I knew the word, but it seemed so inappropriate I looked it up. *Usankusai*: bizarre to the point of being suspicious, of doubtful wholesomeness, tainted. That week I stayed away from class. I felt excluded, and I was bitter.

I did make one friend, a misfit in his own right who would become an important person in my life. I knew little about Takehiko Noguchi except that he was among the handful of students to be admitted to the doctoral program in national literature and that he had a history of clashes with the special police as a leader of the student movement during his undergraduate days at Waseda University. In his presence it was hard to imagine him as a former agitprop activist: Noguchi affected a soft, pliant cool, a somehow androgynous hipness that appeared to be modeled on the bisexual heroes in Saikaku's amorous tales of the late seventeenth century. For all that, his keen intelligence was cutting and often contemptuous; Noguchi was a cynic, which was perhaps why we got along. We began meeting once a week, on the second floor of a coffee shop across the street from the red gate that was the main entrance to the Hongo campus, to tutor each other in English and Japanese. He read something by the critic Northrop Frye; I prepared pages from Mitsuo Nakamura's *History of Postwar Japanese Literature* and read them aloud to him. Unlike the others, who either avoided me or exclaimed with overdone admiration at every word of Japanese I uttered, Noguchi would smile mockingly when I misspoke, his thin lips curling, and mimic my mistake before he corrected it. He was just as severe when we were engaged in casual conversation. His eyes would light with pleasure at a mistake and he would hiss, "That's foreigner's Japanese. Is this what you mean to say?" I have known few people in my life who have served me as many helpings of chagrin as Noguchi, but I never felt that he was being malicious; it was rather that he was taking me seriously, convinced that communication between us was possible, and I was grateful for this. More than once he took me with him to a writers' bar in Shinjuku where he was accepted as a regular and introduced me to a coterie of fledgling critics and novelists and, on one occasion, to the novelist's novelist, Jun Ishikawa. On these occasions, as we sat around a table in a tobacco-fouled tatami room upstairs from the bar, Noguchi put me at ease as solicitously as he was critical when we were alone; listening to the drunken conversations about what was appearing in the monthly magazines, my first taste of the literary life, was thrilling to me.

At the end of my first year Noguchi dropped out of graduate school to become a literary critic and, later, a professor at Kobe University. He was a heavy drinker and eventually damaged his liver seriously, but his pen never flagged; for years he produced book after book at the driven, furious pace that Japanese men of letters seem to have in common, critical studies of the Tokugawa philosopher Sorai Ogyū, Tanizaki, Mishima, Ōe, and several volumes of fiction that failed to win him recognition as a novelist. In 1973, he went to Princeton with his wife, Yoshiko, and taught a course in modern Japanese literature, delivering lectures in English he had written out painstakingly in a notebook. The class was a success, but I think Noguchi was unhappy in the United States: for all his cosmopolitan sophistication, he needed Japanese rhythms of life and a public bath and Tokyo bars in the company of his writer friends to feel at home. I saw him infrequently after he returned to Japan the following year, but in 1975, living in Kobe, he completed in two months an elegant translation into Japanese of my biography of Yukio Mishima.

My most intimidating class at Tōdai was Professor Gomi's weekly seminar on the *Kojiki*, the *Record of Ancient Matters*, an eighth-century text that was the definitive Japanese mythology. Written in an impossible tangle of classical Chinese, Japanicized classical Chinese, and Chinese characters used for their phonetic value to represent classical Japanese, the *Kojiki* had been an object of annotation and explication for centuries; a scholar needed a lifetime to master the exegetical writing alone.

At the first session of the class, Gomi assigned a passage to each of the thirteen students around the table. The assignments averaged ten or so lines of text and a dozen pages of notes. From the following week, the two-hour class was devoted to student presentations. When he had settled himself at the head of the table Gomi would dip his head in a bow to us, which we returned. From the briefcase at his feet he would then remove a Japanese fan and gesture with it in the direction of the student whose turn it was. For sixty, ninety, one hundred minutes the presenter would crawl over his assigned passage character by Chinese character, deploying against the meaning cunningly hidden in the ambiguity of the language the full elucidative force of the critical literature he had managed to absorb. There were always handouts, called seminar memos, mimeographed sheets containing in the student's cramped hand page numbers in secondary texts, alternate characters, graphs and charts.

Gomi heard the report with his eyes closed, the fan moving slowly back and forth across his face. As the student concluded he roused himself, snapping the fan shut, and began an interrogation designed to test the presenter's knowledge and emotional stability. What did the eighteenth-century nationalist critic Motoori Norinaga have to say about such and such a line? In what volume of his collected works did his remarks appear? Was anyone on record contradicting his position? Throughout this soft-spoken inquisition the rest of the class slumped over their books with their eyes on their notes in front of them. Abruptly, *Sensei* would call on one of them to respond; as his name was spoken, the student would snap to attention with a barked "*Ha!*" (Yes, sir!). If an answer was accepted it left the respondent panting with relief; failure to answer produced crestfallen silence, pallor, downcast eyes—the tension was indescribable. One day a student named Tamaki paused in midsentence of his presentation and seemed to swoon; he laid his head down on his books, murmured an apology about not sleeping or eating, and closed his eyes. No one moved to help him, or spoke, or even looked at him—we all sat there looking away, as if he weren't there. Gomi's fan kept moving. When he was able, Tamaki straightened up and resumed.

Although I didn't know it when I signed up, this traditional seminar was a special proving ground: of the thirteen students enrolled, five or six were University of Tokyo graduates in national literature who had stayed on in the doctoral program and were concentrating in the Early Period. If they could distinguish themselves here by passing Gomi's ordeal by fire, there was a chance they might be accepted as teaching assistants; this could lead to an eventual position on this most vaunted of all faculties.

The chief measure of excellence was a presentation of such detail that it took not one, or even two, but many weeks to get through the assigned passage. I was told in the hall by one particularly smug bookworm that no presentation under four weeks running merited serious consideration. In view of these standards, what chance did I have? Never mind impressing the *sensei*, how was I going to avoid humiliation in front of my classmates? The humor in this escaped me entirely at the time: I was in earnest.

My passage was ten lines in length and related a decision by the powerful god Ōkuninushi no kami to send a secondary named Amenohohi no kami to govern a region in the newly created islands of Japan designated "the august reed-and-plain-land of numberless autumns and bountiful rice." Ōkuninushi's explanation to the pantheon for his choice of gods was that the region was "tumultuous."

That was it—simple enough on the surface. However, as hundreds of pages of commentary suggested, the passage gave rise to thorny questions: Where in Japan was this region actually to be found, and what was the social-political significance of the characterization "tumultuous"?

By this time we had moved in with the family and I was able

to make the most of Yasumasa's erudition. Weeknights, when dinner was over, we would go upstairs to his study and work on the ancient texts I needed to comprehend if I was to have anything to say. These included *norito,* early invocations, the *Nihon Shoki,* a history written contemporaneously with the *Record of Ancient Matters,* poetry from the *Manyōshū,* and volumes of Norinaga's *Kojiki-Den* and other commentaries written in the eighteenth and early nineteenth centuries. We studied my passage for weeks, night after night, kneeling side by side on the tatami at his traditional writing desk, smoking our cigarettes and drinking Japanese tea. Gradually, I accumulated a substantial understanding of my allotted lines.

The commute to the Hongo campus from the Kyōdō house was a harrowing motorcycle ride across the city that took me close to an hour. On the spring morning of my presentation I remember feeling as I hung my briefcase from the handlebars that I must drive with special caution because on that day of all days I had no right to take a spill. The purpose of life at that moment was fulfilling my responsibility to Gomi's seminar. I wonder if I have ever again felt so identified with any group.

Professor Gomi made his entrance fifteen minutes late, as always, and, flicking open his fan, motioned me to begin. I spoke quickly from my notes and never once looked up until I had said all I had to say. As I concluded I glanced at the clock on the wall; fifty minutes had passed. I had plunged ahead without stopping for fifty minutes.

"Any questions?" Gomi asked. Silence—no one was about to challenge me. "Did you have help preparing that?" he inquired of me. "*Ha,*" I answered, "my father-in-law worked on it with me." "I see—well, *yoku yatta na*"—good job! Had one of the Japanese students delivered such a skimpy report he would have received a tongue lashing instead of these seldom-heard words of praise. But that was all right—everyone understood that I was being rewarded for a gallant effort. My classmates sighed and relaxed, relieved the ordeal was over and pleased for me, as well they might have been: for that brief moment, the wall between me and them disappeared and I felt the exhilaration of belonging to the group. I felt Japanese.

Midwinter of that year, an opportunity to become a literary translator landed in my lap. The editor-in-chief of Alfred A. Knopf, Harold Strauss, phoned to ask if I would like to meet the most famous novelist in the land, Yukio Mishima. Strauss, the only executive in American publishing who had any reading knowledge of Japanese, was in Tokyo looking for a new Mishima translator, and he was in a hurry. In the mid-1950s, before American readers could have named a single Japanese novelist, it was Strauss who had persuaded Mishima, Yasunari Kawabata, and Junichirō Tanizaki to sign on as Knopf writers. In return for exclusive publishing rights, the contract obliged Knopf to publish one new translation by each author every three years. Donald Keene's translation of Mishima's *After the Banquet* had appeared in 1963, but Keene was beginning work on *Seeds in the Heart*, the first volume of his history of Japanese literature, and had declined to divert his energy to translating the next Mishima novel.

I think that the Harvard economist Henry Rosovsky, who was staying at International House while Strauss was there, had told him about me. On the phone he explained that Mishima wanted to meet a prospective translator before a decision was made and invited me to join them for dinner.

Mishima's choice of restaurant reflected his taste for rococo when he was in his Western mode. Le Crescent, in Shiba Park near Tokyo Tower, bar and main dining room on the first floor, private rooms above, was an overblown affair that mustily

58

recalled an era when Japan was frantically aping its distorted notion of European style and manners: thick, worn carpets, heavy draperies and upholstery, rich French dishes swimming in salty sauces. Even in 1964 the place had the feeling of a mausoleum, a French bordello that had survived from the days of Lautrec.

Recently, haunting the past, I went back for the first time in forty years, surprised to find it still open for business. The large dining room was empty except for one table positioned so that I could observe it easily and unnoticed while I ate. A beautiful young woman in an elegant evening dress of dark velvet was dining with two children, a boy and girl I took to be siblings, who were also dressed formally in a suit and tie and party frock. They were such an unlikely trio, I couldn't imagine what they were doing in this expensive restaurant at nine o'clock on a Saturday night. The woman, in her midtwenties perhaps, was too young to be their mother; could she be their governess, I wondered, dispatched to the restaurant by their wealthy parents to train the children in Western table etiquette? I decided that must be it; as they quietly dined on a full-course meal I observed her shake her head when a small hand strayed to the table from its proper station in the lap or gently correct a choice of cutlery. I felt then what I have felt so often in Japan: that I was in the presence of an intriguing and lovely mystery.

Mishima was waiting for us. He led us to the bar downstairs and ordered Beefeater martinis all around; he made it clear that he was hosting the party. As we were heading upstairs to a private room, Frank Gibney appeared, straight from the airport, in a homburg and an overcoat with fur lapels. A limo was waiting outside to take him home after dinner. At the time, Frank was working for Huntington Hartford as president of the short-lived *Show* magazine. He had palled around with Strauss in the Occupation days but had never met Mishima. "How many are we?" I remember him asking Strauss. "Just four." Gibney smiled appreciatively. "A nice elite number."

Mishima ordered food and wine for the table and chatted with Strauss and Gibney in surprisingly fluent English. To me he spoke in Japanese; this was an audition, after all. The only thing I remember about our conversation is that he began talking about poetic images in the Book of Revelation, *mokujiroku* in Japanese, and that I had to translate this for Strauss and Gibney. Harold shot a roll of pictures. He was justifiably proud of his photography, and I never met him when he wasn't carrying a brace of cameras over his shoulder.

The next day Strauss phoned again to let me know that I had impressed Mishima favorably and to ask me to submit a sample translation of the first chapter of his next book scheduled for publication in English, a perversely sordid tale of adultery and death called *Beasts' Game (Kemono no tawamure)*. I worked at night, writing in pencil in a large notebook. I was revising my draft of the chapter when Strauss wrote that he had changed his mind about the next book. In consultation with his advisors, Donald Keene and Howard Hibbett, he had decided it should be Mishima's most recent publication in Japan, *The Sailor Who Fell from Grace with the Sea (Gogo no Eikō)*. The story was vintage Mishima. A man who has spent his life aboard ship in pursuit of a special destiny that awaits him behind the horizon becomes a sentimental landlubber when he falls in love with a beautiful widow. For his transgression he is punished by a gang of malevolent thirteen-year-old boys, the widow's son among them. Critics had been lukewarm about *The Sailor*, and it had sold only modestly well for a Mishima book, 50,000 copies in hardcover. Mishima was enamored with it: he had written it cover-to-cover without serialization along the way, a treatment he reserved for novels that were important to him.

I was too young and too excited to feel daunted. I went

straight to work on the first chapter of *The Sailor*, completed
it in three weeks, and sent it off to New York. It was Mayumi's
mother who came down the hall to our annex to inform me
breathlessly a week later that Yukio Mishima was on the phone
(Yasumasa had been persuaded to install a phone when we
moved in). Mishima announced himself in his booming voice
and congratulated me for what Strauss had assured him was a
"splendid effort." If I could spare the time, he wished to take
me to dinner to celebrate and asked if I were free to meet him
the following evening at the Hotel Okura.

No doubt Mishima had chosen the Okura because it had
just opened with a fanfare and was already establishing itself as
the caravansary for Japan's wealthy and powerful—a cachet it
has maintained to the present day—and as the place to stay for
visiting luminaries in government, business, and the arts. It has
changed little in forty years: the straight-backed chair in which
Mishima was waiting for me, or perhaps its twin, is still there
in the same position, directly across the large lobby from the
entrance. I saw him at once—the first thing I notice when I enter
the hotel is still that chair—sitting up erectly in a white suit and
tie-pin collar, his gym bag on the floor. All over the lobby people
were halted as in a freeze-frame, twisting their necks to stare at
him, and as I approached I was aware of wondering eyes on me.
Mishima stood up—his head reached my chest—looked me up
and down appraisingly, and said, "You have Gulliver-size feet!"
He led me to the Men's Bar on the lobby floor, long gone, and
announced to the plush dimness of the room, turning heads,
"Yukio Mishima! Table for two." We sat at a table at the back
of the bar, and when he had ordered martinis, he congratulated
me again and asked if I had questions about the text. One sentence in particular had baffled me. The widow's son is spying
on her in her bedroom through the peephole in his closet: "She
gazed at herself in the mirror on her dresser table with a vacant

expression on her face, and her scented fingers did not move here and there." I asked what this could mean. Mishima guffawed with pleasure and said in English in his booming voice, "That's *masturbation*!"

We left the bar with all eyes following us and went upstairs to the restaurant on the tenth floor. Mishima had assured me that we were in the only place in town that served "authentic" *crêpes suzettes flambées*, but when he ordered the dish with a flourish the waiter informed him apologetically that he was out of Grand Marnier. Mishima scolded the man for causing him embarrassment in front of the only genuine Westerner in the restaurant and commanded him to find a bottle. Bowing deeply, the waiter retreated. Ten minutes later he reappeared, sweating from his exertion, with a bottle in his hand; I suppose he had raced downstairs to the bar to find one. He drizzled the liqueur on the pancakes and ignited the dish with a match. As it flamed, delight and satisfaction lit up Mishima's face.

On March 31, 1964, he sent me a note on a sheet of stationery from the Imperial Hotel:

> I signed the contract at once and sent it back to Knopf. I am currently incarcerated in *The Imperial Jail* [these words are in English] writing against a deadline. It's hard work, like breaking rocks in the prison yard, but I expect to be released on April 1. As I mentioned, I would like to invite you and your wife out to celebrate the signing, and propose we meet for dinner at The Mikado. In hopes of setting a date, I would be grateful for a phone call from you at my home on Friday, April 3 at 3 p.m. Should that time on the 3rd be inconvenient I shall await your call on the 4th at the same time.
>
> Cordially yours, Mishima.

His note reminds me how meticulously Mishima laid out his life from day to day. It also reveals the importance he placed on securing a translator he had reason to expect might do justice to his writing. It's hard to imagine a Japanese novelist today inviting a fledgling translator out to celebrate the signing of a contract. There were rumors that Japan's turn for a Nobel laureate was coming up. Though he never mentioned it until after *The Sailor* had appeared in English, Mishima was avid for the prize and knew that his chance would depend to an important degree on the quality of his work in translation.

During the ten months it took me to complete *The Sailor*, and for a subsequent year until I offended him, he lavished attention on me. We went out to dinner often, sometimes in the company of our wives, sometimes alone. The Mikado, to which we returned more than once, was billed as Tokyo's first "supper club." A Las Vegas extravaganza that had mutated crazily, it offered guests upscale dining from a Western menu and a continuous skin show: a three-ring circus that featured topless girls contorting in (literally) gilded cages that lowered from and rose slowly to the vaulted ceiling while seven hundred hostesses moved among the diners and sat with those who wanted company and were willing to add their time to the tab. The place was a madhouse of pretentious refinement and garish vulgarity that delighted Mishima. He could never wait for long until he had to try any restaurant or nightclub that had opened with a buzz. When Akio Morita brought Maxim's to Tokyo and installed it in the basement of the Sony Building on the Ginza, Mishima called excitedly to propose that we should go there to see how large a bill two people could run up.

Briefly, until I dropped out, we lifted weights together at his gym. He mailed front-row tickets for Mayumi and me to the openings of his plays. We went dancing at an open-air cabaret on the rooftop of a hotel in Yokohama. (Mishima had no sense of rhythm; his dancing looked like death throes.) And we were frequent guests at the lavish parties he threw on Christmas Eve and the spring equinox, and at more intimate dinners, after which the gentlemen retired upstairs to the round room to smoke Cuban cigars and exchange gossip too coarse for the ladies' ears.

I remember most vividly the evenings I spent alone with him late at night. He would phone to let me know that he had pushed ahead of his writing schedule to create spare time and invite me to drop in at 11:30 or midnight. His wife, Yōkō, would show me to his study upstairs, wheel in a cart of Napoleon brandy and other liqueurs, and withdraw. Mishima did most of the talking; I listened raptly as he recited passages from *The Tale of the Heike* that revealed the fierceness and delicacy of Japan's warrior-poets, or showed me the fine calibration of the Chinese spectrum, or shared gossip about another writer's disastrous love affair. One night he stood up abruptly from behind his desk, asked me to wait a minute, and left the room. When he came back he had changed into a pair of blue jeans and a thick black leather belt. He explained he had been sandpapering the jeans to make them identical to the pair Marlon Brando had worn in *The Wild Ones*, and had been waiting for an opportunity to ask me, an American who could speak with authority on the subject, whether he had achieved the look he wanted. I think I assured him he might have been Brando's double in his sandpapered jeans.

It was clear that Mishima was a dandy, but I never suspected he was gay, even at moments like these. There was one exchange on another occasion that did cause me to wonder about his sexuality. I had just read his 1954 novel, *Sound of Waves* (*Shiosai*), a sunlit tale of first love between a fisher-boy and a diving girl on a small island that he had modeled loosely on the Daphnis and Chloe story. Sitting with him in his study I effused about the innocence of the story and how its simple purity had moved me. Mishima let me run on; when I had finished he laughed and declared, "That was a joke on my readers. Here's how I wrote it." Covering his eyes with his left hand he held his right arm out in front of him and moved it rapidly up and down as though he were filling a page of manuscript with an imaginary pen. I was mortified at having exposed my naïveté; when I returned to the book I did have the feeling that his love scenes, like Proust's, were camouflaged versions of homosexual fantasies.

I was giddy with self-importance to be hanging out with Mishima as though we were friends. I was also uneasily aware that he was counting on me to deliver the goods. Unfailingly, when I thanked him for his solicitousness at the end of an evening, he waved aside my deference and assured me I would more than repay him with a splendid translation. I laid out $200 for a Mont Blanc fountain pen, the stubby cigar model used by every considerable Japanese novelist—my half-share of the Knopf advance was $400–and completed each chapter by hand in a thick notebook before I typed it on my Olivetti. Working at night until dawn, as Mishima did, alone in the hushed house with my manuscript, I reveled in the feeling that I was a literary man, a real writer, an artist in my own right. Or was I? What if the translation exposed me as an imposter? The thought filled me with dread. Was I great or a nobody? At the time I failed to recognize the narcissist's dilemma.

That summer we spent six weeks in the United States, Mayumi's first trip. We flew to San Francisco, which charmed her. On the way to Tucson we stopped for gas in Yuma, Arizona; she reeled from the blast of heat from the desert furnace and returned howling to the car. From Tucson we drove across the country with my sister, Nancy. At the rim of the Grand Canyon Mayumi squatted, circling her legs tightly with her arms, and burst into tears; the vastness of the canyon, unimaginable to a Japanese, had overwhelmed her.

We stayed in New York for a week at the Waverly Hotel just off Washington Square Park. I had my manuscript with me and worked at my typewriter in the afternoons while Mayumi wandered around the Village. I showed a few chapters to one of my closest friends from Harvard, Tom Weisbuch, a poet who had earned praise from Robert Lowell. Tom read the pages with his head cocked to one side and a quizzical look on his face. When he had finished he had only one comment: though he didn't know Japanese, he could sense the presence of the Japanese language just beneath the surface of my English. I took this to mean that he had found my attempt at translation awkward, and I was shaken. My poet friend had perceived what I had been at such pains to conceal: that I lacked the gift of words. For years, whenever I wrote or translated anything, his judgment returned to trouble me.

I took pleasure in showing Mayumi New York and Boston; her curiosity and enthusiasm gratified me. Visiting with my friends at their homes was harder. She was shocked at how wasteful we seemed to be, choosing taxis instead of the subway, leaving food on our plates, and neglecting to turn off lights.

It wasn't simply our complacency about the comforts of life—our ungratefulness, as she put it—that offended Mayumi. One day I found her crying at the end of the hall in an apartment in Cambridge where my friends had gathered. I was sure we had all been having a good time and couldn't imagine what was troubling her. When she explained I was dumbfounded: wherever we went she had observed our friends walking into our host's kitchen and helping themselves to what they wanted from the refrigerator. She couldn't understand how we could be so disrespectful in someone else's home. I tried to explain that our behavior meant we felt at ease with our friends, but she was unconvinced.

We returned in time for the 1964 Tokyo Olympics, the first to be held in Asia. The Japanese government had spent $3 billion in preparation to host the world for the first time since the war in a manner that befitted a nation on its way to becoming a superpower. The frantic preparations had the comic aspect that seemed to me to typify all of Japan's convulsive forays into Westernization. Large billboards had been installed all over the city, but no one in the planning bureaucracy had bothered to check the English with a native speaker: in bold letters three-feet high, the signs proclaimed WELCOME IN TOKYO!

My completed translation was due on January 1, 1965, and I was still struggling to contrive an English title for the book. Mishima's title was an untranslatable pivot on the word "tugging," as in tugboat. Literally it meant "tugging in the afternoon," *Gogo no Eikō*. The Japanese word for "glory," written with different Chinese characters, is a homonym for "tugging" that every Japanese could be counted on to register upon reading the title. In the closing line, as the sailor drinks the drugged tea that will deliver him into the murderous hands of the children who plan to "tug" him back to the glory he has renounced, the narrator sardonically evokes the double entendre: "Glory, as anyone knows, is bitter stuff."

All I had to show for months of worrying this was "Drag-out" or, more cleverly, as I thought, "Glory Is a Drag." I sent my solutions off to Strauss, who responded in a comic note dated December 2, 1964:

> I think you are on the right track with your proposed title, DRAG OUT, but not quite in that form. It lends itself to cheap jokes. Why does Mishima *drag out* the story? I wouldn't be surprised if the key word

were "drag" and something could be worked out with it. Using one word from the original title, what would you think of AFTERNOON DRAG ? Come to think of it, a lot of homosexuals might be misled into buying the book.

There isn't any reason that we have to stick to the original, which is untranslatable. The word "Peep–hole" comes to mind, if the implications are not too sensational. I think in any case whatever we decide on ought to be discussed with Mishima.

I went to see Mishima, who seemed to relish the challenge. "Let's come up with a long title, like Proust," he said. Then he astonished me by rattling off half a dozen such titles in Japanese. I wrote them down as he spoke them. One seemed to translate itself: *Umi no megumi wo ushinawarete shimatta madorosu— The Sailor Who Fell from Grace with the Sea.* I conveyed this "authorized" title to Strauss and he was delighted.

I sent the manuscript to New York on December 28, 1964; the next day Mayumi and I took our first ride on the bullet train, in service for just a few months at the time, to Kyoto. There we had trouble finding a place to stay; we slid open the entrance door to one Kyoto inn after another, calling out *Gomen-kudasai!* to announce ourselves; when the proprietress appeared in her kimono her face clouded and she informed us curtly that no rooms were available. What she saw when she beheld us was an American flyboy with a Japanese tart, an image retained from Occupation days that augured possible trouble, a drunken row or shoes on the tatami mats or who knew what. It was the same preconceived vision that had troubled Professor Takagi and others when Mayami and I had announced our marriage. (Years later, I included a similar scene of rejection in the script I wrote about American deserters from Vietnam, *Summer Soldiers.*) We eventually found a place and spent two peaceful days in Kyoto visiting Buddhist temples. New Year's Eve day we took the train to Ise; the following morning we watched the first sunrise of the year at the Ise shrine and ate conch grilled in the shell with miso sauce over a charcoal fire at an outdoor stand. It felt like an auspicious way to begin the new year.

On February 9, 1965, Harold Strauss wrote to Mishima: "Dear Yukio—I am very happy to tell you that John Nathan has done an absolutely outstanding job in translating *Gogo no Eikō*. He is particularly good at catching the English idiomatic equivalents of a 13-year old boy." Mishima called to read the letter to me on the phone (he must have given it to me, as I still have it). He was very excited, and I was thrilled—how could I have doubted my prodigious gift! He proposed we go to dinner to celebrate and invited me to meet him at Hamasaku, a Japanese restaurant patronized by the writing establishment, where unfamiliar faces were not welcome. We ate at the polished wooden counter, small dishes of delicacies that Mishima ordered for us, and drank a lot of sake, chilled and heated. Mishima had brought along his new novel *Kinu to meisatsu (Silk and Insight)*. At some point he declared that we were an "unbeatable team," and asked me to help him win the Nobel Prize. My head spun—the Nobel Prize! I promised on the spot to translate the novel he handed me.

The book was difficult to read, and unrewarding. It was a melodrama about the owner of a textile mill whose meddling in the lives of his young employees provokes them to organize a strike. There was something elaborately artificial about the story and the writing that made me wonder if this might be another joke Mishima was playing on his readers. I knew before I had finished that I didn't want to spend a year wrestling the novel into English.

I should have told him at once, but I lacked the nerve. That summer I saw him only once, at a buffet dinner at his house in honor of Howard Hibbett. In August he took his family south to the beach at Shimoda. In September he and Yōkō left the country. I have a letter he wrote me from the Rama Hotel in Bangkok dated October 18, just days after the Nobel Prize for Literature had been awarded to Mikhail Sholokhof. He describes his efforts to promote *The Sailor* in New York and quotes Dominique Aury, an editor at Gallimard: "She kept exclaiming 'It's a marvelous translation; it's marvelous English.' Thanks to your translation two or three people have even told me they thought *The Sailor* was my best novel. I've read a lot of the reviews, but the one in the *English Yomiuri* is the most extravagant in its praise and that makes it the best. Like a woman being told 'You're the most beautiful person in the world.'"

Mishima's excitement troubled me. I resolved to tell him the truth: not only that I didn't want to translate *Kinu to mei-satsu* but that I had contracted with Grove Press to translate Kenzaburō Ōe's *Kojinteki na taiken (A Personal Matter)* and was already at work on the manuscript, a development I shall have more to say about. I went to see him in early November 1965. He was waiting for me upstairs in the round room, the brandy cart in place. He poured me a drink and I confessed. He was polite but unsparing.

"You changed your mind about the book?"

"The style seemed so rich, I don't think I could do it justice in English."

"I've never changed my mind about a book once I've read it."

I said nothing.

"And you made a promise. A samurai doesn't break a promise."

I considered protesting that I was a Jew from Thompson Square Park and not a samurai, but I was too cowed to speak. I'm thankful for that. Yes, I had rendered my promise in a moment when I was giddy with my own accomplishment and with Mishima's reliance on me. In my world that was an extenuating circumstance. But not in Mishima's, I realize now. From where he stood, already well along the path that would lead him to ritual suicide by *hara-kiri* five years later, I was guilty of disloyalty, an inexcusable offense.

That was the last time I was in his house. Months later, he came to a going-away party for Mayumi and me and politely wished us a safe journey. I never saw him again.

4

Kenzaburō Ōe

Mishima's parties were a doorway to the community of writers the Japanese call the *bundan*. The word is scarcely used nowadays, because it has lost its resonance. Today Japan's prominent novelists encounter one another regularly on literary prize juries or at lavish year-end parties hosted by publishers. But they are unlikely to be friends, nor are they conscious of themselves and one another as fellow artists engaged in a high calling. In the 1960s, the postwar *bundan* was in its heyday. Writers who acknowledged one another's seriousness and importance sought each other out, aware of the fundamental loneliness of their métier, to drink and talk together. The *bundan* was not only a cohesive community; its exclusive membership during that decade comprised the most gifted group of novelists the country has produced before or since.

I happened to be living in Japan at this most vibrant moment in its postwar literary history. I can't claim to have been admitted to the *bundan,* but it was certainly my great good fortune as a young man to have had access to a number of its celebrated figures. I met many of them at Mishima's house, where I was frequently the only foreigner in the room. It wasn't simply that I was a foreigner. Being Mishima's translator gave me a special cachet that made me worthy of interest beyond mere curiosity. The pioneering American translators, preeminently Donald Keene and Edward Seidensticker, were actively on the scene and very connected. But these men were fifteen and more years older than I. There was perhaps no one else my age who had my fluency in the language and who possessed—was rumored to possess—the ability to render Japanese writing accessible to Western readers in translations worthy of the original. Over time, I worried that I hadn't truly earned and didn't deserve the friendships I enjoyed. My own gift as a translator, paltry in comparison with theirs as real authors, was hardly more than a circus trick, like balancing on one finger atop a bowling ball. Despite my chronic insecurity, I reveled in the time I was privileged to spend in the company of genuine artists.

Some of the writers who befriended me remain untranslated and little known in the West: Morio Kita, for example, a charming eccentric who was forty-two when we met. Kita was the second son of a renowned poet, Mokichi Saitō, who was also a neurologist trained in Vienna and Munich and the founder of one of Japan's earliest mental health clinics. The Japanese will tell you that second sons turn out happy-go-lucky, unburdened by responsibility for living out the family legacy. There was nothing carefree about Kita. A doctor who had worked for his elder brother at the family clinic until he began writing after the war, he was a self-diagnosed, and self-medicating, manic depressive. The first words out of his mouth were invariably a report on his condition. "I'm in my low cycle today," he would tell me despondently on the phone, "so I hope you can go out drinking." At other times he would announce, no less gloomily, "I'm feeling manic today, so I hope you can go out drinking." In person he always seemed more or less the same, sweet and wry and self-deprecating. Kita had earned his literary credentials by winning the Akutagawa Prize in 1960 for a novel about a Jewish psychiatrist practicing in the shadow of the Nazis. When we met he was working on *Dr. Manbo's Space Launch*, the fourth or fifth installment in a series of comic novels about an eccentric doctor's misadventures around the world. Kita himself was a restless, compulsive traveler; he had journeyed to Cape Canaveral to gather material for the book. His Dr. Manbo novels were best-sellers, but the purists in the *bundan* dismissed them as "popular literature" and condescended to Kita. This wounded him. "I'm just a joker with a nimble pen," he would say with a thin smile. In fact he was a gifted writer. His fifteen-hundred-page saga of a family very like his own over three generations, *The People in the House of Niire*, is keenly observed and mordantly funny.

One summer day Kita phoned to ask Mayumi and me to accompany him to his house in Karuizawa. He apologized for the short notice; his wife and children were away, he was too depressed to stay alone, and it was urgent that he get out of town. Karuizawa nestles in a pine forest on a cool plateau eighty miles northwest of Tokyo; in those days it was a four-hour drive (today it is a fifty-minute ride on the bullet train that was built for the Nagano Winter Olympics). In the chauffered car on the way Kita explained that he was fleeing from the *tantōsha* assigned to him by his publisher. *Tantōsha*, "responsible party," designated an editorial assistant who was responsible for managing the relationship between his author and the publisher. The job required two very different skills: the ability to read an author's illegible scrawl and the tact and pertinaciousness to pry loose the installment of a work in serialization in time for the monthly publishing deadline. Success at this required the cunning of a repo man or a process server.

Kita's house in Karuizawa, a legacy from his father's day, was a grand manor in the old part of town, which was known as the "writers' colony." Mayumi had become good friends with Kita's wife, who treated her like a younger sister, and we had often visited here and enjoyed congenial meals served by the family cook in the Victorian dining room. This time the house echoed emptily and Kita was very nervous. He confessed that he was more than a week late with his Dr. Manbo installment; he was grimly certain that his man, finding the Tokyo house deserted, would appear in Karuizawa.

The next morning Kita staged a theatrical scene that might have come from a Dr. Manbo novel. On a small table just inside the vestibule he laid out an antiquated blood pressure gauge and cuff, a hypodermic syringe in a metal case—a relic, he told me proudly, from his father's days in Vienna—and a phial of German medicine whose effect would be, as he put it, "to cool the fire raging in his brain." As he had predicted, the *tantōsha* arrived at around noon and knocked at the heavy wooden door. He was a rotund, balding fellow carrying an oversized leather valise that gave him the appearance of a Fuller Brush man. I stepped outside, closing the door behind me, and explained that Kita had passed a terrible night in the grip of his illness and was still too distraught to receive company. Then I led him to a window on the veranda, as I had been coached to do, and stepped aside so he could look inside. Sitting at the table, his hair disheveled, Kita was injecting himself with the German drug. The *tantōsha* was shocked, and my looming presence and his puzzlement about who I might be was adding to his uneasiness. Backing away, he asked me to convey his best wishes to Kita and to tell him he would be staying at a hotel in town that night in hopes of seeing him the next day. I went back inside and we all had a good laugh. The following morning we returned to Tokyo.

※　※　※

Living Carelessly in Tokyo and Elsewhere

Mayumi and I drew inspiration from many new friends in those early years, but none who broadened and would continue to enrich our lives so profoundly as Kenzaburō Ōe (pronounced oh-way) and Kōbō Abe (ah-bey). They were unlikely friends. Abe drove one of the first BMWs in Japan and donned Italian leather driving gloves before he took the wheel. Ōe, self-consciously unfashionable in all things, was a country boy from Shikoku who got around on a bicycle. As writers they couldn't have been less alike. Abe, Yves Tanguy to Ōe's Jackson Pollack, etched his surreal allegories with surgical precision; Ōe hurled words at the page from buckets of language to create visceral montages. What they did have in common was a sense of their own superiority and a fiercely exclusive admiration for each other. Abe, eleven years older, offered knowing, fraternal advice and was Ōe's severest critic, pushing him up the slope of his talent. Ōe chafed at his role as kid brother but heeded Abe respectfully. They were, in John Donne's phrase, "one-another's best."

I met Ōe first, at Mishima's Christmas party in December 1964. Ōe and Mishima were never friends, and when Mishima veered into ultranationalism a few years later they would become political enemies. But Mishima was an astute critic who recognized Ōe's talent. I don't think Ōe ever took Mishima seriously as a writer; as a young man (and to this day) he could be dismissive and condescending. He had accepted Mishima's invitation to the party out of vanity and possibly his country-cousin curiosity.

He was standing in a corner behind the buffet table, drinking steadily as he observed the raucous room through his thick glasses and looking ill at ease. I approached him to express my admiration for his novel *A Personal Matter,* which I had just finished reading. In the course of our conversation Ōe told me he had been invited to participate in an international writers'

Kenzaburō Ōe

seminar to be led by Professor Henry Kissinger at Harvard in the summer. He intended to deliver a talk about the heroism of Hiroshima's survivors; he told me he was worried about his English, and I offered to coach him.

That spring, he came to our house in Kyōdō two mornings a week. We faced each other on the floor of our living room in the annex and spoke in English about books he chose, essays by James Baldwin, Bellow's *The Adventures of Augie March*, Henry Miller's *Tropic of Cancer* and *Sexus*. Ōe had a large English vocabulary, but he had never spoken the words he understood so well and had trouble pronouncing them. (To this day, though his English is more than serviceable now, it is no pleasure to the native ear.) Even so, he had an uncanny gift for comprehending English meaning, even in poetry: he taught me more about how to read Robert Frost and W. H. Auden and William Blake than any teacher I ever had in school.

Over time, overwhelmed by his erudition and his terrifying memory, I struggled to come up with an author or a work he didn't know, but always failed. Once I sprang *Rabbit, Run* on him, having just read the book; he asked if I had seen Updike's poems about basketball in *The New Yorker*. I hadn't, so he brought them to our next session and we read them together. When I mentioned Norman Mailer's *Deer Park*, he drew parallels to "The Time of Her Time," a story I hadn't read from *Advertisements for Myself*.

Ōe was twenty-nine when we met; his complete works to date, including a number of best-selling novels, were about to be published in a six-volume edition, but he was still unknown in Europe and the United States. In January 1965, just as Mishima was asking me to help him win the Nobel Prize, I translated Ōe's 1957 story "Lavish Are the Dead." The story appeared in the April–June issue of *Japan Quarterly*, an English-language journal published by the *Asahi Shimbun*. I ended my "Translator's Note," "A translation of *A Personal Matter* worthy of the original would be a significant contribution to the canon of modern world literature."

I felt certain I was the man for this worthy job, and Ōe seemed to agree. Knopf was the obvious choice for publisher. Late in April I wrote Harold Strauss, who was pressing me for a commitment to *Silk and Insight*, to convey my excitement about *A Personal Matter*. Strauss replied in a letter dated May 14, 1965:

> And now it's time to stop playing the peculiar kind of poker game I have been playing with you about Mishima's next novel. The real truth about *Silk and Insight* is that I don't like it very much, and that I had been hoping you would say you do. . . . In the long run I think it will be very much worth your while to become Mishima's official translator—some first-rate European publishers such as Bonnier of Sweden think that Mishima will win the Nobel Prize some day. This will mean a lot to all of us, including you as his translator.
>
> If you want to switch your allegiance from Mishima to Ōe, you should make a clear-cut decision to that effect. If you do make this decision, I think we quite likely will take on Ōe, even though it looks as if I don't have room for him within the self-imposed limitations of the Japanese program, to the effect that we will publish only two novels a year. We will continue to publish as much as Abe writes. Tanizaki is getting old, and I don't expect much more from him. We shall go on publishing Mishima regularly, regardless of your decision, although your decision will force me

to find another translator for him if you opt for Ōe. I hope you will see fit to make this decision very soon, because I do have to write Mishima about it without delay.

Meanwhile, *Newsweek*'s bureau chief in Tokyo, James Truitt, had sent "Lavish Are the Dead" to Grove Press in New York recommending it for publication in Grove's *Evergreen Review*. On May 13, I received a letter from Barney Rosset, Grove Press's founder and president:

> In reference to Mr. Ōe, not only do we like your translation of his story, but we would like to go ahead and publish your translation of *A Personal Matter*. . . . We would like you to contact Mr. Ōe and ask him if he is agreeable to our publishing the translation—pending agreement on the actual terms. I would also like to know what you would consider a fair arrangement for your work on the translation. We look forward to your reply.

I had not heard of Barney Rosset at the time. Ōe knew that he had won the right to publish *Lady Chatterley's Lover* and *Tropic of Cancer* in long court battles and admired him immoderately. When I showed him Rosset's letter he became very excited. But Kōbō Abe counseled him to choose Knopf, pointing out that Strauss had been loyal to his Japanese authors, including himself, and that Knopf under Strauss's influence had been more receptive to Japanese literature than any other American publisher. Ōe allowed himself to be persuaded. On June 4, I wrote Rosset that I was not in a position to negotiate with Grove Press about *A Personal Matter* because Ōe had decided to work with Knopf. On June 9, Rosset replied: "I am very disappointed and confused by your letter of the 4th. Furthermore, we have offered Ōe an advance of $5000 for American rights to *A Personal Matter*." Five thousand dollars was handsome money in those days. (Knopf had paid out $800 for *The Sailor*, to be split by Mishima and me.) Advancing such a sum to an unknown writer for a book he hadn't read, an act of reckless extravagance, was characteristic of Barney: when he decided he wanted something there was never any stopping him.

Ōe came to the house to show me the cable he had received from Rosset. He was flattered and very proud. It wasn't the money so much; he viewed Rosset as a cultural revolutionary and, beyond that, an incarnation of his archetypal American hero, Huckleberry Finn. He listed for me the writers Barney had championed and published for the first time in the United States: Henry Miller and Norman Mailer, Kerouac and William Burroughs and Allen Ginsberg, Ionesco, Robbe-Grillet, Samuel Beckett (godfather to Rosset's second son), Che Guevara and Malcolm X. Ōe had changed his mind; dizzy at the prospect of being included in Rosset's pantheon of novelists, he was now determined to sign with Grove Press and said he would break the news to Harold Strauss himself. I never saw the letter he wrote, but Strauss quoted it back to me in a flabbergasted letter he wrote on June 21:

> Dear John:
> I have received several copies of Ōe's *A Personal Matter* and am well into it and like it very much. One of the copies came from Ōe himself, so he must have at one time contemplated being published by us. But today I received a most astonishing letter from him, telling me is going to accept Grove Press's offer. "As an admirer of John Updike and a close friend of Abe, I appreciate highly Alfred A. Knopf Inc. But I

don't hope to wedge myself into the line-up of Abe, Mishima, and Tanizaki. That is the reason of my determination." Does he really mean this? If so, it is certainly false modesty. I have never encountered an author who was unwilling to be published by the publisher of other well-known authors. . . . At any rate, as you are partly responsible for my interest in Ōe, I hope you will do me the great favor of tactfully trying to sound out the situation. And where does this leave you in regard to us? If Ōe goes to Grove, will you translate for them? I certainly hope not. I'd like to keep you busy on translations for us.

I hope you'll try to answer this letter promptly, since I am quite uneasy about the situation.

As always, Harold.

Strauss's confusion was understandable; Ōe's explanation was disingenuous. I replied to Strauss that I intended to honor Ōe's decision to contract with Grove Press, and continued:

You suggest in your letter that I must make a clear-cut decision as to where my allegiance lies. As I am interested in particular novels rather than authors, I fail to see the question as one of allegiance and would prefer to opt for both Mishima and Ōe, to feel that I would be free to translate any novel I liked and thought I might do well. But if I must choose one to the exclusion of the other, let it be Ōe.

I wince a little at the note of haughtiness in this: I must have been pleased with myself, and reassured, to be standing in the middle of these literary goings-on.

Living Carelessly in Tokyo and Elsewhere

As Ōe and I became easier with each other, I began spending evenings at his home, sometimes with Mayumi but often alone. He lived just three stops away on the Odakyū Line in Seijō-gakuen, an affluent, tree-lined residential district that was also home to the actor Toshirō Mifune; the novelist Shintarō Ishi-hara's superstar brother, Yūjirō; the conductor Seiji Ozawa; the recently retired chairman of Sony, Nobuyuki Idei; and a number of older writers, including Shōhei Ōoka. Ōe's house, unchanged today, was modest by neighborhood standards. The first floor was a single Western room where the family did most of its living together; at the far end was a couch and coffee table and the armchair in which Ōe sat to read or write during the day, a clipboard and manuscript paper on his lap, reference books and dictionaries on shelves mounted on the wall, and a box full of scissors and paste and fountain pens on a small table. The dining table was just off the kitchen at the other end of the room. In forty years of visits I have never been upstairs—the Japanese wonder at the house tours that are part of American hospital-ity—but I know the bedrooms were there, and a study Ōe used at night, and a small library with floor-to-ceiling bookshelves.

The pattern of our visits became a ritual we observed for decades. When I arrived at the house, a ten-minute walk from Seijō Station, Ōe would call a cab and take me with him to shop for dinner at Meijiya, the first postwar gourmet food store spe-cializing in Western delicacies. Invariably he would buy wedges of Camembert and brie; fruit and produce not yet available at an ordinary supermarket, including avocadoes, fresh aspara-gus, and honeydew melons; and steaks he would have cut to a thickness fit for an American carnivore (Kobe beef was sold in hundred-gram units in those days). Home again, he would cook up a Western feast while his wife, Yukari, looked on uneasily, heaping my plate and serving himself and Yukari the meager-est portion of steak or oxtail stew, a day-long preparation he

82

Kenzaburō Ōe

claimed to have learned from his father that required a bouquet garni of herbs and mountain grasses. I knew that, alone, neither of them would have chosen to dine on beef and cheese, but my hunger for food that was hard to come by in Japan bore away whatever self-consciousness I might have been feeling. When I had cleaned my plate with genuine exclamations of pleasure, we moved to the couch to talk and to drink the vintage wine and rare whiskies he had received as gifts. Yukari never joined us, sewing at the dinner table and serving us throughout the evening coffee and French cake or plates of melon and Japanese grapes as large as ornaments on a Christmas tree. Ōe's firstborn child, Hikari, born with severe brain damage—we called him "Pooh"—was an infant in the early days; later he would sit at the television set, squinting at the screen, and, still later, a full-grown adult who depended on his mother for his daily needs, he would sprawl at his father's feet with his nose pressed against the pages of a sumo magazine. Sometimes as we drank we listened to opera, a taste Ōe had acquired in the company of Donald Keene. Sometimes we played a translation game: Ōe would show me verses of American poetry he had rendered in Japanese; I would translate them back into English and we would compare my versions to the original. As we talked, Ōe would bring books downstairs from his study on the second floor, including dictionaries that we would rifle for alternate definitions of words in both languages. These long evenings about language and narrative and style—which ended near midnight, when I took my drunken leave and rode home half asleep in a taxi—are among the happiest memories of my life.

Over the years Ōe's sobriety has deepened and he has grown remote, reclusive even, leaving his home infrequently except to commute to his swimming club. In the early years of our friendship I knew him as a headlong man who laughed heartily and whose solemn, owlish intensity concealed an appetite for lewd and imaginative mischief. One day I accompanied him to lunch at the Australian ambassador's residence, where we drank several bottles of Australian wine. Afterward, the ambassador put us in his official car to take us home to the suburbs where we both lived. As soon as we were out of sight, Ōe instructed the driver to take us instead to Ikebukuro, then a seedy district. By way of explanation, he produced from his inside jacket pocket a slim envelope containing two crisp 10,000 yen notes and proposed that we spend the money at a Turkish bath. I remember thinking he was being reckless; the gossip magazines would have enjoyed catching Kenzaburō Ōe at a Turkish bath in broad daylight. He suggested that I should pose as a Middle Eastern merchant who spoke no Japanese, and I happily agreed.

At the entrance we separated, following our hostesses in bathing suits to their private rooms. I had received my bath in the tub of very hot water and was sitting naked on the massage table when the phone rang. The girl answered and listened intently, nodding and eyeing me apprehensively, and finally said, thinking I would not understand, "Then get me out of here!" A minute later there was an urgent knock on the door and the manager peered into the room and scowled at me. Ōe was standing behind him fully dressed, a huge grin on his face. He had reported that I was known to become violent when aroused and might endanger the girl. Out on the street he collapsed with laughter.

One evening he showed up at our house with Kōbō Abe in tow. Abe had brought a bottle of Bulgarian brandy, which he asserted was better than French, closer to the earth. Abe was interested in Jewish identity because it transcended national borders. He had grown up in Mukden, where his father was a professor at the Manchurian Medical School. At the end of the war he recalled watching Cossacks on horseback trample his father's garden and ride into the house, breaking open bottles of vodka against their saddle horns. Before his eyes the Japanese state of Manchukuo and everything it had seemed to represent shattered into chaos and with it his own identity as a Japanese national. When he began to write after dropping out of Tōdai medical school, the illusory nature of identity was his theme. And so the Jews, our pan-nationalism, intrigued him. That night we spoke about I. B. Singer, Philip Roth, and Malamud. Ōe was quieter than usual; I think he was eager for Abe and me to connect.

Evenings at Abe's house in Wakabacho usually included Mayumi and his wife, Machi, a tall, graceful woman who was an established set designer and an artist who illustrated a number of his novels. Machi joined in a conversation in a way that Ōe's wife, Yukari, rarely did, arguing heatedly with her husband. Mayumi was never reticent herself, then or now: our time with the Abes was more animated than visits with the Oes. I recall our frequent evenings together in blurred impressions with an occasional moment still in focus. Abe never showed me his study, but one night shortly after we arrived he proudly brought out a contraption he had ordered from Germany. Like a large toaster oven, it was a paper incinerator that reduced manuscript pages to dust in the flash of an electric arc. Ōe was a cutter and paster. Abe wrote and rewrote and reworked again each page; by his own account he typically rewrote the opening page of a new novel dozens of times, a hundred times before he got it right. Now the Germans had provided a solution—an unfortunate phrase—to the heaps of crumpled trash that had oppressed him while he worked. This variety of shoptalk from a real writer, a great writer, filled me then as it does now with wonderment.

Abe was a large-hearted, demonstratively affectionate man. He was also an epicurean. He once drove me several hours into the mountains to a restaurant that specialized in game birds that were roasted on a spit. (In his memoir, Donald Keene recalls a similar journey in quest of a carp dinner.) The house sake was a blend available nowhere else, and it was served in clay pitchers kilned by a local potter; Abe admired their rough textures and earthy glazes. When we ate in town it was usually sushi. Abe was a regular at Kuro-zushi, a breathtakingly expensive establishment that catered to business executives and celebrities in the arts. (Seiji Ozawa liked to stop on his way home from the airport when he returned from a tour abroad.) Sushi with Abe challenged my palate: to educate me he ordered delectables that required a cultivated taste: roasted tuna cheekbones, salted fish guts, and raw sea urchin hunching soggily in a bowl with miso sauce and spring onions instead of on top of rice. Abe would observe me worrying the shell fish with my chopsticks and shake his head. "John," he would say in the solemn voice he used when he was disapproving of Ōe, "you'll never understand Japan if you can't appreciate the taste of sea urchin." I worked hard at this and got over my distaste, but *uni* remains absent from my list of favorite things to eat.

I can still recall my excitement sitting between them in the back of a cab the night Ōe and Abe took me to their favorite bar for the first time. The giant flywheel that drove the postwar recovery was beginning to turn; the streets of the Ginza were alive at night with company men drinking on their expense accounts. By the mid-1970s, if you wanted a cab to pick you up at closing time, you had to stand in the street with two, or three, or eventually four fingers raised to signal the cabbie you would pay four times the meter. Today the Ginza feels like Wall Street after dark; cabbies hate to get stuck there at night.

Bar Gordon (after the gin) was on a side street lined with other bars not far from Shinbashi Station. There were any number of upscale establishments that catered to executives and VIPs from out of town. The Gordon was not one of them. If you wandered in and weren't recognized, you would be politely turned away. The Gordon was a writers' bar run like a private club for members of the *bundan*. The proprietress, or *mama-san*, was a charming, elusive chatelaine in her midforties who always wore kimono and was said to have graduated from Kyoto University with a degree in French literature. She was certainly backed by a wealthy patron, a Diet member perhaps, but she was discreet above all things, her métier required it, and I never learned who that benefactor was. She employed twenty or so young hostesses and paid them well; they were all comely, dressed in expensive kimonos or fashionable European dresses, and were required to stay current with the monthly literary magazines. The clientele wasn't limited to writers; in the course of many evenings I spent at the Gordon I was introduced to baseball stars, popular singers and actors, and, occasionally, a business leader. But the regulars, who were seated in the salon behind the piano bar just inside the entrance, were writers: Kawabata, Tanizaki, Mishima, Shūsaku Endō, Kita, and Ōe and Abe. On any given night, some of this elite company was invariably there, amusing the girls at separate tables or conversing with one another across the room. The hostesses circulated, deferring to the most celebrated customers by lingering longer at their tables or returning promptly when they were summoned away by a request from someone else. Our table always drew and held a bevy of them. Sometimes they listened quietly while we spoke among ourselves, but they were always ready for flirtatious bavardage. They laughed at your jokes, lit your cigarette before it reached your lip with a gentle touch of a manicured hand atop your own, and kept your highball glass full without waiting to be asked, a Japanese custom that made moderation impossible, like drinking from a magically replenishing glass.

There was none of the pawing that would have been standard behavior at a cabaret, but there seemed to be a tacit and titillating understanding in the air that the girls were available for liaisons. I wondered if some of my friends might be involved, but I never detected any signs of special intimacy when we were together. I wasn't yet aware of the Japanese genius for concealment. I stumbled on evidence of this any number of times, but never so mortifyingly as at a bar on the Pontochō in Kyoto several years later. I was there with the director Hiroshi Teshigahara, the rogue Noh actor Hideo Kanze, and Shintarō Katsu, then at the zenith of his fame as the star of the *Blind Swordsman* film series. It got very late, and somebody proposed that we invite some geisha over for an after-hours drink. Three or four of them showed up in their street clothes, jeans and T-shirts, and we sat around past closing time drinking and gossiping. Kanze was a surly drunk; abruptly he began abusing one of the girls, manhandling her and finally throwing an arm around her neck in a headlock that had her gasping for breath. I rose to the full height of my American indignation and commanded him to unhand her. An awkward silence fell over the table like a net. Teshigahara took me aside and explained that Kanze and the girl had been lovers for years and frequently engaged in rough play. I had spoken out of turn and felt very much a fool.

My friendship with Teshigahara began at the Gordon. He was a close friend of Abe; as young men in 1948 they had belonged to a coterie of writers and painters, Marxists and surrealists influenced by Baudelaire and Rilke, who called themselves "the Century Society." At the time, Teshigahara was preparing to film *The Face of Another*, Abe's adaptation for the screen of the second novel in his trilogy that began with *Woman in the Dunes*. Shortly after we met he invited Mayumi and me to participate as extras in a day-long shoot at the Beer Hall Munchen. It was the pivotal moment in the film, when the protagonist, played by Tatsuya Nakadai, ventures into public for the first time to test the mask that has become his new face. We were seated at a table with Abe and his wife, the composer who scored all of Teshigahara's films, Tōru Takemitsu, and Teshigahara's wife, the actress Toshiko Kobayashi. The main action was being shot at a table in the center of the hall, but roving crews moved among the tables all day, filming the crowd. Teshigahara had invited us to enjoy ourselves as if nothing out of the ordinary was happening, but this turned out to be an ordeal: every thirty minutes we had to help ourselves again from platters heaped with sausage and sauerkraut and to refill our steins from pitchers of beer as if we had just arrived. By the end of the day we were bloated and sick to our stomachs. Since we were seated with people the audience would recognize I assumed we wouldn't appear in the edited film and was surprised at the first screening to see several inserts of myself swigging beer or lighting a cigarette. In my suit and skinny tie and short hair I looked like Jimmy Olsen.

When Ōe left for Harvard in July 1965, Mayumi and I saw him off at Haneda Airport. That summer I received a postcard from him:

> A few days ago I was introduced to Norman Mailer at a bar late at night. He ignored me as if I were a small dog, or maybe a visiting dentist from an underdeveloped country. Alas!

By the time Ōe returned I was working on *A Personal Matter*, but apparently not hard enough to suit him. Several years ago Barney Rosset gave me a folder of his correspondence with Ōe over the years. The letters contain a number of references to me, many of them uncomfortable, and these I feel justified in using where they are relevant. The following was included in a long letter Ōe wrote to Rosset on December 18, 1965:

Living Carelessly in Tokyo and Elsewhere

Nathan is not so diligent about our work, but he will be diligent soon, we are often talking about this problem. He is very much devoted to my works, but also he find out something other to which he is devoted. He played a role as an actor in the great theater in Tokyo. He played as an officer who visited old Japan 100 years ago, and he raped a couple of girls. Some critics were very much approval to his performance. Anyway, I hope Nathan will recover his diligence as a translator.

5

The Theater of Tears

My debut on the Japanese stage, the performance Ōe disparaged to Barney Rosset, was Mishima's doing. In September 1965, *Newsweek* sent me on a tour of the snow country four hundred miles north of Tokyo to research an article on the rice harvest. I traveled with a photographer named Toda. From Sendai we hired taxis for the day to take us from one rural town to the next. I watched farm families working in the paddies from before sunrise to after dark; we joined the farmers for their noon meal and tea later in the afternoon, struggling to understand the north country dialect the Japanese call *zuzuben*. More than once, at the invitation of a local mayor, I spoke in English to school children in elementary and junior high schools while Toda took pictures. Evenings, we stayed at a local inn. After dinner, which was served to us in our room, Toda would settle in for the night with a stack of weekly magazines, his cigarettes and a squat bottle of Nikka whisky within reach, and I would excuse myself and, over his objections, set out on a nocturnal prowl.

One day, as Toda and I returned from the fields in the late afternoon we were surprised to see two prefectural police cars parked in front of our inn, red lights revolving on the roof. As

Living Carelessly in Tokyo and Elsewhere

I stepped out of the taxi an officer emerged from the entrance and saluted me. "Are you," glancing at his notepad, "John Nathan?" I identified myself and he sighed with what appeared to be relief. "Yukio Mishima-*sensei* is looking for you. Please call him at home right away." The policeman handed me a slip of paper with Mishima's home number on it. I was astonished that I had been found: Toda and I were roaming the northern prefectures with no itinerary. I suppose it was still a simple matter in 1965 to locate an American traveling in the countryside. Anxiously—had there been an accident? I wondered—I dialed Mishima's number; the maid answered and put me on hold and I listened to the familiar chime, "London bridge is falling down," and then Mishima was on the phone explaining that I must return to Tokyo at once to play the part of Townsend Harris, the first American consul general in Japan, in a Shimpa play that was opening in four days. *Okichi the Barbarian,* a soap-operatic variation on *Madame Butterfly,* written in 1933, was the story of a young geisha, Okichi, who falls in love with Harris and is cruelly ostracized after he leaves Japan. The lead would be played by the Helen Hayes of the Japanese theater, Yaeko Mizutani. The director had been looking for a foreigner to play Harris, and Mishima had recommended me. There would be twenty-eight matinee performances.

I had observed Mayumi's mother and grandmother watching Shimpa performances on television. Sitting side by side in front of the screen on a Sunday afternoon, they cried silently, dabbing at their tears with their kimono sleeves. I was unmoved. The dramas turned on the hackneyed Confucian double bind between duty and passion; the exaggerated performance style, a convention the troupe had adopted from the Kabuki theater, to which it was a kind of country cousin, put me off. But I fancied myself an actor, and the prospect of taking the stage in Japan tugged at my vanity.

Toda and I returned to Tokyo the next day; a copy of the script had been hand-delivered to our house before I got home. Reading the play, I had a presentiment of embarrassment. Harris's character as cast in fractured English was fatuous and brutish. I would be playing the caricature of a "hairy barbarian" as perceived by the Japanese who first encountered Westerners; the boos and jeering I elicited from audiences every day for a month as I chased the hapless geisha around the stage were evidence that early convictions about foreigners had been retained beneath the surface of Japan's fledgling internationalism.

Yaeko Mizutani charmed me from the moment we met. She was sitting with the script in her lap on one of the long tables pushed back against the wall in the basement of the old Shinbashi Enbujō Theater, where rehearsals were being held. She was a smallish, compact woman, younger looking than her sixty-one years, her hair cut short like a boy's to accommodate the wigs she wore onstage. As I approached she stood up and bowed and thanked me graciously for interrupting my "vacation" to participate. She was dressed in work clothes, slacks and a deep green sweater with short sleeves. From a photo in a newspaper clipping I have retained I see that I had dressed up in a tie and white shirt, straight as a young Mormon on his mission abroad, and she was probably amused; there was certainly a twinkle in her eye as she greeted me. I learned later that I was there because she had insisted that a real foreigner be cast as Harris.

The role of Harris's interpreter, a Dutchman named Huesken, had gone to Ryūnosuke Kaneda, "Kinryū" to his fans, a thirty-seven-year-old actor who had a burgeoning parallel career in film and on television melodramas. For the run of the performance I shared Kaneda's dressing room backstage and we became good friends. Kaneda was an exemplar of a character type the Japanese call *yakusha-baka*, an "acting fool." He loved the theater, practiced his craft with single-minded dedication, and became so identified with his characters that he sometimes wore his costumes on the street. True to type, he was also a heavy drinker and a womanizer (imagine a Japanese version of the players in Marcel Carné's film, *Les Enfants du Paradis*). A thickset man of medium height with large hips and rear, he was possessed of a resonant barrel of an actor's laugh that rose from his belly and rolled out of him whenever he was amused or delighted, which was frequently. The man loved to laugh; sometimes he laughed so long and hard, usually in the course of a lewd conversation we were having, that he had to remove the glasses he wore offstage to wipe the tears from his eyes with his fist. He was a painter and had moved his oils and portable easel into the cramped tatami room we shared. He was also a reader and a bibliophile. One wall of the room was lined with his paperback books, mostly Japanese translations of European novels and plays. (Years later, he would realize his life-long dream and open a secondhand bookstore in the suburban neighborhood where he lived with his wife and children.)

Our four days of rehearsal were mostly about the players learning their lines, which no one managed to do except in a vague way. In rehearsals and afterward, during the performance, though they relied heavily on the hooded prompters lurking around every blind corner, the actors continually made up their own lines or, often enough to amaze me, interpolated whole speeches from other plays. No one seemed to mind or even to notice. As in the Kabuki theater, the audience is familiar with the repertory and pays little attention to the in-between scenes that transport the drama. When music or lights or the staccato rapping of the wooden clackers signal a key scene, a "spectacle moment," they look up from the lacquer lunch boxes on their laps and are instantly engrossed, grieving with the heroine when she is abused and, when she cries, weeping with her.

The Theater of Tears

The curtain for *Okichi the Barbarian* went up at 11:30, and the house was always packed: Mizutani's fans were legion. Besides, the papers were carrying stories about the "first foreigner to appear in a Shimpa play," the "blue-eyed" Shimpa actor. (My eyes are hazel, but the term was used generically to describe foreigners.)

I recall vividly two moments from my month of performances. One day as I pursued Okichi lustily around the stage a gentleman who must have been seated in a front row threw his chopsticks at me and shouted *"Kuttabare!,"* which translates roughly to "Burn in Hell!" Calling out an actor's name or the equivalent of "Bravo!" in the pause that follows a dramatic moment is an audience convention in both the Kabuki and the Shimpa theater, but I doubt that anyone had used this epithet before. My second memory concerns a bit of stage business that was not in the script. In our bedroom scene—a "spectacle moment"—Okichi exits in search of a pitcher of milk that Harris has requested to calm his nerves and leaves him alone on stage. Restlessly he gets out of bed and walks stage left, tracked by a spotlight, to sliding shōji doors that are meant to open on an adjoining room, where his interpreter, Huesken, is supposed to be sleeping. In his only Japanese lines, Harris inquires urgently through the paper doors, *"Huesken, nani wo shite oru ka, okite oru ka?"*—Huesken what are you doing, are you awake? In the script, Huesken replies, *"Nete orimasu"*—I'm asleep. A week or so into the run, Kaneda, attempting to crack me up alone onstage in a spotlight in full view of the audience, responded in English, in a stage whisper that resounded through the hall, "I'm fucking!" Thereafter, in some performances only so that I would never know when to brace myself, he would choose other pungent phrases from the list of English vulgarities I had provided him in exchange for his list of Japanese equivalents. I can report with a professional's pride that he never unseated me, but his mischief helped keep the daily performances from going stale.

Kaneda was in four of the six plays on the Shimpa program that month, two in the matinee and two at night, and he had moved into the theater for the duration of the run. Backstage, sitting cross-legged on the tatami-mat floor of our cramped room with his cotton *yukata* hiked up around his waist, he applied or removed his makeup in front of a small mirror he had brought with him (the players carried their own makeup kits), painted, read his André Gide, or, at greater length as the days passed, engaged with me in conversations about the differences he perceived in Japanese and Western theater. (Sartre's *Le diable et le bon Dieu* was playing to packed houses at the Hibiya Theater.) A sentimental man, moved to tears as easily as he laughed, Kaneda preferred what he called the "wetness"—sentimentality—of Japanese drama, which was what drew him to Shimpa, though he earned more money day for day by acting in serial dramas on television or playing secondary roles in samurai movies, in which, he lamented to me, he was always the first to fall by the sword.

At night, when the theater closed, we went barhopping. Kaneda's bars, in Asakusa or Ryōgoku on the eastern edge of the city or in the cross-hatch of narrow streets in Kabukichō behind Shinjuku Station in the West, were nothing like the seedy cabarets or the elite writers' bars I knew. These establishments were for serious drinking. When you slid open the wooden door at the entrance you stepped into a cramped, smoke-filled space just large enough for a five- or six-stool bar. There were no white-collar workers here: the clientele were other actors or vaudeville comics, journalists and critics, and the odd university professor easily identified by the worn leather briefcase on his lap as he drank. The atmosphere in these ramshackle wooden bars that had survived the firebombing of Tokyo must have been very much as it was during the early postwar years, when the only available drink was a firewater distilled from sake dregs, and the novelist Osamu Dazai, the postwar troubadour of self-pity, had drunk the night away in these very places, surrounded by his admirers.

Riding cabs from one district to another, Kaneda and I lurched down streets from one small bar to the next. We began with beer, then sake and inexpensive whiskey; to ease along our drunkenness we ate squared chunks of tofu swimming in soy and topped with green onions in chilled glass dishes and chewy strips of dried and salted squid. Sometimes we stopped at stands on the street for noodles or a plate of the Japanese stew called *o-den*. It was from Kaneda that I learned the expression, *"Yoi no kuchi da!"*—literally, "It's the mouth of the night," meaning "It's still early." More than once the Tokyo sky was dawning when I put him in a cab and took another home to Kyōdō.

Kaneda was a son of Osaka. On a weekend after the Harris play was over he took me to his hometown and introduced me to a boyhood friend, Monya Kiritake. Monya's adopted surname signified that he had been accepted into the Kiritake dynasty of Bunraku puppeteers, a lineage that reached back to the late 1600s, when the puppet plays were first produced. Monya had been apprenticed to the troupe when he was thirteen; for the past ten years he had been operating the dolls' feet as they moved across the stage and was hoping to be promoted to the left arm and hand in another three years. The rank of puppet master, the wizard who brings the three-foot dolls to life with his left hand operating the head and his right arm on their arms and hands, lay another fifteen years beyond that promotion. Monya was a slight, frail-looking man with a pockmarked face, oily black hair that he combed straight back, and nimble, darting movements; if Kaneda was a bear, Monya was a mongoose. But his unremarkable presence concealed stamina and a fierce dedication to his métier that always moved me. Months later, we ended up in the same room in a business hotel after a night of carousing. Monya had come down with a terrible flu and spent most of that night vomiting into the toilet. Even so he was up at 6:30, before sunrise, and set out for the theater to lay out the elaborate wardrobes the dolls would wear in that day's program. Calling in sick was unthinkable.

I began traveling to Osaka frequently to watch rehearsals and, after hours, to spend time with Monya and his friends. Wherever we went the puppeteers were welcomed with respect and deference; drinks and food were always on the house. Bunraku was already in financial trouble, and members of the troupe had to get by on pennies. (Today the theater must be subsidized by the Agency for Cultural Affairs to remain solvent.) But it was clear to me that these performers, unschooled except in their own gorgeous art, were revered and supported by the entire city of Osaka for preserving a tradition of merchant entertainment over two hundred years old.

The word *bunraku* translates literally as "enjoying the text," and from the beginning it was the reciters, *tayū* in Japanese, who cast a spell on me. The language of the plays is rich in intricate wordplay that deepens its resonance and makes it difficult to read and even harder to understand when performed; even literate Japanese familiar with the plays take the texts with them to performances so they can follow along. At the beginning of a scene, the reciter bows to the audience and opens the handwritten text on a lacquer stand in front of him; in the manner of a conductor who knows his score by heart, he turns the pages as the scene progresses but rarely glances down at his libretto. For as much as thirty minutes at a time, until a second and often a third performer seated next to him begins where he leaves off, he intones the narrative sections and plays all the parts in voices appropriate to each character. As the drama unfolds he rages, laughs, weeps, and scolds volcanically, his voice shifting from deeply resonant legato to shrill, jabbering staccato, from whispers of despair to tempests of anger, fits of laughter, sobs of grief. Wiping tears from his eyes and saliva from his lips with a silk cloth, he gives heroic voice to cadenzas of sound and feeling that transport the drama gripping the dolls on stage just beneath where he sits. I was enthralled; I wished that I were four years old again and could sit at the edge of the stage as the reciters had at that age, listening and gradually absorbing into reflex memory those difficult texts, practicing and perfecting for years until I too could deliver those symphonic performances. Then as now I cherished my illusions, but even I knew that the art of the Bunraku reciter was out of reach.

The comic monologues called *rakugo* (comic monologues), on the other hand, seemed worth a try, and here there was a precedent: in the closing years of the nineteenth century, an Englishman named Black had established himself as a *rakugo* performer and had appeared regularly onstage at the vaudeville theaters in Edo. If Mr. Black had managed this, why couldn't I!

I had watched *rakugo* on television, but I wasn't hooked until I had the opportunity to interview, for a radio program I was producing at the National Broadcasting Company (NHK), one of the greatest masters of the art then living, Kinba Sanyūtei. My coproducer, Shinichi Yamashita, accompanied me to the interview; on the way in an NHK car with a driver we got lost in the labyrinth of streets in the Yanaka district downtown and had to stop at public phones for more detailed directions. Kinba lived in the small, two-story wooden house where he had been born and raised. When Yamashita slid open the door at the entrance and announced that we had arrived, his wife appeared, bowing and smiling, and led us up a steep flight of stairs to a small tatami room where he awaited us. On the tiny balcony at his back I saw potted flowers and his undershirts and long cotton knickers drying on a bamboo pole; I remember song birds in bamboo cages, several of them, and a meshed cage of crickets.

In his seventies at the time, Kinba was a rotund man with a shaven pate like a Buddhist monk and magnificently bucked teeth. It was very hot; he was dressed in a summer kimono of linen, which he wore opened above the sash, exposing his white cotton undershirt. As we talked we drank glasses of chilled barley tea. His voice rasped out of him, gnarled as an old tree, and the language he spoke was pure Edo dialect, brusque and clipped and contracted with rolled *r*s, the language of classical *rakugo*. He was at once modest and completely self-assured; I have rarely met a man who radiated such delight, infectious delight, in his own art, which was consummate. Yamashita asked for a demonstration. Before our eyes, Kinba became two old codgers deaf as stones:

"That be Yotarō on his way to the barber shop."

"The hell you say—that's Yotarō going to the barber."

"You're blind as a bat—I reckon I know Yotarō when I see him. He's off to the barber shop."

At Kinba's invitation, Yamashita and I went to the theater to watch him perform one of his signature tours-de-force, *Izakaya,* a dialogue in a local pub between a customer and a teenage boy who is a journeyman waiter. The customer tries to order food from the long menu scrawled on the wall. Increasingly befuddled by his sake, he misreads, mispronounces, or otherwise garbles every dish he requests while the novice waiter struggles in vain to comprehend the order. Frustrated, the drunk is by turns cajoling and abusive; the stymied boy loses his patience and returns insult for insult in a stammering, apoplectic jabber. (Kinba told us he had modeled the boy's attitude and falsetto on an apprentice barkeep famous for his insolence whom he had known as a young man.) At the end of the piece, the customer points over the boy's shoulder and requests "an order of whatever that is over there." "Standing in the doorway?" the boy squeals, "With a butcher knife in his hand?" "That's right—bring me an order of that." "That's the proprietor, we're not serving him!"

From beginning to end, the audience howled with laughter. Having studied the text in advance until I could follow the express train of punning and malaprops at the heart of the piece, I laughed too. As I watched Kinba conjure this hilarious encounter with his voice and gestures and flawless timing, I felt myself wanting to try my hand at this comedic art in the language I loved. I knew it wouldn't be easy—imagine a Japanese student of English trying to deliver a set piece in the pure Cockney of a costermonger or a chimney sweep in eighteenth-century London. Never mind; I resolved sitting there in the theater to ask Kinba to accept me as an apprentice.

I practiced *Izakaya* in front of a mirror every night for weeks, mimicking Kinba's performance, which I had on tape. When I felt ready I tried it out in front of the family, and they laughed and clapped appreciatively. I wrote a letter to Kinba and submitted it to my father-in-law for corrections. Kinba responded promptly with a postcard in cursive script I needed help to read. He had agreed to hear me. Maybe he was amused, and perhaps I had impressed him with my fluency during our interview.

I was very nervous when I presented myself at his house on a designated Sunday afternoon at three. Kinba did nothing to put me at ease; he greeted me cordially, but this time he was all business. The low table in the room upstairs had been moved against the wall and we sat facing each other on *zabuton* cushions. (Even then, as a young man, I had trouble sitting for more than a few minutes in the formal position, with my legs folded beneath me, but on that day I thought I managed well enough.) Kinba had his fan on his lap; at his side on the floor was a bowl of red *azuki* beans. I knew what these were for: in the Sanyūtei

Living Carelessly in Tokyo and Elsewhere

School of *rakugo*, the master let fall to the floor a single *azuki* bean each time a disciple's rendition displeased him. I remember regretting my rashness and wishing ardently that I was safe at home with Mayumi. But there was no turning back now.

Before he signaled me to begin with his fan, Kinba scooped a handful of the beans from the bowl—apparently my audition was to be conducted in strict observance of tradition. Struggling not to let this disconcert me, I bowed and launched into the opening lines: *Yopparai wa, yakkō-dōfu ni samo nitari; hajime wa shikaku de, ato wa guzu-guzu* (A drunkard is very like tofu in soy sauce, square-cut and firm at the beginning and later soft as mush). Kinba let me go all the way through the piece without interrupting. Once or twice he may have smiled, but he never laughed. I delivered the *ochi*, the punchline—"That's the proprietor, we're not serving him!"—and bowed again. Kinba looked hard at me for what felt like a long moment, then opened his hand and let all the beans fall. I can still hear the sound they made as they hit the tatami mat between us. "If you're not an Edo man you're probably not cut out for this," was all he said. I was dismayed, and shaken. Mercifully, his wife slid open the *shōji* door at just that moment—she had probably been listening outside—and came in with cups of tea on a tray. We sat there awkwardly for a short while—thinking back, I realize that only I was feeling awkward; Kinba was unruffled by the experience—and when I felt enough time had elapsed I thanked the master for his time and patience and excused myself. I never saw Kinba again. Over the years I have listened often with great pleasure to his performance of *Izakaya* on the audiotape I have with me to this day. I confess that each time I hear it I can't help feeling he was mistaken to dismiss me. If Mr. Black could do it, so could I.

6

Home Again

After close to five years in Tokyo, we left Japan in May 1966. Mayumi had graduated in February; I had kept my promise to her mother. I had been admitted to the PhD program at Columbia. I had no desire to go to graduate school, but my draft board had informed me that I would have to be enrolled in an American university if I hoped to renew my student deferment. I had turned twenty-six in March, which should have meant that I was safe, but I had heard horror stories. At my request, the chairman of the department at Columbia, Theodore de Bary, had written to the draft board on my behalf.

We sailed from Yokohama on a Japanese ship bound for Vladivostok. Kōbō Abe and his wife, Machi, were among the friends and family who came to see us off. Mayumi was eager to begin our new life in New York, where she intended to study lithography at the Pratt Institute; she was also apprehensive. In her chronicle of her life after we separated, *I Opened the Gate, Laughing*, she recalled the departure: "I remember the day I left for America. I stood at the Yokohama port wearing a yellow summer suit, leaning against my big American husband, feeling like a canary chick leaving the mother's nest, to enter the world unknown."

From Vladivostok we took a train north to Chabarovsk. The

Living Carelessly in Tokyo and Elsewhere

Russian plane waiting to fly us to Moscow was gargantuan, like a dilapidated tenement building that had been turned on its side and fitted with four propeller engines. I took one look and retreated to the airport bar to gulp down a carafe of vodka. We spent three bleak days in Moscow being herded around the city by disgruntled Intourist guides. Everyone seemed angry, furious. At the hotel, I went down the hall to the *babushka* sitting behind her desk on the landing with keys dangling from a belt around her matronly waist to request a stopper for the tub and had my ears pinned back by an outburst of expletives in Russian. My only pleasant memory is tea one afternoon with a professor from Moscow University who was Abe's translator.

We rode the famous Chopin Express to Vienna from Moscow. As we crossed the border into Czechoslovakia the world seemed to brighten, as if the sun had broken from a lowering sky. In Prague we were told curtly that no rooms were available. Abe's Russian friend had predicted this and had instructed us to ask to speak to a "Madam Chartovska." Apparently this was some sort of code; no such person existed. We tried it and were given a room in a pleasant boarding house. We saw Vienna through the eyes of a Jewish student we had met in Japan who took us on a tour of bookshops to show us the shelves of anti-Semitic publications; he maintained bitterly that Vienna was the most anti-Semitic city in Europe.

From Vienna we traveled south to Yugoslavia and spent a week in Dubrovnik with a charming family of dock workers who were paid by the government to take tourists into their home. Mayumi left the house early each morning to buy bread with the two daughters and learned from their mother how to roast lamb shanks with potatoes. One day as we walked along the beach she found a sea urchin, broke it open against a rock, and bit into it with the excited pleasure of a child while the family looked on in amazement. At night we sat around the kitchen table drinking slivovitz, and I amused the family by repeating the one sentence I managed to learn in Serbo-Croatian: "One paprika (stolen), five years (in jail)."

Donald Richie, the noir film director and author living in Japan, had given us the name of his friend, the poet James Merrill, who escorted us around Athens. He took us to the Parthenon, to a Greek lunch at which Mayumi discovered taramo salad, and then back to his airy apartment on a hillside where we sat out on the balcony sipping ouzo on ice and discussing what Merrill called "the poet's obligation to be difficult."

Before I left Japan, I had been commissioned to write an article on Mishima for the Asian edition of *Life* magazine. The job had been arranged for me by my good friend Jerry Schecter, *Time* magazine's Tokyo bureau chief in those days. I had met Jerry at a dinner party at Mishima's house just before the Olympics, and shortly after had gone to work in his office as a stringer for *Time* and *Life*. (I believe Jerry paid me out of pocket money.) I began writing on the Greek island of Paros and finished the piece in St. Gall, where we were staying with a friend since high school, Ruedi Mettler. I was feeling angry at Mishima. After our last meeting at his house he had described me in a weekly magazine as "an American hoodlum who has been seduced by our Japanese Left." I retaliated with a snide article for *Life*. "Reading a Mishima novel," I wrote, "is like attending an exhibition of the world's most ornate picture frames." The piece attracted attention in Japan; when Mayumi and I reached New York, Ralph Graves, *Life*'s managing editor, called to say he wanted to run my article in the domestic edition and added matter-of-factly that he would pay my fee a second time for the privilege of reprinting it. I was overjoyed— I had been given an opportunity to appear in print on home ground and had doubled my money into the bargain. We lived for months on what the article earned me.

Living Carelessly in Tokyo and Elsewhere

Ōe mentioned the article in a letter that reached us shortly after we arrived in New York: "Your article on *great* Mishima"—he used the English word—"angered Mr. Keene and overwhelmed the writers who went out of their way to lay hands on the magazine. It brought smiles of happiness to the faces of all of us who know J.N. That was a superlative piece of work." I'm sure I read the letter gloatingly, but today I regret my disrespect.

We moved into a railroad apartment on the third floor of a brownstone on Ninety-sixth Street just off Central Park West. The living room faced Ninety-sixth Street and the bedroom overlooked a small fenced-in garden at the back of the building. The landlord, Dr. Albert Jablons, used the garden apartment as his office. Jablons was a crusty seventy-year-old, Jimmy Durante and George Burns in a single body. He smoked cigars day and night and was covered in ashes. From occasional remarks we learned that he had a home and a family somewhere nearby, but he frequently stayed in a bedroom behind the office. His nurse and constant companion looked like an aging Olive Oyl; it appeared she sometimes spent the night too. Jablons had been under contract to the Merchant Seaman's Union for decades: his practice was limited to sailors who were ill when they docked in New York. Every so often we saw one of these unfortunates sitting in dismay at Jablons's desk as he took their blood pressure or administered an injection, a smoldering cigar within reach.

During the year I spent at Columbia I was a resentful graduate student. When I arrived, the department insisted I take a language placement exam, and that rankled me; when I placed out of the language program no one seemed surprised, but neither was I told what I expected to hear, that this was a mere formality in my case. I took and enjoyed Donald Keene's class on the early thirteenth-century text *A Chronicle of My Hut* (Hōjōki), but after the first week I rarely attended his 9 a.m. lectures on

106

modern Japanese literature because my spastic colon made it difficult for me to leave home early in the morning. Apparently Keene noted my absence and assumed mistakenly, because I postponed going to see him until the end of the semester, that I wasn't interested in what he had to say on the subject. When I finally explained, he commiserated with me, and even recommended an internist and wrote out his name. This may have been the warmest moment we have ever shared, although our paths have crossed many times since. (For years we had close mutual friends in Ōe and Abe.)

Ivan Morris, Keene's colleague in those days, was as cordial to Mayumi and me as Keene was distant. I attended his seminar in legal documents from the same period that had produced *The Tale of Genji*, his passion and specialty. The texts were impossibly difficult to read and often stumped Morris himself, a fact he cheerily admitted. Unlike his mentor, Arthur Waley, whom he described as "incurably frumpy," Morris was a stylish Englishman, an art connoisseur and a collector of antique chess sets, which were on display on inlaid chess tables around his living room. He presided over a salon of writers and musicians who gathered for dinners at his luxurious apartment on the Upper West Side, and Mayumi and I were frequently included. Sometimes Morris would call to ask me to bring along my alto recorder because Frank Conroy was coming that evening. Conroy, who was working on his memoir, *Stop Time*, played excellent jazz piano; after dinner he would sit down at Morris's Bösendorfer and we would improvise together.

Mayumi was encountering a brand-new world; I had been away from Western culture for so long I was often able to experience her wonder as my own. We discovered Bob Dylan together. The lyrics were hard for Mayumi, but I helped her understand them and she was enthralled.

Our closest friends in New York were the volatile Rossets:

Living Carelessly in Tokyo and Elsewhere

Barney, who was forty-five at the time, and his twenty-two-year-old wife, Cristina. They had met when Cristina began baby-sitting for Barney's son, Peter, while she was still in high school, and they had been married for two years. Cristina was pint-size, even smaller than Mayumi, and very game in a gallant way. Young as she was, she managed Barney and the compulsive craziness of life with him with extraordinary aplomb. She was well-loved by many of Barney's celebrated friends, including Samuel Beckett, who openly adored her.

Rosset was a Greenwich Village man who rarely ventured north of Fourteenth Street. He lived with Cristina and their two German shepherds, named, in honor of Ōe, Suki and Yaki, in a townhouse on West Houston Street. Before we left New York, he moved the family across the street into a former warehouse he had converted into a paranoid fortress; there was an expansive garden at the back, but the windows facing the street were narrow as gun ports. Grove Press was nearby, a six-story building on the corner of University Place and Eleventh Street. Barney's office was on the top floor; he worked at a large white Knoll table in the center of the room, scribbling queries and ideas as they came to him in his cramped lefty hand on sheets of paper his secretary typed up at the end of the day, and conferring combatively with his principal lieutenants: Fred Jordan, an Austrian who was managing editor of *Evergreen Review*, and Richard Seaver, an editor who had spent years in France translating the Marquis de Sade, Marguerite Duras, and others, and would later become a publisher with his own imprimatur at Doubleday.

At the end of every business day, Barney crossed the street to his newest acquisition, the Black Circle Bar, next door to the Black Circle Theater, where he showcased the X-rated films he was importing from Europe. The bar leaked money, partly because the bartenders and waiters were constantly looting the

108

register, but Rosset was a man of habit and he was comfortable there. For an hour or two he read the papers, all of them, and munched on celery sticks and drank Tanqueray martinis. Grove staffers stayed away—a day of swimming upstream against Barney's current was more than enough for them—but friends dropped in to chat, knowing they would find him at his invariable table at the back of the room. I never saw him do business at the Black Circle except with Cy Rembar, his favorite among the battery of lawyers he retained; lawsuits were a pastime.

Dinner was likely to be at Casey's on Tenth Street, a precursor of Elaine's. Casey was a tall Chinese man with missing teeth and a graying ponytail down his back. It was rumored, preposterously I realize now, that his wealth came from uranium mines his family was said to own in China. Casey had little to say other than a gummed "Right on!" (he spoke with his lips folded tightly over his teeth, I suppose to conceal the gaps), but he ran his establishment imperiously: if he didn't know you and approve, you would be made to feel uncomfortable at one of his tables. (Years later, Casey visited us at the farmhouse we were renting in Princeton. He arrived with a car trunk full of caviar, smoked oysters, and frogs' legs in beautiful jars and tins. In the middle of the night he got up and drove away, leaving a note: "Great evening; too quiet out here.") There was always a crowd at Barney's table, friends and freeloaders whom he found interesting for the moment. While his dinner guests ate, Barney picked at his food, too busy arguing and drinking to eat. I never saw him pay any attention to his plate at Casey's or anywhere else. His wiry energy was partly due to speed, which he had been using since high school; he carried a silver pillbox, a family heirloom, in his jacket pocket. At the end of the evening he paid the bill as a matter of course; I have never known a man possessed of wealth and generosity in such equal measure. Something usually happened: incidents, and not infrequently catastrophe, seemed to coalesce around Barney. I remember an evening when a shiny black dress boot landed in the middle of the table. It had been flung by Maurice Girodias, the smarmy owner of the Olympia Press based in Paris and Barney's archrival as a publisher of Victorian pornography. Barney sprang from his chair and lunged across the room at Girodias. They grappled, and Casey had to intervene.

The Rossets spent weekends and holidays and most of the summer at Barney's house in East Hampton. Until we had a car, a VW bug I bought from a fireman in Brooklyn, Mayumi and I rode out on the train, a comfortable journey, as the Long Island Rail Road was still using a club car said to have belonged to Diamond Bill Brady and Barney had coupon books full of reserved seats for summer weekends.

The main house on the Rosset compound was a sunken Quonset hut that had been Robert Motherwell's studio. There were two guest houses, the larger with its own indoor pool and a smaller cottage where we stayed. The refrigerator was stocked with breakfast food; we joined the Rossets midmorning. Our daily routine began with reading manuscripts Barney brought from the city in a battered leather suitcase. I remember sitting across from him at the dining room table, reading a typescript smudged with penciled changes of Herbert Selby's *Last Exit to Brooklyn*. Mayumi and Cristina went to the beach or into town to shop for clothes and groceries. They had bonded quickly and spoke of themselves as sisters.

Afternoons we played endless rounds of croquet on the broad lawn in front of the house or doubles on Rosset's tennis court with neighbors, the *New Yorker* writer Berton Roueché and his wife and Fred Praeger of Praeger Books. Rosset was ferociously competitive, a cunning player who infuriated his opponents with sneaky lobs that dropped just over the net.

There was always some new toy to play with. Rosset's

friend Ledig Rowohlt, who had inherited his father's publishing house, Rohwalt Verlag, sent him a slender rocket two feet long that was fired with a charge from a car battery. For weeks we spent Saturdays on the beach launching the rocket in a screaming arc over the ocean. Later he discovered the chainsaw; Barney had purchased an East Hampton ranch house in a stand of birch and hemlock, and for a time we worked together in the hot sun felling young trees in no pattern I could discern. As I tugged at a pliant tree to allow Barney's blade to bite deeper, I felt ashamed: Why was I pretending to enjoy his obsessive craziness? The thought led me to a shadowy place. There was a large cast of characters in orbit around Rosset who struck me as ordinary except for some eccentricity that qualified them as offbeat. What if I were the same genus, ingratiating and mediocre? I had experienced the same disquiet with Mishima, though Barney and I were surely closer than Mishima and I had ever been, and it would trouble me again.

In the later afternoon we opened the liquor cabinet. Mayumi and Cristina were never drinkers; I drank scotch three fingers at a time until I could feel it, and Barney, watching the evening news on all three networks on multiple screens, sipped rum and Coke from a tumbler that wouldn't leave his left hand until he went to bed. We ate dinner at home. More than once the dogs made off with thick steaks before they had been grilled; Mayumi was dismayed, but the Rossets laughed and exclaimed, "How sweet!," and we had to make do with leftovers from the night before.

At night we went to parties, often in Springs, the artists' colony where, among others, Lee Krasner and Willem de Kooning lived and worked. (Rosset's first wife was the painter Joan Mitchell, his high school sweetheart in Chicago, and in the 1950s he had been a patron of the Abstract Expressionists.) Barney stationed himself in a corner with his perennial glass in hand and waited for someone to engage in intense conversation, ignoring the melee around him. Cristina gossiped with other young women in the glitzy crowd. Mayumi danced with abandon all night. I can picture her dancing with Isamu Noguchi, de Kooning, Mick Jagger, and the partner most intimidating to me, the "jolly green giant" from Trinidad, Geoffrey Holder. She seemed to disappear in Holder's huge embrace, and as I watched, my heart hammered. I felt out of place at these high-octane gatherings and I couldn't believe how completely at ease she seemed. Before long she had bewitched de Kooning, who later presented her with three of his drawings, inscribed "To the mystery known as Mayumi."

Two Labor Days in a row Barney took us to the annual writer-painter softball game played on a field in Springs. The painters in particular were prone to hurl their bats angrily into the crowd when they struck out; when Larry Rivers was up, people backed away to protect themselves. Arthur Kopit, whose play *Oh, Dad, Poor Dad . . .* was on Broadway, was the longest hitter. At second base, Saul Bellow cursed his teammates when they fumbled a ball; the art critic Harold Rosenberg insisted on playing shortstop in spite of a pronounced limp and triggered Bellow's rage. For someone like me who wanted desperately to feel like an artist, the game was an awesome spectacle, but there was nothing good-natured about it; I have rarely observed such a primitive display of consuming ego.

Occasionally the Rossets threw their own parties. One night we were playing hide-and-seek on the pitch-dark lawn with pencil flashlights Cristina had provided when someone spiked the punch with LSD. By the time Mayumi and I got back to our cottage I was on a terrifying voyage. Mayumi seemed to be enjoying her hallucinations: she curled up on the bed with her eyes closed and a blissful smile on her face. I spent the night peering into the bathroom mirror at a reflection of two distinctly different faces that were both mine (one was smug, the other cowering). I fell asleep briefly at dawn, and when I woke up I rushed to the bathroom to confirm that the faces had merged into one that I recognized as me. Deeply relieved, I stepped out into the freshness of the morning. Croquet mallets and balls were lying on the lawn where we had left them in the middle of a game the previous day. Vacantly I struck a ball with a mallet; it rolled across the lawn away from me and, as I watched, snowballed into a huge ruby roundhouse and rolled me into itself. I felt fear and despair; I spent the rest of the morning in front of the mirror. I never knew what happened to Rosset and Cristina that night; if they had been tripping they didn't let on, and I was embarrassed to ask.

Shortly after we arrived in New York, Barney invited me to write a monthly column in *Evergreen Review* meant to be a "Talk of the Town" for anti-Establishment readers, and offered me a $3,000 advance for six installments. The column would be called "Notes from the Underground." I accepted the offer without pausing to consider that I knew so little about the cultural scene in New York that I might have been a tourist. I was reluctant to ask Barney or the *Evergreen* editor, Fred Jordan, for leads; instead I relied on Allen Ginsberg.

We had seen Ginsberg for the first time when he appeared with Alan Burke, a TV talk show host whose popularity was based on his skill at making his controversial guests squirm. That night, Burke attacked Ginsberg the minute he took his seat, inquiring with a sneer if it was true that he used his public talks as an opportunity to scan the audience for young men, and did his "wife," Peter Orlovsky, put up with his promiscuity. In the face of hostility, Ginsberg was serene. He responded with a soft voice and a beatific smile, and as we watched in wonder he disarmed his convulsed host and gently led him to a tolerant place inside himself he didn't know he possessed. At the end of the segment, as Ginsberg recited a sutra, marking time with a pair of small Tibetan prayer cymbals, Burke concluded with a pious aside to the camera that Allen Ginsberg was, after all, a genuine and a remarkable man.

I described the experience of watching Ginsberg to Barry Farrell, a fine writer and friend at *Life* magazine who had written cover stories for *Time* on Thelonious Monk and Jeanne Moreau that were held to be exemplary. At a party at his apartment on West End Avenue Farrell led us down the hall away from the crowded living room to a bedroom with the door closed. Grinning at me he knocked on the door and opened it. Ginsberg was sitting on the floor with Peter Orlovsky and someone else, smoking from a large hookah with three separate pipes attached. Farrell flattered us with an introduction, and we joined them. It was the first time Mayumi and I smoked marijuana. (As far as I knew when I left the United States in 1961, the drug was used exclusively by black musicians in Harlem.) It was a long evening, and by the time we left I felt sufficiently acquainted with Ginsberg to call him for advice about my *Evergreen* column. It seemed there was nothing likely to be of interest to *Evergreen* readers he didn't know about. He led me to Tiny Tim, the androgynous singer with the eerie falsetto who would later marry Miss Vicki on the *Tonight* show, and to the performance artist Raphael Ortiz, a charming fellow who strummed a guitar with a live chicken until he had sliced it to ribbons ("Solo chicken on guitar") or demolished a grand piano with a long-handled axe ("Piano"). One morning on the phone Ginsberg mentioned a small band of daffy ecstatics who painted their noses with oatmeal; they were hanging out in a storefront on Third Avenue and he had a feeling they would be attracting attention before long. I followed his lead and wrote for *Evergreen* what may have been the earliest account of the Hare Krishna movement in America.

Home Again

▪ ▪ ▪

Mayumi was studying etching and lithography at the Pratt Contemporary Printmaking Center. A number of her etchings from this early period, *Beauty on a Starry Yet Windy Night,* for example, which anticipates the abundant "goddesses" that would shortly become her principal theme, are among her best work.

We were both busy in our new lives, but we missed Japan and we were missed. I have a letter from Kōbō Abe dated October 4, 1967, that conveys his warmth and unflagging goodwill:

> John:
>
> I'm so sorry you had an unpleasant time in the U.S.S.R. We have just returned and had our own terrible moments. . . . Happily for us, *Woman in the Dunes* has created a sensation there and we benefited richly from that. *The Face of Another* is about to be translated as well. Congratulations on completing your translation of Ōe's novel. Ōe is like a tiger with his prey before him, crouched to spring. People are still talking about your article on Mishima in *Life*. In any event, now that you are gone I am feeling keenly that I have lost a truly valuable friend. It's as if America itself has moved a vast distance away along with you. I must now settle down again and resign myself to life as a bug drenched in ink. Please convey my very best to wonderful Mayumi.
>
> With true friendship from the bottom of my heart,
> Kōbō.

On October 9, 1967, our first child was born in Mt. Sinai Hospital across Central Park. We named him Zachary Tarō. I drove

115

Living Carelessly in Tokyo and Elsewhere

Mayumi and the baby back from the hospital in our VW at five miles an hour, ignoring the horns blaring at us. We laid our swaddled son on the bed and looked down at him in wonder. What now? Experience doesn't alter the joyful bewilderment of that homecoming; I have felt it at the birth of each of my four children. Mayumi silk-screened a birth announcement, a baby boy suspended tranquilly in a starry sky. Ōe sent us an apostrophe to Zachary on a large sheet of mounted rice paper impressed with tracings of silver and gold: "To a man child born into the furor of the Vietnam War—may he thrive."

We were in Tucson with the baby at Christmas when Rosset called from New York with a mission: he wanted me to go to La Paz for a secret meeting with a general who had defected from the Bolivian army. The general had managed to acquire the diary of Che Guevara, who had been killed the day Zachary was born. He had agreed to deliver the manuscript to Grove for publication, bypassing his own government, in exchange for $5,000 in cash. Posing as a professor of Latin American studies, I was to deliver the cash and pick up the diary. Barney was wildly excited; next to court battles, this kind of intrigue was his favorite tonic.

Listening to Barney I had a presentiment of dread, but in the end I acquiesced, and he wired me the $5,000 for the general and an additional $5,000 for tickets and the professorial suit I was to wear as a disguise. The money arrived and I cashed it dutifully. Mayumi was upset; she reminded me that I was not an espionage agent and refused to go with me to shop for a suit. That night I had a horrifying dream. I was walking in a park with Mayumi and Zachary, who was a toddler. A man with a moustache approached and inquired if I were "Señor Nathan." I nodded; he removed a device from his jacket pocket. *Pffft!* A dart embedded in my forehead; my chest constricted as the cyanide took effect. I awoke in a cold sweat and phoned Barney to say I couldn't do it. He was angry; if I hadn't wanted to go I should have said so on the phone. I had cost him precious time, not to mention the expense of wiring a large sum of money. I suppose he was right. But I have never been much good at taking a stand that might diminish me in the eyes of people I admire. In fairness to myself, I should add that the general was under surveillance and was arrested several days later, just before we were supposed to meet. Had I accepted the assignment, I might have ended up in a Bolivian jail. We said nothing more about the matter, but Rosset must have deplored my behavior to Ōe, who referred to it in a letter. "Barney, you have said once 'we must *be present* with the political situation' when you talked me John Nathan's cowardly escaping the chance to visit Bolivia. I recollect the words 'be present there.' I must be present amidst the political winter of Japan, and I must testify everything." I won't deny my cowardice; nonetheless I wince to think of Barney and Ōe joining in judgment about me.

That winter, partly to be closer to Pratt, we moved downtown to a loft on Henry Street, just a block away from the offices of *The Jewish Daily Forward*, where my grandfather had worked. It was a commercial building—we were living there illegally—and the heat was turned off at 6 p.m. To keep ourselves and the baby warm at night we turned on the oven and blew hot air into the loft with a small electric fan. It was hard to concentrate in our unpartitioned loft when Zachary was awake and Mayumi was spending long hours at her lithography press at Pratt, so we hired our first nanny, a devout born-again Jamaican named Rosalee Gromley, a grandmother who lived alone in the Projects east toward the river in a darkened, perfumed apartment that was part voodoo temple and part sacristy, heavily draped with bead curtains and filled with relics that gleamed dully in the candlelight. More than once Zachary spent the night there, sleeping with Rosalee in her bed beneath a portrait of Jesus.

Living Carelessly in Tokyo and Elsewhere

Midmorning she would come to the loft and take him out with her for the day. When we wanted him back I would look for them in Tompkins Square Park or, in the later afternoon, at one of the bars she frequented along the Bowery. I would find Zachary perched on top of the bar in his baby seat, grinning with the attention lavished on him by Rosalee and the barflies who were his fans. I suppose it was reckless of us to entrust the baby's care to Rosalee, but she was adoring and fiercely protective of him, and she managed to make us feel that he was in reliable hands. There were unsettling moments, particularly for Mayumi, who found Rosalee's creole accent incomprehensible. One afternoon I came back from shopping and found her hysterical. Rosalee had brought Zachary home covered from head to foot in yellow grease, glistening like a newly tallowed candle and screaming with discomfort. Mayumi had failed to comprehend a word of Rosalee's explanation, which she repeated to me: "I keep tellin' her, it be lamb fat foh to gentle de chile's fevah!" I deciphered this for Mayumi and she calmed down and gave Zachary a bath in the sink.

I had dropped out of Columbia and was commuting to Princeton three mornings a week to teach my first class in modern Japanese literature. I was also working on last-minute revisions of *A Personal Matter*, which was now finally in page proofs. Ōe's ending troubled me; in a three-page coda that felt appended to the novel, the protagonist, Bird, rescues the brain-damaged infant he has been trying to destroy and transforms into a responsible father and an upright man. The turnaround struck me as abrupt and unconvincing. I expressed my concern in a letter to Ōe and he replied, "The end of *A Personal Matter* elicited the same criticism [in Japan] as in your letter. Please discuss this with Barney; if you are in agreement about the last three pages please feel free to delete them. I have no desire to rewrite the ending. I shall leave the final decision to you and

Barney." How many times since then have I thanked my lucky stars for having had the good sense to leave the book alone! Rereading it over the years I see that the final paragraphs are not as sanguine as they might appear.

Late in May 1968 Grove flew Ōe to New York to help promote the book. For two weeks we met with reviewers every day. Our objective was to direct their attention to the slim volume by an unknown Japanese novelist in the stack of unread books on their desks. To amuse ourselves Ōe and I ordered eggs Benedict every day at lunch at a different restaurant and compared notes; at the end of two weeks we agreed that Sardi's East served the best. Soon enough, we developed an effective routine. At a pause in the stilted table talk about forks and chopsticks or *The Tale of Genji*, I would turn the conversation to an American novel, *Huckleberry Finn* or *The Invisible Man* or *The Adventures of Augie March*. This was Ōe's cue to display his command of American fiction. It made me proud to watch him perform, speaking in his mispronounced but expressive English. By the end of a lunch or a round of drinks at the Black Circle, critics were so dazzled they couldn't wait to get back to the office to read *A Personal Matter*.

The book received enthusiastic reviews everywhere that mattered, with one exception. Writing from Singapore for *The New York Review of Books*, the British poet and Asian traveler D. J. Enright, whom we hadn't met, pounced on Ōe's ending:

> The only thing about *A Personal Matter* that might be said to be "revolutionary" is its happy-as-possible ending. The pity is that this is wholly incongruous; it is simply inconceivable that Bird could turn over so many leaves in the space of the book's last few pages. Even the most avid admirers of the happy ending in fiction will find this one a miserable fraud.

Living Carelessly in Tokyo and Elsewhere

But Enright's nastiness was chaff in a bracing wind of admiration. Our triumph was Eliot Fremont-Smith, the influential reviewer for *The New York Times*. When he showed up at lunch Fremont-Smith seemed distracted, as though wondering why he had come at all, and could scarcely be bothered to ask the usual polite questions. Then the conversation turned to opening lines in great novels; Ōe proposed that first sentences were half the battle and engaged Fremont-Smith in a debate about what Melville had accomplished with "Call me Ishmael." It was clear when we parted that the *Times* reviewer was intrigued; the following week he titled his review in Books of the Times, "Two from Japan—a Curiosity and a Discovery." The "curiosity" was Mishima's *Forbidden Colors*, a variation on the Miss Havisham theme: an aging homosexual novelist uses a handsome homosexual youth as his agent in exacting revenge against womankind. Fremont-Smith wrote, "The step from *Forbidden Colors* to *A Personal Matter* is like emerging from an impossible perfumed hothouse into the clear, real world." He continued: "The book is original, different, tough in its candor and beautiful in its faithfulness to both intellectual precision and human tenderness. We shall be reading more of Ōe—hopefully in as fine a translation as John Nathan here provides. Alone, *A Personal Matter* is something very close to a perfect contemporary novel."

Fremont-Smith's praise was sweet music to us; I won't pretend that our exhilaration, Ōe's and mine, wasn't spiced by the fact that Mishima had fared so badly in the same review. Thinking back, I wonder how Mishima felt. Perhaps the review was of small interest: at the time, June 1968, he was at boot camp with his private army of young nationalists, the Shield Society, already on the road, though no one knew it, to a martyr's death by his own hand.

Home Again

Before Ōe left the country he joined us in East Hampton. Barney had brought along a packet of reviews; we read them aloud at the dinner table and toasted *A Personal Matter* and one another. Ōe got very drunk and proposed other toasts, and we raised our glasses to Mao and Fidel Castro. Barney observed that the dogs, Suki and Yaki, were looking forlorn, so we toasted them too.

7

Summer Soldiers

When we arrived in Tokyo early in July 1968, Ōe and Abe were no longer speaking. I was dumbfounded. Their friendship had been sustaining to both of them and perhaps in particular to Ōe, who was already feeling isolated and subject to fits of despair about his writing and the political situation in Japan, which he viewed as baleful. Neither of them ever spoke to me about their quarrel, but a letter Ōe sent us in March before he came to New York suggests that their estrangement had to do with politics:

> I meet Abe from time to time. Recently, Mishima badgered him into adding his name to a protest about China's Red Guard based on a comical reactionary *humanism*. It was signed by Mishima, Jun Ishikawa, Yasunari Kawabata and Abe. I believe Mishima intended this as an advertisement designed to please Harold Strauss at Knopf. Abe's participation was a blow and deep disappointment to our leftist intellectual community. As someone who loves him, I felt sadness and anger, but I also had to smile. Abe is a good-natured genius. But he doesn't study, and his bizarre

world-view has led him to misunderstand completely what is going on in the outside world. This time he fell into Mishima's ill-intentioned trap. The statement drafted by Mishima was a *laughing matter.*

I tried unavailingly to arrange the kind of evening together we had all enjoyed in the past; I know that Donald Keene was also attempting to mediate. Abe asked me how Ōe was doing, wistfully I thought, but Ōe never said a word. As far as I know, the rift never healed.

Our two months in Japan were hot and listless. Mayumi was trying hard to wean Zachary and was irritated by her mother's doting, permissive approach to the care of her first grandchild. To escape the heat we rented a cottage in Karuizawa and drove there with the family in a vintage Cadillac I borrowed from the director Hiroshi Teshigahara. Riding in the back, Mayumi's mother felt that she was being chauffeured by a New York gangster. It was the first, but not the last time I have been likened to a mafioso. Teshigahara's father had used the car as his chauffeured limousine, but it had been retired to the garage for years. When I picked it up it was scratch-free and shiny from weekly feather dustings by the devoted drivers in the family's employ. I returned it ten days later looking like a battered stovepipe, with incinerated brakes: it was a behemoth of a vehicle, much too large for an amateur driver on Japan's twisting, narrow roadways. Teshigahara must have been appalled as I rattled the car into his garage, but he was a generous man and said nothing.

In September 1968 we moved to Cambridge. I had been appointed a junior fellow in the Society of Fellows at Harvard. Professor Reischauer had nominated me, and I had subjected myself to the interview in March. I sat in a chair facing an intimidating semicircle of senior fellows, professors in the humanities and sciences who grilled me for an hour about my study plans. I was proposing a comparison of narrative persona in Japanese, French, and American fiction. Someone, possibly Ruben Brower, the crankily fastidious reader of Robert Frost, asked whether I had considered learning Russian, in order to extend my critical reach to the Russian novel. I believe I replied off-handedly that I was determined to learn German and hoped to acquire Russian as well if time permitted.

The Society of Fellows had been endowed in 1933 as a *jardin potager* for Harvard faculty. The appointment was for three years at a stipend equivalent to an assistant professor's salary (today it pays $56,000). Additional funds were available for travel and research, including the acquisition of a library, and there seemed to be no limit on what you could spend. (The elders balked only once during my tenure, when a composer named Peter Winkler who was comparing the Beatles and Mozart submitted a bill for hundreds of records.) Junior fellows, men only in my day, were discouraged from teaching or taking classes; our only obligation, when we were in town, was to attend the weekly Monday night dinner in a private dining room in Eliot House. There was little small talk at these cerebral evenings. Among the dozen or so senior fellows who showed up regularly were James Watson, the double-helix man; Paul Doty, a Nobel laureate in chemistry who traveled in celebrity circles and brought Shirley MacLaine to dinner more than once; Judge Charles Wyzanski Jr. of the Sixth District Court; the constitutional law scholar Paul Freund; a Nobel laureate in physics named Edward Purcell; and Willard Van Orman Quine, revered as the father of mathematical logic. Curious and erudite, Quine could stump any one of us with questions in our own field. One evening at sherry before dinner he asked for my help in clearing up something that had been troubling him: Why was it, he wondered, that the suffix *maru*, written with the character for "circle," was appended to the names of Japanese ships? I admitted I had no idea and confess that if Quine's genial ghost appeared before me today with the same intriguing question I would still have to plead ignorance.

Away from the dinner table I spent little time with the other junior fellows in my group, which included an economist, two cellular biologists, a theoretical physicist, an architect, a city planner, and a Byzantium scholar. Then there was Joel Cohen, a baby genius and terrifying polymath who was at work on a comparative study of the dynamics of community in microbes, monkeys, and native islanders. Cohen was an accomplished harpsichordist; one day he inquired of me whether I could sight-read Handel trio sonatas *at tempo* on my alto recorder. I thought I could and we tried, with a cellist friend of Cohen's playing the viola da gamba part. I managed to keep up, and for several months we met on Saturday afternoons to play through the trio repertory. I let my music lapse decades ago but I imagine that Cohen, a long-standing professor at Rockefeller University, continues to play.

I made one close friend in the society, Terrence Des Pres. Terrence had grown up in the back woods of Missouri, the son of a fire-breathing preacher who had moved the family year after year in his Studebaker jalopy from one rural congregation to the next. He had studied philosophy at Washington University in St. Louis and was working on a book that stands today as a classic in Holocaust literature, *The Survivor: An Anatomy of Life in the Death Camps*. Terrence and I were united by an outsider's ironic view of the society's self-seriousness. Monday nights, when it was time for dinner, we sat together at the far end of the kidney-shaped table, outside the flux of discourse, and exchanged sardonic remarks about the youthful prodigies holding forth while we savored the excellent wine Terrence had chosen as the society's designated sommelier. Occasionally, the society chairman, the economist and Nobel laureate Wassily

Leontief, would summon us to the center of the table: "Gentlemen," he would call out in his heavy Russian accent, "would you mind favoring us briefly with some of your recent and no doubt provocative thinking about your work?" As we were both showmen we acquitted ourselves plausibly at these command performances, which we referred to privately as singing for our suppers.

I don't know if I realized at the time that what held us apart from the others and drew us toward each other was a fear of taking ourselves seriously. Terrence hid his erudition and the sophistication of his wonderful mind beneath sardonics and self-disparagement and a hillbilly befuddlement about the world that he affected disarmingly; in truth there was nothing naïve about him. Nor was he the insouciant rake he appeared to be; recalling our time together, I am aware of the darkness that was already building inside him beneath his apparent joviality. I suppose a source of the darkness was the subject that gripped his imagination; the philosophy of survival. In 1973, the year after we moved to Princeton, Terrence came to interview for a teaching post in the Philosophy Department and was unaccountably—unimaginably—rejected. He was crushed and very bitter and exiled himself to a job at Colgate College in rural upstate New York. There he became a venerated teacher whose course on the literature of the Holocaust drew hundreds of students every year. But his isolation deepened. In 1987 he killed himself. I had heard from him occasionally and had often thought to visit him but never got around to it. I wish I had.

Our first year in Cambridge, I was preparing to take oral examinations for a doctorate in Far Eastern languages. The status the society conferred allowed me to place myself in candidacy for a PhD without having attended graduate school. The general examination comprised four fields; I elected classical and modern Japanese literature, Japanese history to 1868, and the English novel. I worked at the Japanese fields desultorily, reading my way through a list of books several afternoons a week in my study at Adams House. Reading the English novel with William Alfred as my tutor was the most inspiring academic experience of my life. Alfred's verse play about Irish American life in the 1920s, *Hogan's Goat*, had just completed an extended run on Broadway; his annual course on *Beowulf*, lectures he delivered to rapt students in the paneled amphitheater in Memorial Hall, was a jewel in Harvard's diadem of once-in-a-lifetime experiences. He held his tutorial sessions in his study in the small house on Athens Street in workingman's Cambridge, where he lived his bachelor life. There I sat with him one afternoon a week drinking the tea he served me on a small tray and discussing the English novel from Defoe to Iris Murdoch. (Alfred was a passionate Catholic who went to Mass every morning at St. Paul's Cathedral.) We were frequently interrupted; his door was always open to people in the neighborhood, poor people it appeared, who needed him. I remember a small boy in particular who stored his shoe-shine kit beneath his desk and was constantly in and out to fetch or replace it. When we got to *Dubliners* and *Portrait of the Artist* late in the spring, Alfred read me passages aloud in a full-throttled Irish brogue to allow me to hear the music of Joyce's language. At our last session before the general examination he suggested with a twinkle in his eye that I think about the function of time in George Eliot and, in particular, in *Middlemarch*. When it was his turn to interrogate me that was the question he posed. The two-hour exam was painless and even pleasurable: it felt like a chat about subjects of mutual interest with elders, including my former professor, Howard Hibbett, who had already accepted me as one of their own. That at least was what I chose to feel.

Mayumi was working hard at her art and discovering the feminist in herself. She built a print studio in the basement of our rented house on Hancock Street and rushed downstairs to work whenever the baby took a nap. Her sister, Hiromi, had come to live with us that year, and she helped with the house and took Zachary down the street to the park, but it was hard for Mayumi to find the time she needed, harder, I fear, than I realized. In New York she had made etchings and lithographs, but now she turned to silkscreen and was beginning to create the naked, full-figured goddesses that have been her subject ever since. In November 1968 she held her first one-woman show, in the Senior Common Room at Adams House. The centerpiece was her first *Goddess Calendar*, a dozen goddesses, one for each month, installed in 12"-by-18" silkscreen prints, majestic or comic or lascivious against backgrounds she developed from traditional Japanese seasonal motifs. Her work was well received by the community; she sold every print on the wall, and Henry Rosovsky's wife, Nitza, and her partner, Linda Abegglen, offered to represent her in their new gallery. In the space of a few days Mayumi became an established Cambridge artist, and before we left Cambridge her work hung in galleries in New York, Cleveland, and Tokyo as well.

Our closest friends were Alan and Pamela Berger, a couple who had married just after graduation, whom I had known well during our undergraduate days. They lived around the corner on Merril Street in a two-story walk-up apartment that Mayumi had found for them while they were away in France (and where they live to this day). Alan was an aspiring novelist who had been a graduate student of Paul de Man's; a New Yorker who had come to Harvard from Fieldston, he wore a signet ring on his left pinky, smoked cigars in the privacy of his attic study, and went to the racetrack every Saturday afternoon. Pamela was an art historian and an obdurate feminist who was a member of the team of women who edited *Our Bodies, Ourselves*. It was Pamela who opened the book of feminism for

Summer Soldiers

Mayumi, who read its pages hungrily and began to discover the fiercely independent and often resentful woman in herself. I felt proud of her growing dissatisfaction even as I observed it with concern. Together with the Bergers we marched in Cambridge and in Boston against the Vietnam War.

There was more in the air in those days than opposition to Vietnam; the shibboleth among the hip was "Let it all hang out!" This call to internal emancipation threatened me. I had no idea what "it" was that I was meant to be hanging out; even if I had been in touch with my deepest feelings I was committed to the dissimulation that was my family's legacy. Mayumi's family was also in some ways repressive, but Mayumi turned out to be a natural-born free spirit. The Zeitgeist beckoned her and she responded with the same exuberance that radiated from her exultant goddesses. I remember a performance we attended with the Bergers by the Living Theater, a company of revolutionary ecstatics led by Julian Beck and Judith Molina, looming figures in the acid subculture. The players invaded the audience and shouted abuse in our faces as an incitement to freeing our minds. Mayumi threw her arms around the experience with a passion that was clearly awakening something in her. I remember experiencing a sinking of the heart as I realized that my beautiful and talented wife was preparing to take flight with wings I didn't have. I am sure that the performance that night in Cambridge in the winter of 1969 was the beginning of a shift beneath our feet that would split us apart ten years later.

I have a disturbing memory from that time that suggests to me that things between us were already awry. Our second son, Jeremiah Jirō, was born at Cambridge Hospital on December 11, 1970. New Year's Eve, Terrence came to the house with some horse capsules containing "organic" mescaline. Mayumi abstained because she was nursing the baby. Terrence and I got high and sat at our dining table watching a candle flame attenuate toward the ceiling in a spindle of light. Before midnight we left the house and tiptoed across a white blanket of fresh snow to the Orson Welles Theater on Massachusetts Avenue. The theater had opened its doors to the community for a New Year's Eve event, a psychedelic sound and light show that was both ahead of its time and attuned to the sensibility of the moment. As we watched and listened in a blissful trance, quart bottles of soda that almost certainly were laced with LSD were passed down the rows from seat to seat. Remembering my ordeal at the Rossets' country retreat I passed the bottle along without drinking from it, but the mescaline was still active in my brain and the contact high was stroboscopic. The importance to me of this episode is not its details but the fact that I left my wife and infant son on New Year's Eve in search of diversion outside the family. Recalling the moment, I wonder how I could have been so focused on myself. I can't help feeling that the carelessness I perceive in myself that evening has been a determinant of my life's course.

In the fall of 1969 Grove Press forwarded to me a bid for an option on *A Personal Matter* and a film treatment from Burt Lancaster Productions. The treatment was a plodding, literal rehash of the book's plot. Reading it, I stepped effortlessly into a fantasy so full-blown it must have been waiting in a corner of my imagination to be summoned forth. I would write a screenplay and direct the film myself: I would become a Hollywood auteur. I asked Grove to turn down the offer—Ōe had appointed me his representative for film rights—and began to work on my own adaptation. I transposed the story from Tokyo to Cambridge and Boston. Bird's reality, his wife and newborn baby with a damaged brain, were in a Cambridge hospital; his escape into fantasy beckoned to him from his lover's apartment on Beacon Hill across the Charles River. I added scenes between Bird and his wife and expanded the role of the drag queen who entices Bird momentarily in the first chapter of the novel.

I worked obsessively on the script all winter. I was possessed by film fever and the fever burned away my intention to produce a magnum opus on narrative modes in fiction. One Monday evening after dinner, Leontief informed me that a screenwriter from Yale had been nominated for the society. I inquired about his chances. "None whatsoever!" he replied with an emphatic shake of his head. "First junior fellow, then butterfly—never other way around!"

Leontief's innuendo bounced off me and I continued writing. I spent six months on a draft and sent it to a few people I knew in the film business. The writer-director Abraham Polonsky, an enfant terrible in Hollywood until he was blacklisted in the McCarthy era, urged me to press ahead. "It's a good story, full of intriguing twists and turns," he wrote. "In any event it will break apart like Humpty-Dumpty when you begin to film it and you'll have to piece it together again. Congratulations and condolences. I always feared you would come to no good, and now I see you have fallen all the way down to making movies. I welcome you to our lamentable brotherhood." I also sent the script to Arthur Miller's agent, Kay Brown, whom I had met in Tokyo when Miller and his wife were there visiting Kōbō Abe. Kay claimed to be "excited" by the script and promised to send it on to her West Coast office to see whether they would represent me. The script ended up in the hands of Howard Hausman, a senior agent at William Morris in New York. Hausman was an early film packager with a reputation for getting a film produced by assembling a team from among his clients, who included directors, writers, and stars. Like every player in the film business I have known, he had his own act: when I was shown into his office he was always in choleric conversation on the phone. "I don't care what Dustin says, Meryl is right for that part," he would be shouting, gesturing at me to take a seat, or "If Barbra says her hairdresser has to direct, that's how it has to be. With her ego she'll have him in a body bag the minute he screws up." For half a year I was in his office frequently; this pattern was so invariable I began to suspect he was yelling into a dead phone to impress me, though I couldn't imagine why he would go to the trouble.

At our first meeting he said he thought the script was produceable but not with me in the package as director. I surprised myself by assuring him that Hiroshi Teshigahara was interested and wondered if he would do. Until that moment the thought of approaching Teshigahara had never occurred to me, and I had no reason to suppose I could enroll him. But Hausman grew visibly excited; he considered *Woman in the Dunes* a spectacular film. If Teshigahara came on board he thought the project might fly.

In mid-April we returned to Tokyo, intending to stay through the summer. I called Teshigahara's office and learned that he and his wife were in traction in the hospital: he had slammed his BMW into the back of a truck at ninety miles an hour on the freeway heading north to Sendai. I visited him at his bedside and explained the project and what Hausman had said. He knew Ōe's novel and was enthusiastic about collaborating with me to turn it into a film. He asked for a treatment in Japanese and I prepared one for him.

I hesitate to spatchcock my sister's death into an account of my first film folly. But it occurred just at this time, and it is here, linked to the events I am recounting, that it resides darkly in my memory. One night in May I returned drunkenly to the Kyōdō house after a night on the town and found Mayumi waiting up for me, though it was well past midnight. "Something terrible has happened," she said grimly in Japanese and handed me a letter from Tucson. It was from my mother and had been five days in transit. For years, decades, her note haunted me, turning up at the back of desk drawers I emptied as we moved from one house to the next until finally I managed to lose it. But I can still see her handwritten words on the folded sheet of paper:

May 22, 1970

Dearest Nick [my family nickname]:

Tragedy struck us today. Nancy was shot and killed by a madman. We shall try to raise the children as well as we can. You needn't come.

Love, Mom.

These words numbed me as though a drug had entered my veins, but even then I wondered why my mother had chosen to write instead of calling on the phone or at least sending a cable. And what did she mean, "You needn't come"? This shocked me at the time, and confounds and appalls me now as I reflect on it. Was she hoping I would stay away because she feared I would find her in the grip of emotions she could not suppress in her usual way? As I never asked her for an explanation while she was alive, this will remain one of our troubling family mysteries.

I called home and got my mother on the phone. I learned that Nancy had been driving to Mexico with her two children, Jacob and Natasha, four and two years old at the time. On a desolate stretch of highway just past a truck stop called Five Corners, the killer had pulled alongside her and fired a bullet through the window into her neck. Her car had swerved off the road and rolled down into a shallow ravine; the killer had parked his car, walked down to the ravine and shot her again. He hadn't harmed the children; they were found wandering in the desert by Mexican *vaqueros* on horseback. My mother's account on

133

the phone was flat; I adjusted my own listening and responses to the impassivity that was our default mode of communication—what passed for communication—about all things.

For several days I wandered vacantly around the Kyōdō house, which was suddenly empty. In fact, Mayumi's family was there, all seven of them living under one roof, but somehow they managed to stay completely out of my way. I was aware of the Japanese gift for allowing privacy in close quarters, but the Odas' disappearing act was the most dramatic example I have ever experienced. Mayumi stayed close by; I could feel her supportive presence, but even she was reticent and withdrawn.

I prepared for my trip to the United States by cutting my tangled hair short; I was afraid of attracting attention to myself. Nancy had drawn someone's attention and had paid for it with her life. The violence of the remorseless desert where I had grown up, palpable in the shimmering heat, renewed itself in my memory as a sensation of terror. On the JAL flight to Los Angeles I felt grimly resigned: I was flying back across the Pacific Ocean to a land of death.

When I arrived at the house in the desert where I had grown up I hugged my mother and father wordlessly. There were no tears and no one spoke about Nancy or what had happened; my family didn't know how to mourn. The next day I saw my father cry for the first and only time; abruptly tears burst from ducts behind his eyes and flooded down his face. "You're hysterical!" my mother scolded as though angry. Could not she allow him his grief or say something comforting? And what was she feeling? There was no telling; perhaps she was as disconnected from her pain as I was from mine.

The killer was still at large, and the local paper had reported that the children, the only witnesses, were staying with their grandparents and had disclosed their address. My parents were afraid to remain in town; I loaded them into our car and drove the family to Los Angeles. It was a nightmarish trip: every time a green pickup truck passed us on the road the children became hysterical and threw themselves to the floor. We had arranged to stay at the Bel-Air home of my mother's cousin. The killer was apprehended a week later, convicted of three murders and given consecutive life sentences.

I had film business in Los Angeles. An actor friend named Paul Price who had lived above us on Ninety-sixth Street had read my script and taken it to an acquaintance of his in the movie business, Rudy England. Paul and Rudy wanted to produce the film together and were assuring me they could raise the money. Rudy was no more a producer than Paul, but he had worked as a production manager on two films and knew enough about the business to talk a plausible game. He was a determined and charming huckster, younger looking than his thirty years, like an Eton schoolboy, poor in experience but rich in shtick: in New York he drove around in an old yellow schoolbus that he had fitted out with velvet seats.

Rudy had flown to L.A. to work out the details of a production agreement with me, and we arranged to meet in front of Tower Records on Sunset. He drove up in a rented Mercedes convertible—I suppose he couldn't find a schoolbus—with three suntanned chickadees in the back seat to whom he had touted me as a hot screenwriter on the way up. He proposed breezily that we combine business and—with a leering wink at me and a nod at the girls—pleasure, and asked me to follow him in my car. We drove into the Hollywood hills, through a wooden gate that one of the girls unlocked with a key, and down an unpaved service road past palm trees and dazzling bougainvillea hedges to a small cottage. It was sparsely furnished and appeared to be uninhabited. The girls spread a beach blanket on the wooden floor and laid out a picnic of wine and deli sandwiches. Rudy rolled a fat joint and passed it around. I should have known

135

better than to smoke in my condition; even under clear skies I felt apprehensive when I got high. But I was eager to break away from my reality that day, and the scene in the cottage with Rudy and his companions was already so unreal it inspired me to recklessness and I dragged deeply on the joint. I don't think we had touched the food when the girl with the key moved to a window and said, turning toward me, "Do you know where we are?" I must have known before she answered her own question: I felt myself submerging in icy water. "This is Sharon Tate's place; the main house is over there." The space in the room seemed to shift; I could see Rudy and the girls observing with dismay what must have been the horror on my face, but I was alone in a cavern and creatures with gnashing teeth were wheeling above my head, winged bats or black buzzards of death. I stood up and bolted from the cottage without a word and drove away with my demons in pursuit. I got lost in those hills for what seemed like hours. By the time I emerged on Sunset and drove back to Bel Air the sun was setting.

A few days later Mayumi arrived from Tokyo with Zachary and we all sat down for a family meeting at the pool of the Bel Air house. My parents asked if we would take the children if they turned out to be more than they could handle. Their father, a Canadian journalist who was a drunkard and an epileptic, had abandoned Nancy and their infant son, Jacob, and disappeared into Canada without a trace; Natasha had been born in my parents' house. Speaking to me in Japanese, Mayumi said she was unwilling to accept the responsibility. We had one small child and our second was on the way; she wanted time to devote to her art and raising our own children was all she could manage.

"Why is she speaking in Japanese?" my father demanded to know.

I would have taken the children even then, but I felt I had to honor Mayumi's feelings and so I covered for her. I explained that our circumstances prevented us from making any promises about my nephew and niece but assured my mother and father that if they became ill or died, we would not allow them to grow up in a foster home. To this day I regret not having taken a stand about the children in spite of Mayumi's opposition. Taking them on as our own would have been the right thing to do. Though we never spoke of this again, the wound it inflicted on the family, unattended, never healed.

That summer we fled to Europe. Home again in late August, I optioned the film rights to Ōe's novel from Grove Press for a token $1,000 of my own money and secured a letter of intent from Teshigahara, who agreed to work for a salary of $1,000 a week not to exceed fifteen weeks, principal photography to begin "on or about June 1, 1971." I exchanged long letters with Price and England about production details and even devoted weeks to preparing a budget in spite of my ignorance of the process; it added up to a grand total of $405,000 to produce the film (including a 15 percent contingency to cover overages!). I was in earnest and failed to see that this preoccupation in advance of any leads to money was misbegotten. That fall I received a visit at home from James Ivory's producer, Ismail Merchant, who expressed interest in acquiring the property. Our meeting was a disaster: for some reason I had gotten stoned before he arrived (I ask the reader to believe me when I avow that my smoking was infrequent, however poorly timed), and I found that the dope left me unable to move a muscle and aphasic. Merchant, elegantly mannered and spoken, must have thought he was encountering a madman and hurried out after thirty minutes. In any event, I was too intent on my fantasy of collaborating with Teshigahara to have accommodated him. Briefly Mayumi and I were also wined and dined in New York by a wealthy rug merchant named Joseph Saleh who was contemplating a move into the film business—I remember a dinner at Le Cirque—but he must have changed his mind about my script and disappeared from sight.

Around Thanksgiving Howard Hausman called from New York to say he had found an investor, Joseph Levine, a mogul who had made a fortune acquiring movie theaters all over the East Coast. Hausman wanted Teshigahara in New York, and he flew in a few days later. We had a meeting with a cameraman Hausman felt would be perfect for the film, Victor Kemper, who had admired *Woman in the Dunes* and was excited about working on the project, and we were introduced to a young line producer with a track record, Roger Rothstein. Rothstein walked into Hausman's office and exclaimed, with a gesture of his signet-ring-fingered hand in our direction. "We'll need a million dollars apiece of key-man life insurance on these guys!" Somehow, miraculously, it was all starting to feel real, though we had yet to meet our angel Levine. It turned out he was only considering putting up the money, but Hausman was confident he was hooked. I was behaving insufferably, smoking little Dutch cigars from a tin and dragging Mayumi to Mercedes Benz showrooms.

Teshigahara was still in New York when the mirage vanished; rereading the screenplay, Joe Levine had decided it was too dark to make a successful film. Hausman went cold and stopped taking my calls. I was devastated; I had devoted a full year to the project and had nothing to show for it but an unproduced screenplay. Teshigahara was also despondent. As I drove him to the airport, we discussed briefly a very different film, about American deserters from Vietnam hiding out in Japan. I don't remember who brought it up, but I think it was me.

On November 25, 1970, Yukio Mishima stunned Japan by committing *hara-kiri* following an appeal to troops in the Self-Defense Force to join him in an imperial restoration. Like many others in and outside the country who felt they had known him, I was shocked and bewildered. Shortly after the incident, which was headline news in newspapers around the world, Professor Reischauer urged me to consider writing Mishima's biography; he said he had never understood Mishima and could think of no one better equipped than I to elucidate the mystery of his life. Reischauer's encouragement inspired me to write a proposal for a book. I showed it to an associate of Kay Brown, Phyllis Jackson, whose most famous client was Dr. Seuss (Theodore Geisel), and she quickly sold the book to Little, Brown.

Near the end of February, Teshigahara called from Tokyo to say that he had secured funding for the film we had discussed briefly as he was leaving New York and wanted me to come to Tokyo to research and write the screenplay. Since the story would be focused on American soldiers, he would be counting on me to help him direct. Mayumi was agreeable to going; she had been in correspondence with a Tokyo gallery owner named Yoshii about a major show of her silkscreen prints, her first in Japan. In mid-April we packed up and left Cambridge with Zachary and baby Jeremiah. The contract with Little, Brown was waiting for me in Tucson, where we stopped on the way; Phyllis had negotiated a kingly advance of $12,500. The deadline in the contract, which I extended twice, was October 1, 1972.

Summer Soldiers—the title, a gift from my friend Marilyn Young, was lifted from Thomas Paine's invective against deserters— was based on actual events. For several years a group of Marxist intellectuals calling themselves the Peace in Vietnam League, Beheiren in Japanese, had been picking up GIs who were AWOL in Japan and shuttling them every week or two via an underground railway from one Japanese family to the next. The host families were upright citizens opposed to the war who considered themselves warriors in what they referred to, in English, as "the Movement." The deserters were viewed as young revolutionaries in the making; the idea was to find them jobs so they could support themselves, assimilated in Japanese society, while speaking out against the war. The operation was enabled by an agreement between U.S. forces in Japan and the Japanese government that prohibited the Japanese police from arresting American GIs who had left their bases.

The league's lofty vision turned out to be a pipe dream. The uneducated, traumatized soldiers on the lam found themselves in a world they were unequipped to understand; in most cases their political convictions were not sufficiently developed to help them withstand the ordeal. Some stole from their host families, others came on aggressively to wives and daughters—there were incidents of rape. Bewildered and lonely, many ran away from the haven they had been provided and turned themselves in within thirty days, before they could be court-martialed for desertion.

By the time we arrived in Tokyo, the Peace in Vietnam League had shifted focus, from harboring deserters to counseling GI dissidents on the base about applying for conscientious objector status. But they had kept journals and hundreds of hours of taped screening interviews that were made available to us by Yoshiyuki Tsurumi, the Leftist historian who was the Movement's principal ideologue. At our first meeting at Teshigahara Productions, Tsurumi introduced us to a young married couple, Ken and Junko Tsukasa (they later told us their real name was Yamada; everyone had at least one code name), students at Tōdai who had spent six disheartening months looking after a deserter named Alan, code name Jim Hatakeyama. Alan had broken all the rules, clowning conspicuously in the streets of Tokyo, bringing home girls he picked up in bars, and quitting the job they had found for him at an auto mechanics shop after the first week. The Yamadas had come to feel that Alan was vain and selfish and a dissembler, pretending to be against the war to manipulate his hosts and protectors; when he finally disappeared from sight with a girl he had met at the Kamakura train station, they dropped out of the movement in disillusionment. I modeled my protagonist on Alan.

For a month, accompanied by Ken and Junko and a gentle, warm-hearted stoner in rings and beads named Nori Tanaka, I interviewed former host families in Tokyo and Kyoto, sat in long sessions with grown-ups from the league, and listened to sad stories told by girlfriends the GIs had picked up and discarded as they traversed Japan.

I traveled alone to the Marine Corps Air Station in Iwakuni, a feudal town on the Inland Sea thirty miles southeast of Hiroshima. The fourteen-hundred-acre base was the doorway to a fugitive life for a number of the GIs whose stories I was tracking. The base itself was off-limits, but there was plenty to see and hear in the bars and eateries, pawn shops and strip joints that lined the unpaved roads just outside the gates.

During the month I devoted to uncovering material for the film, Teshigahara accompanied me infrequently; when he did drop in he was often distracted. This was partly due to his limited English, which required me to interpret for him. But I soon realized that he was preoccupied with what he referred to sourly as the "flower business."

In 1927, the year he was born, Teshigahara's father, Sōfū, founded a new school of *ikebana* he named Sōgetsu (grass/moon). The Sōgetsu School blossomed gorgeously all over Japan; thousands of young women preparing to become accomplished wives by acquiring the art of *ikebana* paid for lessons with local Sōgetsu instructors (who had paid the school to be licensed), subscribed to the monthly Sōgetsu magazine, and attended exhibitions of Sōfū's recent creations at department stores across Japan. Revenue rose up the pyramid to the founding grand master at its apex and made Sōfū a wealthy man. (The year before we began work on the film, 1970, the Tax Bureau had fined him $2 million for neglecting to add the value of several Picasso paintings to his net worth.)

Hiroshi Teshigahara grew up in the elegant environment Sōfū created, surrounded by beauty and cosseted by maids and retainers who served his father and referred to him as "the young master." As Sōfū's first-born child and eldest son, he was expected to succeed his father as grand master; from childhood, he was taught to appreciate not only flowers but painting and ceramics and calligraphy. In 1950 he graduated from the National University of Fine Arts and Music, Mayumi's alma mater, where he had studied painting and become an accomplished potter. After graduation, resisting pressure from the family to work at Sōgetsu, he apprenticed himself to the avant-garde sculptor and painter Tarō Okamoto, who had studied with Arp and Mondrian in Paris in the 1930s. In 1959 he went to New York with a wind-up 16 mm Bell and Howell and shot his first film, a kinetically vivid documentary portrait of a Puerto Rican prizefighter named Jose Torres who was briefly a hero of the Peoples' Rights Movement and was championed by a gang of New York writers led by Norman Mailer. In 1962 Teshigahara directed a surreal tale of murder and ghostly possession written for him by his friend and mine, Kōbō Abe, with a score by another member of their modernist coterie, Tōru Takemitsu; *Pitfall* was awarded the NHK New Director's Prize. In 1964, Teshigahara made *Woman in the Dunes* from a script adapted for him by Abe from his novel of the same title. The film was awarded the Special Jury Prize at Cannes and was nominated by the Academy of Motion Pictures for best foreign film, establishing Teshigahara in the eyes of Western critics as an important director. He sub-

142

sequently filmed the second and third volumes of Abe's trilogy from adaptations by Abe, but neither film had the graphic brilliance or the dramatic tension of *Woman in the Dunes*.

Teshigahara was determined not to accept the crown of his father's kingdom, but if he hoped to demonstrate to his family that he had found a worthy métier he needed a new film to direct. By the time I asked him to collaborate on *A Personal Matter*, he had been in search of a new project for close to three years. In *Summer Soldiers* he foresaw the promise of a fresh start: Americans clashing with Japanese, largely in English, in a documentary style that would thrust the unvarnished reality in the viewer's face.

Early in May, with a briefcase stuffed with tapes and notes, I incarcerated myself in a room in the New Japan Hotel in Akasaka, leaving Mayumi and the children with her family in the Kyōdō house. This variety of self-exile, "canning" in Japanese, as in canned peaches, was common practice among Japanese writers who were working against deadlines (I have cited Mishima's letter to me from "the Imperial Jail"). I stayed in my room through the interminable summer, for the better part of four months. Teshigahara showed up occasionally to drop off expensive melons and grapes and a bottle of Johnny Walker Black and to inquire about my progress with an uneasy smile. But I saw little of him or anyone else; the idea, and his expectation, was that I would work around the clock without distraction. In truth, I wasted many hours prowling the lobby and wandering down bar-lined streets in the middle of the night.

It took me a month to outline a story in eighty scenes; by the end of June I had a draft of a script. I wrote in English, typing out the Japanese dialogue in roman letter transliteration. As I worked, Yoshiyuki Tsurumi translated the script into Japanese but returned his pages to me; I wanted Teshigahara to read the draft when it was completed. I see by my pocket calendar for that year that I delivered it into his hands on June 30, and that we celebrated with a costly, delicious meal at Kittchō. He called me at home the next day to say the draft was interesting but too talky and not visual enough. I asked if he wanted to meet to discuss the script in detail but he was on his way to Kyoto and preferred to leave revisions to me. I returned to my hotel room and finished a second draft on July 20, less didactic perhaps and more visual. This time I had to wait a week until Teshigahara called to ask me to join him for a working session at his summer house on Lake Yamanaka. We drove there the next day with the producer Yukio Tomizawa and an assistant director named Osawa who had been with Teshigahara on all his films since *Pitfall*. The house was large and luxurious. We sat down in an airy room with windows that looked across the lake toward Mount Fuji; Osawa began pinning numbered scene cards in order to the white wall. I watched, speechless: Teshigahara had unraveled my story, transposing the order of my scenes as though randomly, omitting some that I considered crucial and adding scenes of his own that were like daydreams with no bearing on the plot. Worst of all, the scene cards trailed off in the middle of a story that seemed to be heading nowhere. Osawa sat down grimly and we all stared in silence at what was literally the handwriting on the wall. Finally, Teshigahara asked me what I thought. I said I didn't know what to think because I couldn't imagine how the film would proceed from where he had left it. "That's your job to figure out," was all he said.

We argued for two days and nights, never leaving that beautiful house. Breakfast, lunch, and dinner we ate canned sausages and cabbage over rice, apparently the only meal Osawa knew how to prepare. It became clear that Teshigahara and I had different films in mind. I was committed to the documentary realism we had discussed; I wanted to reveal my characters as complex, sympathetic individuals by grounding the story in the details of their fugitive lives. Teshigahara was halted in the shadow of Kōbō Abe's influence: he wanted an allegory, a film about the deserter in every man. His own life had accustomed him to deference; when crossed he withdrew into himself sullenly. There were long intervals of silence broken only by the incessant click-clack of Tomizawa's cigarette lighter as he thumbed it nervously open and shut. The night before we left, as he lay down on the bed next to mine in the guest bedroom we shared, Tomizawa expelled a long breath, a sigh of hopelessness.

I went back to work in my hotel room. I was angry and offended, and I felt sorry for myself, but I could hardly walk away and lose what I wanted most, a chance to participate in an actual production. I revised furiously, resigned to making whatever compromises were necessary to accommodate Teshigahara. The first week in August, he phoned from New York to report that he and Tomizawa had found a young actor named Greg Antonacci to play the Puerto Rican character, Jose Arakawa, and a singer and songwriter from Memphis, Keith Sykes, who was "perfect" for the lead. He sounded very excited on the phone, and his enthusiasm lifted my spirits and gave me the energy I needed to finish the new script. Back in Tokyo, Teshigahara read and approved it.

A few days later I was working with Tsurumi when Teshigahara showed up at the New Japan to say he had decided, on rereading the script, that he was uncomfortable with the middle. I know it was August 21, a Saturday, because the word "Agony!" with an exclamation point is scrawled in pencil on that date in my calendar. But there was no turning back now; Teshigahara had retained Keith Sykes for nine weeks for $1,800 and expenses, and he was due to arrive in Tokyo on September 1. Fuming, and lacking the confidence to stand my ground, I agreed to attempt a final rewrite.

Living Carelessly in Tokyo and Elsewhere

As I worked I was furious at myself. Was I an utter fool, without talent, to have failed so consistently to engage Teshigahara's imagination and secure his approval? Three scripts sweated out through the summer and now the possibility—it did seem to me that night to be a possibility—that the project might be abandoned at the last moment. If that happened I felt certain it would signify one thing only: that my inadequacy had been exposed.

We began shooting—the Japanese use a fractured English term, "cranking in"—on September 3 in Tokyo, then went on the road to Kyoto and Kobe and finally, exhausted, finished in Iwakuni, where the story began and ended in the second week of November. Though we had agreed that little-known actors or even amateurs in the Japanese roles would help create the documentary feeling we were aiming for, Teshigahara had assembled a cast of stars whose familiar presence in the film had the contrary effect: Tetsuko Kuroyanagi, today a best-selling author and host of her own talk show who was already on her way to becoming the Barbara Walters of Japan; Hideo Kanze, the apostate "young master" of the most famous school of Noh; Tamao Nakamura, daughter of the Kabuki actor Ganjirō Nakamura and married to Shintarō Katsu; and others. He did make one brilliant casting choice: Reisen Lee as the bar girl Reiko who harbors the lead deserter in Iwakuni. Lee was married to the playwright Jūrō Kara and was his leading lady in the wildly imagined, anti-American plays he staged in his Red Tent Theater. An ethnic Korean who had survived poverty and discrimination growing up in Japan, she was a fiercely individual and courageous actress. She spoke no English but memorized the broken GI-speak I wrote for her and performed it authentically, intimidating Sykes in a way that made his subservience to her in the film believable.

Summer Soldiers

Keith Sykes was a country boy who seemed to be as bewildered to find himself in Japan as the deserter he was playing. He was well-intentioned and charming in a diffident way that was right for the part, but I sensed right away that he had plenty of attitude as well and would require careful handling, an unpleasant job I knew would fall to me. The story I have told myself and represented to others about *Summer Soldiers* is that I directed the scenes in English, which made up 80 percent of the film. There must have been a degree of truth in this: shortly before he died of leukemia in 2001, Teshigahara had my film credit changed from "Original screenplay" to "Written and co-directed by John Nathan." But the pages of the intermittent journal I kept during the first month of filming make no reference to my work as a director. Instead, they reveal my discontent, verging on bitterness, at feeling less important to the process than I wished to be. I believe the disappointment that led me to be unsparingly critical of Teshigahara was primed by unrealistic expectations. And I suspect that the aloofness in him that infuriated me was his response to my looming presence on the set, waiting indignantly for him to ask for my input while I silently condemned every choice he made. If there is arrogance in my observations and complaints there is also an abjectness that troubles me. Striving, and failing, to feel superior, I tumble into despair about myself, which blinds me to what I have achieved and prevents me from finding any pleasure in it.

Sunday, Sept. 5
I'm thrilled that this is finally happening, I love the beautiful camera, and working with the crew is a joy compared to holing up in a hotel room. But I have my doubts about the compromised script, Teshigahara, myself.

Living Carelessly in Tokyo and Elsewhere

Wed., Sept. 8

Yesterday we shot # 27, the Kume family sequence. Keith did well enough, Teshi was shockingly bad. It appears he doesn't know how to convey a situation to his actors with any depth or finesse or even interest. He moves through the day arrogantly and forbiddingly, squinting at the world through his view-finder and overlooking the details of performance. It rankles me to sit quietly on the sidelines in my capacity as interpretor and manipulator of our truculent lead while Teshi fucks up the screenplay, what remains of it. I fear the film will be hollow, all surface and no depth.

Friday, Sept. 10

Teshi is so selfish and aloof, the crew tags along behind him instead of participating actively . . . Keith surprises me occasionally with moments of graceful acting. His laugh is lively and appealing. Our script supervisor Eiko Yoshida, wry and competent—she has worked with Kurosawa—who appears enigmatically to have no personal life, has picked up all the filthiest language in the script and enjoys using it at the right moments. I asked at noon what she thought of the garage scene and she shook her head and said only, "Cunt-suck!"

Saturday, Sept. 25

Keith has decided that the Lotus Sutra is "the Devil's language" and says he won't memorize the words because he doesn't want them "hurting his mind" in years to come. *Veh iz mir!*

Summer Soldiers

Sunday, Sept. 26

It's easy enough to look on and criticize silently but very very hard for me to step forward into Teshi's force field and elicit his sullen displeasure by challenging him. But isn't it my responsibility to say honestly what I know and feel without worrying about consequences? Where's my confidence? Where has it ever been? I must try harder. (I sound like Dr. Johnson.)

The journal breaks off at the end of our month in Tokyo. The awkwardness between Teshigahara and me intensified until the crew began complaining about it. By the time we reached Iwakuni we were scarcely speaking. Our last shot the day we wrapped was Sykes slouching toward the gates at the entrance to the base. (We had saved this for the final day because we were afraid of calling attention to ourselves and being rousted out of town by military police.) When Teshigahara called "Cut!" for the final time, he thanked the cast and crew and went straight to the airport, leaving me behind to return to Tokyo with Tomizawa on the train.

Teshigahara took the footage and disappeared into an editing room at the Aoi Studio in Roppongi for three months. Occasionally he called me at home with a question, but he never invited me to join him in the editing room and I couldn't bring myself to barge in. I must have been hurt, but what I remember feeling is detachment; I was caught up in researching my Mishima book, interviewing the members of his family who consented to speak with me and dozens of people he had known across the diverse domains of his labyrinthine world.

It was early April when Teshigahara invited me to a screening of his rough assembly. Tomizawa was there and so was Tōru Takemitsu, who had agreed to compose the music for the film.

Living Carelessly in Tokyo and Elsewhere

(Takemitsu's score for *Summer Soldiers* was incidental in every respect.) Teshigahara had edited here and there some unexpected turns in the story, but the film struck me as jerkily episodic and lacking focus. It wasn't unwatchable, and it had its moments of humor and irony, but it certainly wasn't the film we might have made had we agreed on what it was about. When the lights came up Teshigahara asked me for comments; careful to hide my disappointment, I suggested some interpolations and several deletions, which he incorporated in his final cut.

As we were finishing the film, Saul Bellow came to town and the U.S. Embassy asked me to serve as his Virgil. He was visiting Japan on the same program that had brought Faulkner to Tokyo before him. Faulkner, famously, had latched on to a paramour within hours of his arrival and had sequestered himself in his hotel room with her for most of his stay, declining the appearances at universities that were part of the deal. Bellow was determined to outdo Faulkner, who, as he told me more than once, had persisted in referring to him as "Mr. Ballou." In response to his request, I rounded up some comely writer groupies (the Japanese term is "literature maidens"), but Bellow's fame in Japan wasn't yet sufficient to compensate for his edginess, which put the girls off. Rejected night after night, his mood darkened until he was racing through the paper he had prepared on Joyce at a speed none of the Japanese academics in the audience could hope to understand and storming from the room without waiting for questions. Even so, we managed to have some decent times together; I took him home for an evening with Mayumi's family, which he seemed to enjoy, and we went out drinking with Ōe and Abe. Then at lunch the day he was leaving he informed me that I was "the best squaw man" he had ever met. I was unfamiliar with the term; Bellow explained that it referred to insecure scions of wealthy East Coast families who had attempted to feel special by marrying an Indian squaw and living with her on the reservation. His appraisal felled me like a crowbar. Seven years later, his words were still ringing in my ears when I resolved to distinguish myself with accomplishments that had nothing to do with exoticism and tried to put Japan behind me.

Summer Soldiers premiered at a theater on the Ginza that specialized in independent productions. It ran for two weeks but was largely overlooked by critics. In June we all went to New York to screen the film for American distributors, but no one picked it up; it was, after all, a small work, and at the time there was little interest in the war in Vietnam, over for nearly two years, which most Americans preferred to forget.

On October 1 *Summer Soldiers* was screened at the New York Film Festival at Lincoln Center. The festival had opened two nights before with the last of Eric Rohmer's *Six Moral Tales, Chloe in the Afternoon*. Mayumi and I attended the glitzy opening-night reception at Alice Tully Hall and chatted briefly, champagne flutes in hand, with Rohmer and Nestor Almendros and the female star of the new film, Zouzou, who seemed out of sorts and was sullenly uncommunicative. I think I had some trouble explaining what we were doing there—Teshigahara didn't arrive until the following day—and remember feeling like an imposter who had crashed the party. The film ran for one week at the 68th Street Playhouse and disappeared.

By that time we were already living in Princeton, where I had accepted a full-time teaching appointment. The historian Marius Jansen had been urging me to come for a year but I had resisted; I had no desire for an academic career, and, in my good moments, I was still confident that I was destined to be a director. But *Summer Soldiers* had fizzled, and clearly Hollywood wasn't calling. With a wife and two small children to support and no prospects of a steady income, I had panicked and accepted Princeton's invitation. Barney Rosset railed at me; he accused me of selling out my talent as a writer—*Life* magazine had expressed "professional interest" in me—and predicted I would be bored to death at a university. Over the years I have sometimes wondered whether I shouldn't have listened to him.

8

Full Moon Lunch

For six of our seven years at Princeton we rented from the university a property called Jewel Farm, after the family who had worked the land for generations. The farm was surrounded by hay meadows and soybean fields. In those days, most Americans thought of soybeans as cattle feed; our friends in the Asian community, on the other hand, were pleased to have access to one hundred acres of *edamame* for themselves to eat and dropped in regularly with bushel baskets. The main entrance, off Route 1, which proceeded south to Trenton, led straight to the elm trees that shaded us in summer; a second driveway, easy to miss, traversed a meadow to the back of the house from Washington Road, the main ingress to the campus and the town of Princeton just minutes away. Our eighteenth-century farmhouse, built of local fieldstone, was two stories of oddly shaped rooms with sloping wooden floors, a cellar that was haunted according to Mayumi and the boys—an abandoned tombstone lay face down, half embedded in the dirt floor—and a cobwebbed attic from which bats flitted through the treetops in summer twilight. The property came with a shed of rusted, antique tools and a dilapidated barn and paddock where we kept a mount for Zachary to ride, a $100 nag named Patches, and, I can't think why, a cunning, vicious pony. Jeremiah, just three when we got to the farm, had his own beast of burden, a mongrel St. Bernard named Jessie who pulled him around in a red wagon. Twenty yards from the house there was a small fire pond that was home each spring to a flock of mallards on their way south. One afternoon our friend Gavin Borden, the founder of Garland Publishing, spied the geese; the next morning he drove out from the city with the hunter's wildness in his eye and a brace of handmade Spanish shotguns in a carrying case. We blasted away while the boys looked on, their eyes wide as plates. Gavin stayed to roast duck for dinner. As we were sitting down, the police arrived to issue us a citation for discharging firearms in Princeton Township.

There were often students in the house; I remember affectionately Consuela and Carlos, a lithesome Puerto Rican and her jovial Cuban boyfriend, and a large-hearted bumbler named Larry Baskind. In return for room and board, this gang looked after the boys, helped with chores—our arcadian life included firewood to be chopped, snow to be shoveled, hay to be fetched for Patches and the pony—and in general livened up the house with their good-natured clowning. Children of the times, they were stoned much of the time, and Mayumi often smoked with them.

Though our marriage was broken by the time we left Princeton in 1979, there was something prelapsarian about our life on Jewel Farm, and I remember it nostalgically. Among my happiest memories are the softball game parties we organized on Sunday afternoons on a diamond we laid out in an open meadow behind the barn. Unlike the annual East Hampton softball free-for-all, this was not a celebrity event; we invented rules to enable adults and small children to play in the same game. The teams comprised Princeton families and students and friends from New York, including Japanese visitors who were passing

Full Moon Lunch

through, Kōbō Abe and the fledgling novelist Ryū Murakami (no relation to Haruki), who couldn't get over the fact that we had a softball diamond in our backyard and who, taking a turn at bat, hit the longest home run ball of the day. Watching or playing in the game and listening to music we piped from the house to twin Klipsch speakers installed in the meadow—Dylan and Joan Baez, Mayumi's favorites, and The Band—we drank a lot of wine and cold sake and basked in a sensation of communal well-being that I have associated ever since with those Sunday afternoons. (Recently the modern China scholar Perry Link told me he sometimes recalls our softball parties as he drives out Washington Road and looks across the empty fields to where Jewel Farm once stood.)

Some people always stayed to dinner, which we ate at the cherry table that functioned as our hearth. It had been crafted for us as a display piece by a Japanese painter named Miyazaki, a classmate of Mayumi's in Tokyo who was having trouble supporting himself in New York with his painting. I had asked for a table of heroic dimensions and Miyazaki had complied. The top was nine feet long and four and a half feet across; our friend had fashioned it from beveled cherry boards two inches thick, six inches wide, and of differing lengths, joining them seamlessly in an irregular pattern with inlaid butterfly joints of a slightly paler wood. The massive tabletop was secured, in the manner of a raft, by two transverse beams underneath at either end. These fit snugly with wooden pegs into the leg assembly, two trapezoidal slabs of cherry braced by an arched beam like an oxbow. I wanted benches and Miyazaki provided a splendid pair of them; seven and a half feet long, they were slabs of cherry supported by three smaller trapezoids that echoed the table's pedestals and pegged with square pegs that came flush to the sitting surface. With two chairs at either end, sixteen guests could sit comfortably at our table and, if necessary, twenty could crowd around

155

it. The place reserved for me at the head of that table felt to me like the kingly seat of the patriarch, the paterfamilias I have always longed to be. The table itself, worthy of installment in a mythic vision of abundance and largesse, lives in my imagination today as an emblem of a moment in time that I have lost, a state of grace in which I provide nourishment and protection to my family, pleasure and solace to my friends.

When I wasn't preparing lectures, I was writing hard on the Mishima biography. As always, I worried as I wrote; there was my contractual deadline to fret about, now extended to June 30, 1974, and the more deeply troubling doubt about my ability to encompass and convey the life of such a considerable man. Who was I kidding to think that I was up to such a job? My anxiety was increased by the knowledge that I had a competitor, a British journalist named Henry Scott-Stokes who was at work on his own life of Mishima. In the last years of his life, after we had quarreled, Mishima had anointed Scott-Stokes as his Boswell and they had developed an intimate relationship that served their own interests. (The Tokyo correspondent for *The London Times*, he had broken the story of Mishima's private army in the English press.) On a bright October day in 1974, Henry drove out from New York for a brief visit at the farm. He was as I remembered him from the mid-1960s: bright and self-assured and somehow undeclared about his personal life, a slender, good-looking fellow with slicked-back hair and a lethal air that had always put me in mind of a paring knife. We took a cautious, mostly silent walk across the autumn fields, taking each other's measure. On our way back, as we approached the house, he said to me with a thin smile and a triumphant glint in his eye, "You know, I'll beat you to press!"

As it turned out, Farrar, Straus published Scott-Stokes's *The Life and Death of Yukio Mishima* just weeks before Little, Brown released my *Mishima: A Biography* in December. The unfortunate result was that many major newspapers and magazines ran double reviews. Scott-Stokes didn't steal my thunder as I had feared he might; neither can I say that I fared dramatically better than he. Ours were very different books: I had written a literary biography modeled on Richard Ellman's *James Joyce*; I had also read family correspondence and had conducted lengthy interviews with Mishima's parents and brother. Scott-Stokes, who didn't read Japanese, made little of Mishima's untranslated work, but had benefited from intimate access to the last terrible years. Some critics, Paul Theroux among them, preferred his book. One in particular, a certain M. G. McNay writing in the *Oxford Mail*, deplored mine, citing as an example of my "appalling gaucheness" a line from the preface: "I was the only good translator he was likely to encounter who could actually beat him at arm wrestling, and that mattered, I am certain."

On October 29, in advance of the reviews, I received a letter from Donald Keene in Tokyo: "I received your book last night and read most of it without stopping. I think it is a fine piece of writing and genuinely absorbing throughout. You deserve to be congratulated and I am delighted to do so." Keene went on to point out, "most ungraciously," that I had been "somewhat sloppy on minor points" and cited a number of examples of mistakes in reading Japanese names and, most nettling to him, a French misspelling: "Why couldn't you or someone at Little, Brown catch the error in French, three times repeated of 'compte' instead of 'comte'? The above are of course all minor matters, the sort of stupidities that are the heart of reviews in academic journals, but they should indicate the need to verify even such points. . . . In any case, congratulations on having done a fine job. The translations in the book are particularly felicitous."

At the time, riding high on the book's reception, I fear I may have dismissed the gentle scolding in Keene's letter as querulous.

Living Carelessly in Tokyo and Elsewhere

Rereading it today, I am moved to see that he had bothered to articulate his feelings to me and that his commitment to careful scholarship—never one of my virtues—was genuine.

Princeton treated me well. In the summer of 1974 I was promoted to associate professor with tenure at a salary of $15,500. The tenured position required a PhD, which in turn required a dissertation. Harvard accepted instead a footnoted version of the Mishima biography, in galleys by that time, and granted me the degree. I was of course aware that I had arrived at my PhD by a rare and privileged route, and I'm sure that my success, which I took for granted in those long-gone days, fed into my arrogance. On my own behalf I should add that I took pains to make sure that my graduate students benefited from my experience. Unlike so many of my colleagues then and now, I had escaped the anguish that is commonly the cost of a doctoral degree and was not impelled to make certain that students should taste the same misery on which I had supped. I urged my graduate students to prepare for the general examinations as quickly as possible, defended them at exam time against iniquitous questions from other examiners designed to trip them up, and exhorted them to approach the dissertation not as a dread exercise that might someday be crafted into a book but, from the onset, as an appealing study designed to be worthy of publication. I believe I have been accused of dispensing PhDs from the bottom drawer of my desk, but that is an outlandish charge. The truth is, I was serious about the doctorate but not pious.

As I began my third year at Princeton I was feeling restless about, as I characterized academic life to myself, writing notes in other people's margins; all of a sudden I wanted urgently to try my hand at filmmaking again. I envisioned a series of documentary films about Japanese families going about their quo-

Tokyo University, the department of national literature, May 1963.

Seeing Kenzaburō Ōe off on his first trip to America, Haneda Airport, June 1965.

With middle-school
students in the snow
country, autumn
1965.

Left to right: Cristina Rosset, JN, Barney Rosset, Mayumi, Kenzaburō Ōe, at Ōe's house, June 1965.

As American Counsel Townsend Harris, with Yaeko Mizutani as Okichi, Shinbashi Enbujo Theater, September 1965.

With Kōbō Abe, on the set of *Face of Another*, February 1966.

Left to right: Kōbō Abe, JN, Kenzaburō Ōe, at Abe's house, winter 1966.

With Mayumi's father, Yasumasa, in front of the apartment on 96th Street, New York City, September 1967.

With cast and crew of *Summer Soldiers*, Iwakuni, October 1971. Standing, center, left to right, Teshigahara, Keith Sykes, JN.

With Saul Bellow at the Japan Society, New York, October 1974.

Left to right: printmaker Masuo Ikeda, Mayumi, Li-lan (Ikeda's wife), JN, novelist Ryu Murakami, unidentified, Jewel Farm, Princeton, New Jersey, winter 1974.

Directing *The Blind Swordsman*, Uzumasa Studio, Kyoto, March 1978.

With Shintarō Katsu, Uzumasa Studio, Kyoto, March 1978.

Left to right: Zachary, Mayumi, JN, Diane, Jeremiah, Fairfax, California, June 1994.

Barney Rosset, Astrid Meyer,
Stockholm, December 1994.

Left to right: Diane, Joan Bingham, Barney Rosset, JN, Nobel Prize
award ceremony, Stockholm, December 8, 1994.

With Sony chairman, Norio
Ohga, Sony Headquarters,
Tokyo, May 1997.

With Kenzaburō Ōe, Tokyo, September 1997.

With Noh actor (and living national treasure) Otoshige Sakai, his wife and their three sons; Diane, Emily, JN, Toby, Okura Hotel, Tokyo, August 1997.

JN's sixtieth birthday. *Back*: Diane; Fujiko Hara; Mayumi; Mayumi's sister, Hiromi; Zachary. *Front*: Jay Miracle, unidentified, Toby, JN, Martin Blakeway with Sherlock. March 5, 2000, Santa Barbara, California.

With Otoshige Sakai and geisha friends, Asakusa, May 2001.

With junior high students, Kawagoe, October 2002.

Left to right: Princeton Professor Yoshiaki Shimizu, Ambassador
Tatsuo Arima, JN, The Imperial Hotel, April 2002.

Left to right: Zachary, Emily, Toby, Diane, Santa Barbara, California, March 2001.

Left to right: Toby, JN, Emily, Diane, The Thacher School, May 2005.

tidian lives. I wanted audiences to see for themselves that the caricature that had possessed the American imagination since Pearl Harbor—inscrutable, grinning, vulpine little people—was false; I hoped to convey the Japanese as I had experienced them, wise and foolish, full of contradiction, as confoundingly human as ourselves. I wrote a proposal and took it to WNET/Thirteen, the PBS station in New York; the novelist Robert Kotlowitz, who was then senior vice president of the station's national division, liked the proposal and promised to package it as a WNET project and to include it in funding submissions to corporate and foundation sponsors.

Memory distills from the summer and autumn we spent in Tokyo that year, 1975, an isolated moment of sounds only: my rear bicycle wheel braking and simultaneously my son Jeremiah's scream. I was carrying him on the flat rack behind my seat to his first day in kindergarten at the Wakō Gakuen School. That morning, Mayumi and I had joked about Japanese conformity as we decked him out like a schoolboy in a comic book, in shorts and tennis shoes, a yellow sun hat, and a matching plastic backpack equipped with a regulation pencil box and a Masked Rider thermos of milk. The family waved us off as we pedaled away on our twenty-minute ride. Then Jeremiah's foot caught in the wheel and the bike skidded to a stop with a sickening squeal. From the blazing sun in a perfectly blue sky raven light poured remorselessly down upon us; in my panic, as if I had gone deaf, I couldn't hear my son's screaming. A crowd gathered, someone called an ambulance, we were rushed to a local clinic a few blocks away. I helped pin down Jeremiah's thrashing body while a doctor swabbed and probed the wound, stitched it up—the tendon had just missed being severed—and encased his foot in a plaster cast that reached above his ankle.

I was uneasy about having entrusted Jeremiah's care to a local clinic. At the time a great divide still separated Japanese doctors who had been trained in the West, principally the United States, and the local neighborhood variety. Western medicine as practiced by the Marcus Welbys around the corner was still an arcane, exotic science. No matter what the malady, treatment came in single-dose paper packets of unnamed white powder or, more commonly, injections of yellow fluid drawn from glass ampules; doctors who had never left Japan took down their medical histories and clinical notes in scrawled German, a disconcerting custom that invoked the late nineteenth-century Japanese pioneers who had studied their medicine in Leipzig and Berlin. In 1965, a Rightist fanatic leapt the embassy wall and stabbed Ambassador Reischauer in the thigh as he sat in his garden. His aides wanted to fly him in a helicopter to the army hospital in Tachikawa, but Reischauer insisted on being taken instead to a local Japanese hospital just down the hill, where he was given contaminated blood transfusions that damaged his liver.

Recalling this, I grew apprehensive as Jeremiah got worse instead of better, feverish and crying in pain. On the afternoon of the third day I confronted the doctor, who admitted he was a bit "perplexed." "This antibiotic at this dosage works for a Japanese child," he said, "but I'm not certain it works for a foreign child." That was all I needed to hear. I strode into the room where a second doctor and two nurses were attending Jeremiah as he lay in bed and bellowed a no-nonsense imperative in Japanese: "Stand away from the child!" The physician looked at me in disbelief; even Mayumi and her father regarded me in dismay—no Japanese patient would have dreamed of questioning his doctor's authority in any way. But there was no mistaking the angry determination on my face, and everyone stepped back from the bed. I lifted Jeremiah in my arms and took him downtown in a cab to St. Luke's, a teaching hospital that I knew from Donald Richie was staffed by superior doctors, many of whom had been trained at the University of Chicago Medical School. The first thing the internist did when he saw the cast was cut it away, exposing an infection that was spreading up his ankle. He said the wound had to be bathed and dressed freshly once a day; I could leave Jeremiah in the hospital or commute with him from our house in Kyōdō. I chose to make the daily trip; every afternoon for a sweltering late-summer month I pulled him in a wagon to Kyōdō Station and then carried him on my back up and down stairs as we changed trains twice on the fifty-minute ride to Higashi Ginza near the hospital. Under the young internist's care, the wound finally healed and Jeremiah was able to walk without a limp.

By the end of the second semester, 1976, I had managed to raise $50,000 in foundation grants, just enough to make a pilot film for my series. I returned to Tokyo in June. The family stayed behind in Princeton. I don't remember discussing this with Mayumi, but the growing distance between us must have affected her decision to remain at home.

In correspondence, Teshigahara's assistant director, the one-meal cook at his mountain retreat, had agreed to manage the production for me. The day after I arrived he showed up at International House hours late for our appointment and stayed just long enough to beg off the job, claiming he had decided on consideration that he was unqualified. (It was clear to me, though he didn't say so, that he had signed on with someone else.) In a panic I called Yukio Tomizawa, the producer of *Summer Soldiers*, who introduced me the following day to a production manager named Yōichi Ukita, a singular, sometimes maddening character who was my constant companion that summer and for an entire year from the following July, when I returned to complete the series. Forty-two at the time, Ukita had been in the business since high school; a fixer and a *hondler*, he knew every freelancer in Tokyo and every vendor, and he knew costs down to the nickel. Disdaining to use a calculator, he carried in his jacket pocket a small abacus; as I discussed a shoot with my crew in bars and coffee shops, he would sit apart, clicking the beads on the abacus, reducing my vision to dollars and cents and, depending on the total he calculated, nodding his approval or scowling. His self-esteem was founded on bringing in a production on or under budget, but he placed his own impediment in the way of success by pocketing occasional money from the kitty. Every week I gave him cash to deploy as he saw fit; in the first batch of receipts he returned to me I found a statement for an overnight stay for a party of two at a "love hotel." When I pushed the receipt in his face, reminding him that I read Japanese, he shrugged and said it wouldn't happen again. He doubtless continued to rob me unindictably now and again, but I understood that he considered the extra cash a bonus for the economies he achieved.

In temperament and habit Ukita was the model of an old-fashioned Japanese movie man. (In all weathers he wrapped himself in a cotton bellyband that caused his trousers to bunch around his waist.) Fiercely proud of his métier, he was irascible, a heavy drinker though he flushed an angry red after a single glass, an incorrigible gambler lethally adept at mah-jongg, indefatigable and indolent by turns, shiftless in his good-natured way. He sometimes disappeared for days at a time; when he finally showed up, often as not looking haggard after a sleepless night, he offered no explanation, nor did I ask for one. I knew that, like his brethren in the trade, he was moonlighting though I was paying him to work for me full time. He vexed me often enough, but over time I came to feel that he was loyal to me in his unreliable way. Certainly the work would have been impossible without him.

I wanted a working-class subject for the pilot film. With Ukita as a guide I met day laborers, carpenters, a man who chiseled playing boards for the game *go*, the merchant owner of an appliance store, and an assortment of cooks. We encountered some colorful characters, but their lives seemed too circumscribed and monotonous to sustain the scrutiny of an hour-long documentary. In the end it was Tomizawa's wife, Setsu Asakura, who led me to the perfect family. For more than thirty years, as far back as Setsu's childhood memory extended, a fishmonger named Sugiura had delivered each morning from his shop directly across the street the fresh sashimi her renowned sculptor father ate for breakfast. After the war, old man Sugiura's son, Masao, who had been a galley cook on a ship in the Imperial Navy, had converted the family business from fish to catering box lunches for funeral parties at the Buddhist temples that were concentrated in the district. When I described to Setsu the milieu I was looking for, she snapped her fingers and declared that I must meet the Sugiuras.

Setsu accompanied me to the shop. When I slid open the doors I beheld a filmmaker's banquet: ten people, the extended family, worked around a long aluminum table in an impossibly cramped space. With long wooden chopsticks, jostling one another, reaching over shoulders and under arms, they packed the compartments of red lacquer lunch boxes with food from large trays: shrimp tempura and poached fish, taro and lotus root simmered in miso broth, pickles, green peas folded into lozenges of rice, small yellow flowers placed here and there for color. From a six-burner stove in the foreground corner where he did most of the cooking, the boss, Masao Sugiura, sixty-one, kept a watchful, cranky eye on the process to assure himself that the presentation was just so. It would take some time to learn the connections around the table, but I saw at once that a portrait of the Sugiuras might illuminate two Japanese arts: packaging and interpersonal relationships.

That afternoon, Masao Sugiura agreed to cooperate. I don't

Living Carelessly in Tokyo and Elsewhere

think it occurred to him to turn me down. Connections count above all else in Japan, and we were drinking tea and eating rice cakes across the street in the stately parlor room that had belonged to his family's oldest and most venerated patron. I also knew there was nothing I could say to prepare him for the degree to which I would invade his life.

For a week I dropped in at the shop by myself early each morning and stayed until after dark. Gradually the Sugiuras relaxed around me. There were six of them in the immediate family: Masao and his wife, Toshiko, in their early sixties; their two sons, Keizō, twenty-nine, and Takashi, twenty-seven; and the brothers' wives, Yoshiko, a Kyoto girl who seemed somehow out of place in this Tokyo family, like a southern belle in Flatbush, and Tōkō, who never let down her guard with me. The family also employed a kitchen manager and three young apprentices, two local lads born and raised in the neighborhood and Shibukawa, a self-proclaimed Marxist who was the son of a Ginza bar owner.

We began filming on July 9 and worked the family hard for three weeks. On our first day at the shop, there were problems. The hum of the air conditioner bothered our soundman, but the heat of the lights with the AC turned off threatened to spoil the rice, which apparently has the fastest "legs," the Japanese idiom for spoiling. Our troublesome solution was to shoot with our lights on and the air conditioning off for no more than fifteen minutes at a time.

Staying out of the way was impossible. There was scarcely room in the kitchen for the Sugiuras, and there were ten of us, not to mention our gear. As we intruded day after day, the cramped kitchen became tense. We considered going out on location on the busiest days—we knew in advance when there were multiple orders to fill—but I wanted to catch the family at full tilt. By the end of our second week, Masao was greeting

164

us in the morning with dismay in his eye; at times the family worked in sullen silence.

The scamps in my Tokyo crew contributed to the tension. One night after work Shimpei Kikuchi, a soundman who had been a friend since *Summer Soldiers*, and our cameraman, a tough Korean Japanese named Shōbun An, took the brothers drinking and to a mah-jongg parlor, where they won from Keizō and Takashi all the money in their wallets. The brothers returned at dawn hung over and broke. Masao didn't say a word to me about the incident—I was after all a foreigner and a *sensei*—but he did ask Ukita to ensure that in future the gamblers in my employ stay away from his family.

I had seen Masao fulminate until he was red in the face but never when we happened to be filming. So I put the good-natured Takashi up to lighting a cigarette while he stood at the stove. Predictably, on camera this time, the boss descended on him like an avalanche, and when he had excoriated Takashi to his satisfaction, he turned to the room and berated the others for smoking "like cigarette salesmen" and in general treating him like a "pushover." To be sure, it would never have occurred to Takashi on his own to smoke in the kitchen. Nonetheless, the old man's anger and Takashi's hang-dog docility as he submitted to the scolding were genuine, and the dynamic of the scene was representative, familiar to me.

Our most serious crisis occurred in the final week, when we tried to film the Sugiura men at the Tsukiji fish market. Early each morning, the boss and his sons drove to the market to bargain for the fresh fish they needed that day. Tsukiji at dawn was a boisterous, kaleidoscopic feast for the camera's eye; Masao in a suit and tie and Panama hat—he was president of the local fish dealers' association and often stayed behind to attend a meeting—was a singular figure as he walked the long aisles with his cane, bargaining with vendors and slipping his fingers beneath

Living Carelessly in Tokyo and Elsewhere

the gills to appraise the freshness of the catch. Normally, the family emerged sleepily from the shop at 5:45 and arrived at the market by 6:10. The night before the shoot, I asked the boss if he would oblige us by leaving at 4:45 a.m, allowing us an extra hour to film the van traversing the empty streets of downtown Tokyo at dawn. We were setting up a shot on the Ginza while we had the Sugiuras wait in the truck two stoplights away when Kikuchi let out a whistle and passed his headphones to me. Unaware that the wireless mike on his jacket was transmitting his words to us, Masao was complaining to his sons about how slowly we worked and wondering how much we intended to pay the family for the terrible inconvenience—a large sum, he reckoned. We managed to get the family to the market on time, but our presence there embarrassed Masao.

When I got to the shop at eight the next morning, Shōbun An was waiting for me looking distraught. The camera had been closed imperfectly and an entire roll of negative film from the day before had been exposed. With a deep bow, An offered to leave the job and to provide me with an excellent camera-man as his replacement. I was horrified and furious, but I knew better than to yell at An: he was taking responsibility for one of his assistants. Later, Ukita told me he had lectured both of them all night and warned them their careers would be over if they slipped up again.

The Tsukiji sequence would have to be reshot; that afternoon we decided a gesture of appreciation would be required before we dared ask Masao to indulge us with a second opportunity to discomfit him. I had heard him express interest in French food. Ukita clicked the beads on his abacus and allowed reluctantly that we could afford one splurge; he would take the money from the "fees and gratuities" item in the budget. I called to invite Masao to join me for dinner at La Belle Époque, a French restaurant at the top of the Hotel Okura. Ukita arranged for

166

a limo to pick him up and return him to the shop. Our meal together, as we both knew, was a social ritual designed to relieve tension by correcting a deficit in the book of our interaction. I ordered the most expensive items on the menu for both of us, and a bottle of Haut Brion that cost $200 (I pictured Ukita's pained look as I chose it). My extravagance did not escape the boss's notice. But he was careful that credits for the evening should not accrue entirely to me: as we sat down he presented me with two Japanese dolls for my boys and an antique copper teakettle that undoubtedly cost more than the meal. The dinner was a success; when I asked to reshoot the scene the next morning he consented.

On our last day, July 31, the family catered a meal for us at the sculptor's residence across the street. Joking that we had spent three weeks with our mouths watering at the sight of food we couldn't touch, Masao entertained us with the most expensive item on his menu, a meal he called "Full Moon Lunch" because it was served in a round lacquer box. I used this as the title of the film.

In just over three weeks we had shot fifteen hours of 16-mm color film. I edited *Full Moon Lunch* in twenty-five days, working day and night with an editor named Suwa and his two assistants in a dingy room at the same Aoi Studio where Teshigahara had cut and mixed *Summer Soldiers*. Suwa used a hand crank to advance our work print from one large reel to another through a desk-top editor with a tiny viewing screen; as we squinted at the image the sound track blared from a squawk box. That summer I acquired the ability to understand the gibbering of Japanese dialogue at fast-forward speeds. I recorded my own narration and we mixed the film in a day; we had our first print, including English subtitles I had prepared, on September 1. The process was primitive by American standards, and I didn't realize that the breakneck pace at which we worked, standard practice in Japan, would be unthinkable at home. On September 2 we screened the film at Aoi Studio; everyone who had worked in the crew, including assistants, showed up to see for themselves that their work was up to standard. I have made dozens of films since, in the East and the West, but don't recall one American, not even a cameraman, taking time from another job to assure himself about the quality of his work for me. The Japanese take singular pride in their métiers.

The film was screened publicly for the first time the following day, Friday, September 3, in the auditorium at International House. I have the poster that was prepared by a young woman who worked in the Program Office. On a large circle of yellow poster paper she had pasted stenciled cut-outs of the letters in the title and my name in a rainbow of colors. I asked what had inspired her to this and she replied it was fitting because I was "color-crazy," a Japanese idiom for lecherousness.

I spent that summer in a luxurious apartment in Denmark House a few minutes from Harajuku that belonged to my friends Johan and Gisella Almqvist, who were away in Europe with their children. Working on the film was exhilarating, but when I came home at night, living alone for the first time in fourteen years, I was forlorn. I missed the boys and our life at Jewel Farm, and I was troubled by the widening rift between Mayumi and me. When I was by myself, I listened to Cat Stevens and my theme song that summer, The Band's "It Makes No Difference."

The song soothed and grieved me, echoing my sentimental longing for something—a tranquil life with my wife and family—that I had failed to nourish and sustain when it was mine to enjoy. I had Kikuchi transfer the album to tape and played it when we were in our van. I taught my crew the meaning of the lyrics, and Kikuchi's assistant, a good-natured young man named Urata, memorized the words and, mispronouncing them unintelligibly, sang along with me.

Full Moon Lunch was received admiringly at screenings at Princeton and the Japan Society of New York and won the Red Ribbon at the American Film Festival and Best International Film at the Washington International Film Festival. I took a print to PBS headquarters in Washington, and a young program executive named Fred Cox agreed on the spot to make the program available to affiliates across the country in March 1977. The film aired in all the major markets between mid-March and mid-April and attracted favorable attention. In his "TV Weekend" column in *The New York Times*, John J. O'Conner wrote "a quietly intriguing documentary" and concluded, "The portrait, intensely personal, affords remarkable insight into the contemporary Japanese condition."

9

Unraveling

To raise money for the rest of the documentary series I went back to the foundations that had sponsored me in the first round. In Tokyo, I had a powerful advocate, Shigeharu Matsumoto. Matsumoto was a gracious, pipe-smoking Meiji gentleman who had acquired flawless English at Yale. A cousin of Haru Reischauer's whose father had been finance minister in the Meiji government, Matsumoto had declined appointments as ambassador to the United States and the United Nation from his close friend, three-time prime minister Shigeru Yoshida, to devote himself full time to founding International House, which he had persuaded another longtime friend, J. D. Rockefeller III, to fund. At this critical moment for me, he happened to be on the board of both the Hōsō-Bunka and Japan Foundations. As I learned later from his successor, the French literature scholar and translator of Pascal, Yōichi Maeda, Matsumoto had convened meetings of both boards when he learned that I was applying for additional funding and had spoken on my behalf. I am sure I am indebted to him for the sizable grants I eventually received from both foundations.

There was also the arcane world of patronage. The leading expert in approaching wealthy individuals with a quantifiable interest in Japan was Rand Castille, the director of the art gallery at the Japan Society of New York. Castille ran the gallery like a fiefdom, funding the costly exhibitions he mounted from sources he cultivated privately. He tended to the patrons on his list, which one suspected ran heavily to heiresses, with unflagging solicitude: flowers on birthdays and, where appropriate, Saint's Days, new books inscribed by the author and hand-delivered—"The mail is for solicitors," he cautioned me. Castille was known to guard his list fiercely from colleagues in the Japan Society with programs of their own that needed funding. But when he saw *Full Moon Lunch*, he decided to grant me limited access to his platinum circle. During the course of that year, he took me to lunch with half a dozen prospects: the midwestern owner of a family pharmaceutical business who had a priceless collection of Japanese swords, a newspaperman from Texas, and several doyennes of New York high society. After each meeting he would call me on the phone and critique my performance disapprovingly. I remember most vividly having lunch—a luncheon, Rand called it—with the heiress to the Aspirin, or was it Bufferin?, fortune. He had given me to know that this eccentric lady was a rare orchid and had assured me that she could fund my project out of her grocery money. I took the train in from Princeton in plenty of time and was waiting for them at Lutece when they arrived in our guest's chauffeured car. I thought the meeting went well; I comported myself with all the charm I could muster, and it seemed clear to me when we parted that the lady had enjoyed herself. When Rand phoned me later he dressed me down smartly. What could I have been thinking to have arrived ahead of them, as though I had nothing better to do than wait around! Had I never heard of an entrance fashionably late enough to have allowed him to sing my praises and create anticipation before my appearance? But this was only one of many gaffes. As we chatted at lunch, instead of dwelling on her every word my eyes had roamed the room as though I was distracted. And what about her cigarette! Over coffee I had obliged her to sit with a cigarette between her fingers without offering to light it for what felt like half an hour, until Rand, with a sinking heart, had clicked open his own lighter. "That's when you lost the money," he intoned gloomily. "I saw it go up in smoke!" That was our last fund-raiser together; I suppose he decided I was incorrigible.

By the time classes ended in early June I had received production grants totaling $145,000: $90,000 from the U.S.-Japan Friendship Commission, $25,000 from the Japan Foundation, and $30,000 from the Hōsō-Bunka Foundation. According to the budget I had constructed with Ukita, I was still $110,000 short. My hopes were now pinned to a decision by the executive director of the Henry Luce Foundation, Martha Wallace. I knew little about Martha except that she had connections to big business and the government—she had been a member of the Trilateral Commission chaired by David Rockefeller in the Jimmy Carter years—and was at home in upper-crust New York society. A tall, angular woman, she wore her hair in a prim bun on top of her head, but facing her across her antique desk and at lunch at the Century Club I had been able to make her laugh, and the twinkle in her blue eyes had led me to suspect there was more good humor in her than she let on. I was sitting in my office in Jones Hall on a Saturday morning when she called and said, "Pack your bags, John, I have your money." Luce had granted me the entire amount of my shortfall, substantial money in those days. I learned later that Martha had created a new fund to make the grant possible, the Henry Luce Foundation Fund for East Asian Research. The Fund is still on their books and active; my project was the first award. As with the other grants, the money was remitted to Princeton and the university passed it on to me.

Unraveling

I now had $255,000 to spend at my discretion and a year's leave from Princeton in which to produce three hour-long documentary films (two were all I was able to manage). Mayumi was reluctant to spend a year in Japan. Her life as an artist was on track, and she had a circle of close friends in New York whom I barely knew. But in the end she relented; I believe she agreed to come because she wanted our sons, ten and seven, to deepen their experience of Japan.

Our production budget allowed us to live high on the hog that year. I rented a newly built house in Shiroganedai, an affluent residential district close to Meguro Station. There was a spacious living room with glass doors that opened on a garden, a modern kitchen with an oven, three bedrooms upstairs—Mayumi converted one into a studio—two proper Western bathrooms, and central heat and air conditioning. We even had our own car, a Nissan Bluebird stationwagon that Ukita picked up secondhand, which we garaged at the house and used all year as a production vehicle. The boys commuted by city bus to Nishimachi International School on a hill above International House in Azabu; the founder and principal, Aya Matsukata, Haru Reischauer's sister, ran the school out of the five-story former Matsukata family manor where she and Haru had grown up. (Tuition was a staggering $3,000 for the year.)

I arrived in Tokyo knowing only that I wanted a portrait of a farm family for the second film in the series. Between July 25 and September 29 I traversed the rice country north and east of Sendai four times with Ukita along, the same Tōhoku region I had visited years before, looking for a family to film. I chose the Tōhoku because I hoped to capture the unexpressed darkness I sensed beneath the harshness of life in that laconic country. I had a letter of introduction to local mayors from the Agency for Cultural Affairs; this secured us access to granges and from there to individual families. As we sat sipping green tea, I imagined

173

Living Carelessly in Tokyo and Elsewhere

a Japanese filmmaker knocking at doors in the Nebraska farm-
land with a request to intrude on a family's life with cameras and
crew for a year and felt certain he would be turned away. The
farmers we met were guarded, but they were also curious about
me and almost always cordial. It was stressful work; I had asked
Ukita to be sure to rephrase what was said in Tōhoku dialect in
standard Japanese, but he often sat silently at my side nodding
and grunting. When I barked at him for his silence he admitted
sheepishly that he himself was having difficulty understanding.
Over the year our ears attuned to the local patois.

I was looking for a multigenerational family of appealing
and diverse individuals. We had visited about thirty households
when we arrived at the Katō farm, and I knew after an hour
that I had found what I wanted. The Katōs were rice farmers who lived in the village of Miyazaki in Miyagi Prefecture,
four hundred miles north of Tokyo and east of Sendai toward
the Japan Sea. Four generations lived together in a sprawling
thatch-roofed house built around a great room under a roof
of exposed cedar beams lashed together high above the dirt
floor. The family grew rice on their two acres of paddies across
the highway and raised horses to be sold at the annual spring
auction in Kawatabi thirty miles down the road. Their annual
income was about $16,000, half of which they spent on fertil-
izer and leasing farm machines. By the time I looked in on them,
they were already representative of a vanishing breed. In 1979
observing the Katōs' life was like viewing museum dioramas of
life in the past.

The patriarch, Asaji Katō, eighty-nine, still exercised the
horses in their paddock twice a day; when he wasn't at work,
he dozed at the *kotatsu* table in the great room, above a charcoal fire used to keep the feet and legs warm during the freezing winter, where the family took its meals. He was always
served first. Asaji's son, Masao, sixty-seven, the titular head of

the household, was a heavy drinker who could become abusive when drunk. Masao's wife, Toshi, fifty-seven, "Grandma Toshi" we called her, was an open, lively woman who was the warm heart at the center of the family's life. Masao's son by a previous marriage, Masashi, forty, had charge of the farm. Known as "the young master," Masashi was a heavy drinker like his father; taciturn at best, he was often sullen in our presence and never warmed to me. Masashi's wife, Hisae, thirty-seven, had married into the family fifteen years earlier but was still known as "the young wife" and expected to work longer hours than anyone else. Masashi and Hisae had three sons. Their first-born, Hiroshi, fourteen, the designated heir to the farm, confessed haltingly to our camera when we finally got him alone that he was prepared to run away rather than shoulder responsibility for eking out a living as head of the family. Hiroshi's younger brothers, Tamotsu and Masayoshi, were in grade school.

The Katōs had never met an American. When I first appeared at the farm, the great-grandfather secluded himself in his room and stayed out of sight for two days. He supposed an American must be a GI and felt certain that GIs were in Japan to kill Japanese farmers. Over time he relaxed around me.

We descended on the farm five times that year: twice in October to film the rice harvest; from December 26 through January 5, a time of year-end rituals and New Year's celebrations; in mid-February, the fallow season, when the young master was away at work at a Nabisco potato chip factory and the house was hushed inside walls of snow that reached to the roof; and in May for the spring planting of the rice seedlings—forty-six days in all. By the time we returned for our second week in October we had installed a power pole and transformer at the end of the road to supply the power we needed for our lights, which we left hanging from the beams of the great room until we said our final good-byes that spring.

Living Carelessly in Tokyo and Elsewhere

All told, there were sixteen of us in the crew. We stayed in a sorry inn fifteen miles down the road toward the town of Kawatabi, whose other guests, when anyone else was there, were telephone linemen and prefectural assayers. At the end of an exhausting day, which often began before sunup, the crew was free to return to the inn to soak away their fatigue in a tub the size of a swimming pool that was fed by hot springs. Most nights the Katō men insisted I remain behind to sit with them at the *kotatsu* talking and drinking sake. It was always freezing in the house—you could see your breath—and the local sake, which they poured cold from a kettle into tumbler-size glasses, had a nasty bite. The twin sensations I recall most vividly, other than exhaustion, are feeling chilled to the bone and the venomous buzzing of the sake in my brain.

The challenge of the film was breaking through the façade the family hid behind to reveal to the camera, and the world at large, their feelings as individuals. Mayumi and our boys, who were with us more than half the time, helped open doors that might have remained closed to me. Mayumi fit in effortlessly, working with the women preparing meals in the kitchen and gabbing with them about life on the farm and life in the city, and the boys played with Hisae's youngsters and endeared themselves to Grandma Toshi. Even so, for a long while the family was reluctant to allow our cameras indoors and particularly into the rooms beyond the great room. The journal I kept that year reminds me how manipulative I was—there is no other word for it: documentary filmmaking is a process of manipulation—in securing the access I wanted.

October 15
  We began badly with teatime in the fields at 3:00, the "little lunch" they call it up here. Normally, Grandma Toshi walks out to the paddies with a basket of rice

crackers and a kettle of green tea which she leaves with Hisae and Masashi (in Masao's day, he tells me, the kettle was filled with *doburoku*, a home-fermented beer distilled from sake dregs). Today, the whole family turned out with tea in the best teapot, the kettle hidden away, and Toshi bearing fancy rice cakes on a tray. To make matters worse—even further removed from the everyday scene I wanted—Masao brought along a local veterinarian whom he had flagged to a stop as he passed in his truck and invited to join the party. The Katōs hold on to their notion that we are here to take commemorative snap-shots; they invite everyone in sight to step into the picture and direct me in the middle of a sequence to step in front of the camera to pose with them. And how quick they are to dress up: turn away for an instant and the frayed rope around a horse's neck becomes a festival halter, rooms are whisked clean or closed to us, fancy food is served up on party plates. This is to be expected (why should they show us their dirty linen) but it makes me anxious to realize how far we must go before they will let down their guard and be themselves.

October 24

10 days and 5000 feet of negative, 2½ hours of film. Last night, heart in my mouth, I tried our first shoot inside the house, our first unequivocal invasion of privacy. We've had power for four days but I wasn't confident the family was ready. Whenever I suggested to Toshi it was time we moved indoors she would cry out in dismay and remind me how messy the house was. But since yesterday was our last day this autumn, I decided we must light the great room

177

and kitchen and film a meal no matter what, to make sure the family understood that the going would get tougher when we return at New Year's. We showed up unannounced at 5 lest a feast be prepared and I asked permission to hang our lights. Confronted, Toshi acquiesced. We shot the women in the kitchen and a meal, too stiff and silent to use but a fine preparation for the close-up work we'll begin in December. When we were finished we turned off the big lights and joined the family around the table for sake and singing and felt greatly relieved on both sides. Yoshida went into Hiroshi's room to help the boy string the guitar strings we had brought him, the first time anyone in our crew had crossed the boundary; I followed Yoshida inside and brought Segawa with me. Toshi hurried in a minute later to protest that the room was a mess and a disgrace for us to see, but we were installed and when I chided her she shrugged her shoulders and withdrew. The barriers were coming down, the easier ones anyway, and I was too excited to breathe. As we were leaving around 9, Toshi drew me aside and asked me solemnly to consider arranging a marriage between our Yoshida and a 29-year-old cousin on a neighboring farm. I said I couldn't make any promises—Yoshida married to a farm girl!—but agreed they should meet when we returned at New Year's.

October 25
Mayumi and the boys were saying goodbye when we arrived. Toshi had presented them a bagful of goodies for the train, three flavors of soda, pickles, some clay dishes etc. And for each child a small parcel

wrapped in tissue. What is it? says Jeremiah. He opens the parcel and discovers money, three crisp 1,000 yen notes, and waves them around while Mayumi and I flush red. "Put it away, Jirō," I hissed in English, but he is too excited to heed me. I was mortified, but Ukita assures me we must simply return the same amount to the Katō children when we return.

New Year's at the farm in the snow country was a festival of year-end ritual and celebration as exotic and enthralling to my Tokyo crew as it was to me. We stayed for eleven days and shot more colorful and atmospheric scenes than I could ever use, but I felt we were still skimming the surface of the Katōs' lives. When we returned in mid-February, I finally struck gold with Grandma Toshi. The previous month she had visited us briefly in Tokyo; in the subterranean safety of the subway she had hinted briefly at the torment she had suffered when she first arrived at the farm in 1943, a war widow, at the hands of her new mother-in-law, Great-grandfather's now deceased wife, the cruel and jealous mistress of the household. The right time to ask her more about that seemed to be the snowbound season, when the house was hushed and there were no chores to distract her. I asked if she would do an interview on camera alone with me, and she agreed. We chatted for a while about nothing special until she seemed relaxed, and when Segawa touched me on the back to let me know the silent Éclair camera was running, I leaned toward her across the tangerines on the table and said softly, "I imagine you had a difficult time at first." Whereupon Toshi told her story with only occasional prompting from me: of arriving here at twenty-three and "wanting to die" when she learned that she had been preceded by four other women all driven away by Mother-in-law's cruelty, of being scorned by the Katō clan as a young widow from the city, "a used bride," of wishing to run away and then actually fleeing for a period of time to her family home in Fukushima, of Masao's drunkenness, on and on.

It was one of those mysterious moments that occur so rarely, if at all, in the making of a documentary film: Toshi was confiding in me and there were five other people in that small room, three huddled over the camera, Shimpei in the corner at his tape recorder, and young Urata standing over us like a statue with a boom just above Toshi's head but certainly invisible to her now. For forty minutes she spoke and no one moved. I willed her to go on, offered thanks to the gods of documentary filmmaking, and wondered if I could justify using any of her intimate revelations.

We returned to the farm for a final week at the end of May. The night before we began filming Masashi and Hisae slogging through the mud as they planted rice seedlings in the flooded paddies, I had a moment of terror. Once a month an itinerant *samisen* player stopped at the village to give the farmwomen a class in the three-stringed instrument. They gathered at the local grange and turned the occasion into a small party, bringing food to share and sake. When we had filmed for an hour the crew left me behind to chat and observe and returned to the inn to prepare for the dawn shoot the following morning. The teacher had departed and I was standing in the makeshift kitchen as Hisae and her friends washed dishes when one of them announced, with a leer in my direction, "Hisae has feelings for John-*sensei*!" Hisae flushed scarlet and grinned, flashing the gold fillings in her teeth. I froze, aware of the titillated, lascivious look in her friends' eyes as they appraised the two of us in their shapeless farm clothes. One false move of either rejection or acknowledgment could easily, I felt certain, land me in big trouble on the farm before we had finished our work. Not knowing where to look or what to say I bowed silently and

180

stepped outside with nowhere to go. I stood there in the pitch darkness, listening to the clamor of frogs from the paddies and cursing Ukita for taking so long to come back for me.

By the time we visited the Katō farm in May, I was already editing the third film in my series, a portrait of the actor Shintarō Katsu. Between 1962 and 1973, Katsu had starred in twenty-five *Blind Swordsman* films, which had established him as a superstar not only in Japan but in Hong Kong and the rest of Southeast Asia. When I met him in the late 1960s, he was disporting himself like a one-man version of Frank Sinatra's Rat Pack, a gang he would have been thrilled to join. Katsu was an all-night boozer and carouser on a heroic scale, a gambler heavily in debt to the Yakuza mob, an unabashed and compulsive womanizer. He was other things: a talented actor, a virtuoso *samisen* player, and a charismatic man with a capacity for gentleness and sensitivity. Alas, he was also hell-bent on self-destruction, which he eventually accomplished.

When I set my sights on Katsu as a subject for my own series, I told myself I wanted his passion and intensity. The families in *Full Moon Lunch* and *Farm Song* were ordinary people, modest and reticent. Lest my audience suppose that all Japanese were mild, I wanted a virulent personality. In truth, looking back, I believe I was enamored of Katsu's celebrity, his libidinous wildness, and what appeared to me to be his unfettered life. I don't think I saw, or acknowledged clearly enough, his vainglory and his desperation. And I remained in thrall to my fantasy about him through the five debilitating weeks of shooting in Kyoto when we scrambled to keep up with him from noon to dawn each day. As a consequence, the film I finished was an homage, largely unironic, which offended and continues to offend many people, female audiences in particular.

Living Carelessly in Tokyo and Elsewhere

My connection to Katsu was his close friend Teshigahara. They were strikingly different—Teshigahara a man of refinement, Katsu a compulsive vulgarian—but they belonged to a distinctively Japanese brotherhood: both were eldest sons of a founding grand master, and both had grown up wealthy, pampered, and burdened by an expectation they had rebelliously disappointed that they would succeed their fathers.

Katsu's father was the head of a school of *samisen*; Katsu had been trained on the instrument from childhood and was an accomplished musician. In the late 1950s after a tour of Hollywood and a meeting with James Dean just before Dean died, Katsu resolved to become a movie star and apprenticed himself at the Daiei Studios. He was still playing minor roles in 1961 when the studio received a treatment for a film about a legendary blind gambler, Zatō Ichi, with a deadly cane sword swifter than any sighted eye could follow. Katsu knew how to play a blind man; his childhood *samisen* teacher had been blind, and he had observed him closely. By the second film in the series, he had established himself and Zatō Ichi as national folk heroes.

I recall a summer evening in Tokyo in the mid-1960s when I tagged along on his nightly round of bars. Katsu was dressed in white jeans and a florescent chartreuse T-shirt from Disneyland. He was accompanied by two aides-de-camp, unsmiling gentlemen in dark suits and sunglasses who were kept busy peeling money from rolls of 10,000-yen notes and communicating his instructions to bar hostesses and occasional runners who would show up at our table to take a whispered message and hurry away with it. I think I supposed at the time that they were placing bets.

We began with the exclusive celebrity bars on the Ginza, L'Amour and Tokudai-ji; Katsu's favorite hostesses would leave their other guests to surround him at our table as we entered, and then they would plead and cajole until he transformed into blind Zatō Ichi, lighting his own cigarette unfalteringly, finding squid on a plate with his chopsticks, or, best of all, holding out a glass to be filled with Napoleon brandy and judging by the sound of the pour just when to withdraw the glass as it brimmed. At each club he introduced me as a friend of Teshigahara and Kōbō Abe; hearing this, the girls became more attentive to me, keeping my own glass full, lighting my cigarettes, and laughing appreciatively and, it seemed to me, coquettishly at my remarks.

When Katsu grew restless, he would stand and announce that we were moving on, inviting one or two of the girls at our table to come along to our next stop as his guests. It was like walking the Ginza streets with a Pied Piper whose magic attracted only alluring bar girls. Somewhere along the way, Katsu caught me eyeing him with what I imagine must have been a kind of awe, wondering, as I was often to wonder, how he was able to keep it up. "John," he grunted, "every day is my birthday, and every night is my birthday party." I would later have occasion to observe him on nights when celebration was the furthest thing from his mind, but at the time I think he believed it.

Our evening ended at two or three in the morning at a private supper club in a high-rise in Akasaka. By that time there were a dozen young women along, and as we filed in Katsu called for T-bone steaks and french fries for everyone. In view of the lateness of the hour and the volume of liquor they had consumed, the girls were impressively animated and attentive. Abruptly Katsu rose from his chair at the head of the long table and said simply, "I have to be at the studio at six o'clock." Then he bent over and kissed me on the cheek—"Bye, John," he said in English—and strode from the room with one of the girls at his side.

The table went lifeless: no one bothered to feign any interest in the only male remaining in the room. I realized that each of them was hoping to be chosen as Katsu's special favorite for the evening; now that he was gone they were alone with their disappointment and their exhaustion and little else. I was mortified; it was not the last time Katsu would unseat me.

We met again in the spring of 1970; Teshigahara had crashed his car and Katsu and I chanced to pay him a visit in his hospital room at the same time and left together. As we walked down the long corridor, I was aware of doctors and nurses crowding doorways for a look at the star as we passed, but Katsu seemed too engrossed in what he was saying to notice. Just before we turned the corner, without missing a beat, he transformed into the familiar figure of Zatō Ichi; his shoulders hunched and his large, shaven head pulled in like a turtle's head and angled crazily up at the ceiling, his body bent forward and his step shuffling as though he were wearing wooden clogs, while he tapped his way along with an invisible cane sword in his right hand. As we turned the corner, I could almost hear the thud of bodies hitting the floor behind us down that long hall as fans fell in a swoon. Then we were out of sight, and Katsu, himself again, went on talking as if nothing had happened.

In mid-December, just before we left for New Year's at the Katō farm, I phoned Katsu in Kyoto, and he said he would meet me at the studio the following night. Katsu Productions was renting a lot at the former Daiei Studios in Uzumasa, on the outskirts of Kyoto. I arrived at 4:30 the following afternoon. The man in a dark suit who motioned me to a couch in Katsu's bare office had been with us for a part of that night in Tokyo, but as he gave no indication of knowing me, I said nothing. At six, Katsu entered dressed and made up as Zatō Ichi. He was reserved; I wondered whether he remembered our meetings in Tokyo seven or eight years earlier. I told him I was making a series of films for PBS and was determined that one should be a portrait of him. He hadn't heard of PBS and asked repeatedly if I meant CBS.

"What's in it for me?" he asked when I had finished. I told him our budget didn't include a fee, but promised to make a film that conveyed his power and originality. I would make him a familiar figure in the United States and Europe, I declared grandiosely, and whet the Western appetite for his feature films. He seemed unimpressed. "Let's see the first film," he said.

I had brought along a print of *Full Moon Lunch*, but I was nervous about showing it to him. How could a family catering business hope to hold his interest. It was bound to be too—ordinary.

By then it was nine o'clock and no one had eaten, but Katsu insisted we screen the film at once. *Full Moon Lunch* began; Katsu laughed aloud from time to time (when he laughed his aides laughed with him) and called out "Excellent!" at my slicker cuts. When the lights came up he shook my hand warmly and said, in English, "You are a good director, John." Then, to his staff, "If he can make a film like that about lunch makers, think what kind of film he can make about me!"

That was how it happened: Katsu agreed to participate on the spot. But he had his own confabulation that I was to hear many times. The first was during an interview with the *Asahi* newspaper: "John came to me and said he wanted to make a film," he began, " and I said what will you pay me? My fee should be ten million yen. John looked down and thought hard for a minute. I could see he hadn't expected me to ask for so much. Then he looked right into my eyes"—at this point Katsu reached over and rested one hand on my knee as I sat there poker-faced—"and he said, 'I can't pay you money but I'll give you my heart!' 'Done,'" Katsu roared, "'I agree.' I knew John meant what he said. So now, I have his heart and he has mine and that's a dangerous situation—we may end up destroying one another!"

Living Carelessly in Tokyo and Elsewhere

At the time, though I knew he was grandstanding, I fear I heard genuine substance in Katsu's preposterous conceit. In truth he was no more an outlaw living by the outlaw code of honor than I. But, as I have said, I was enthralled by his fantasy about himself and eager—determined—to feel that it was also mine.

We began filming at the Daiei Studios in early March as Katsu went into production of the 104th episode of *The New Adventures of Zatō Ichi* for Fuji Television. I had chosen this installment because it was one of five or six that he was directing himself that season and was therefore likely both to absorb him and to provide plenty of fireworks. His costars in the show were Ken Ogata and the winsome Mitsuko Baishō.

The exhausting challenge was managing to be where the action was and ready to film it. Katsu was perversely unpredictable; we had to be in standby mode all day, and after dark was even harder. I was welcome to go wherever Katsu went at night; indeed, he seemed to grow dependent on me and began to demand that I accompany him. The problem was that our crew could not follow us with their cameras and lights and tape recorders in and out of nightspots all over Kyoto; I had no choice but to send them back to our hotel with instructions to wait for a call from me. This was vexing to them and created tension between us.

As I worked, whirling in the maelstrom of Katsu's life, I began to ape his mannerisms and overbearing attitude. My language coarsened in a simulation of his rough Edo speech; I spoke deep in my throat with a growl, and I learned to bark orders and to expect that I would be unquestioningly obeyed. This worked magically: a Japanese crew is conditioned to expect the director to be a tyrant on the set. I began to take for granted authority and compliance. And I relished the satisfaction of feeling that I was self-assured.

We chased Katsu around Kyoto for a month, the only month

in my life without a decent night's sleep. Before a week was out I was running a fever from exhaustion and my crew was spent and jittery. One headlong, frantic day followed another indistinguishably. The following entry in my scribbled journal sums up the experience. I am tempted to doctor it—it reveals how unaware I was of living inside Katsu's melodrama—but I shall hold my nose and set down what I wrote.

Sunday, March 12

At four I went over to the Fujita Hotel and learned that Katsu had risen at noon and was already at the studio. In the restaurant downstairs, more from habit than hunger, I ate the special T-bone he always orders for himself and me. I sat alone, eating, still in a daze from the night before, then waited in the lobby for Ukita to pick me up and watched a graduating class of college girls in bright spring colors chirp and twitter through their tears as they said good-bye to one another. This normal little moment seemed to me to be occurring at a vast distance—we have come a long way offshore.

Ukita arrived with Usui and we drove out to the studio. In his dressing room I asked Katsu if we could film the serious interview I wanted that night and he agreed. What I needed, as ballast to a film that threatened to float away without it, were Katsu's direct and concise answers to questions about his struggle to disengage from the persona of Zatō Ichi and his desire to win acknowledgment as a full-fledged director of serious films. I intended to ask these questions and would interrupt only when I sensed him wandering off the subject. Katsu was silent a minute, then grunted his assent.

In his hotel room we discussed where he would sit and where he would be free to roam. I wanted him full-face into the camera and relatively at rest for this sequence—he half agreed to keep still; in principle he would sit on one of the two beds and talk directly to me.

At eight o'clock I left the hotel with the key to Katsu's room and instructions to pick up a bottle of Remy Martin for all of us to drink during the interview. Katsu went off to dinner with Baishō and Ogata but before he left I had his solemn promise to be back by ten, sober and ready to do the interview.

At 9 we lit the room and positioned our cameras; we were prepared to shoot up to three hours of film. Miyashita and I went downstairs for a drink; Miyashita confided his concern that Katsu, once he has begun to drink at dinner, may not be disposed to honor his promise. I was confident he would show up.

About 10:40 Usui came into the bar to deliver a phone message: Miyashita and I were to hurry over to a nearby club called Hikari where Katsu and his party were waiting. I should have packed up and gone back to the hotel; to accommodate his willfulness would be to lose an important round. But how could I be certain that refusing to join him would not provoke him into walking off the film? I decided to go and see—it wasn't altogether that I lacked the courage: the man was free, he asserted his freedom against all constraints, and that battle, after all, was part of what I most admired in him. I asked the crew to wait at the hotel and walked to the nightclub Hikari with Miyashita and "Andy" Matsumoto, Katsu's publicist.

At Katsu's table upstairs, I encountered the standard array of bar girls and Baishō, dazed and dreamily placid. Katsu was off in a corner with Ogata—when they returned to the table he announced that the actor had just become, in gangster (yakuza) parlance, his "little brother," and Ogata proclaimed this the happiest night of his life. Katsu, in Ogata's leather cap, was drunk and speeding, beyond reasoning with. I sat there glumly, wondering what to do—what unsettled me most was Katsu's slurred insistence that he would do the interview at sunrise with light pouring through his hotel window. This of course was out of the question: by dawn, at this rate, he would be useless.

Katsu rose abruptly and staggered out of the bar. We followed, to the Bel Ami, one of his regular stops, a posh Kyoto cabaret. I sent Usui back to the hotel with instructions to pack the crew home—there would be no filming that night. We were at the Cabaret about an hour, surrounded by hostesses, Katsu loud and abusive and throwing money at everyone in sight. For a pleasant enough ten minutes I danced closely with Baishō, who always managed to rise above Katsu's turbulence into smooth air of her own. Then Katsu ordered us all up and out.

At the entrance to the Club we encountered two Americans in business suits. Katsu walked up to them and shook their hands; then Andy stepped in and did the honors in English: "This is Mr. Katsu, big Japanese movie star like Sammy Davis, Jr.!" The Americans were impressed; they explained they were from Nebraska, "in fertilizer." This seemed to go over Andy's head, but I didn't help him out. For a moment we all stood there, the Nebraskans eyeing me and wondering who I was. How could I explain?

Miyashita pulled up in the Jaguar and a dozen of the girls bowed us off and clapped their hands when Katsu kissed the lady proprietress goodbye. Then we roared off to the hotel, Katsu drunkenly at the wheel, Baishō beside him, Miyashita and Ogata and I in the back, Miyashita nervously reminding Katsu to keep his hands on the wheel.

At the hotel we all went up to Katsu's room for a nightcap, and the moment I had been dreading most arrived: Katsu turned to me and said, "Now we'll do the interview."

"No," I said, "you're drunk and this has to be sober."

"I'm free," Katsu roared, "no one tells me what to do!"

"I'm going home," I said, "I'll see you tomorrow."

"Maybe not. If I feel like it I throw away everything, my movies, even my life!" What he meant in this case, I felt certain, was not his life but mine, my movie at any rate, which he was threatening to walk out of. But there was no backing down now.

"If we are really brothers as you say, then my going home tonight won't change anything, and when you see the movie you'll know I was right."

Silence. All eyes on Katsu. He stood there swaying on his feet, glaring at me. I bowed, said good night, and walked out of the room. Katsu followed me, with Baishō and Ogata. We all got into the elevator and started down. Suddenly he spoke in English: "Everything is terrible now, my family, my work. Sometimes I want to cry." He pounded the wall of the elevator with his fist and there were tears in his eyes. "And who helps me? Nobody helps me—This is the

190

real me" he shouted, "film this!" We faced each other in the elevator with tears in both our eyes. I grabbed him and hung on like a bear, and then we were at the lobby and I bowed again and left.

Out on the street, as I stood waiting for a cab, Miyashita ran up and waited with me. We said nothing. As the cab pulled up he opened the door for me, and bowed deeply as I drove away.

Working with Shōhei Imamura's editor, Hajime Okayasu, I cut the Katsu film in five weeks. The second week in May I screened it for Katsu as I had promised. He had been charged with possession of opium and was holed up at the Tokyo Prince Hotel. I snuck in late at night with Kikuchi and the equipment we needed. We had agreed he would have no say in matters we chose to call "aesthetic," but could object to scenes he considered damaging to himself and his family. His only objection was to several cuts of himself and Baishō dancing flirtatiously at a Kyoto discothèque to the music of Stevie Wonder's "Superstition." (Baishō was married to a fearsome Brazilian Japanese pro wrestler named Antonio Inoki.) He watched the film in silence and when it was over said nothing. No one moved; his staff was careful not to react until they knew how Katsu felt. Finally he turned to me and said quietly, "I feel as if I've met myself for the first time. I'm a hell of a nice guy. But very lonely." At the time I took this as a genuine compliment. Reading Donald Richie's *Japan Journals*, I wonder whether Katsu's praise in fact was disingenuous. In an entry dated January 9, 1979, Donald noted en passant, "Bested, Katsu turns into a lonely little boy and talks to his pals. And to me, since I am on his side of the table. I know he hates John Nathan's film about him, and I try to tell him why it is good. This is difficult because the reason it is good is that it shows him to be a lonely little boy."

Living Carelessly in Tokyo and Elsewhere

I spent June and most of July editing *Farm Song*. It was exhilarating to be alone in the editing room without having to worry about my subjects and crew. I rushed to the Aoi Studio every morning and fretted on days when we were supposed to be resting. I screened my rough cut for Tōru Takemitsu, who liked what he saw and agreed to compose music for the film. His score, written for Japanese percussion, *shakuhachi,* Noh flutes, and Western harp and bass flute, was sublime, among his masterpieces of movie music. I was astounded by his unexpected choices of scenes to orchestrate, but when he had recorded the score and we put it up against the picture his music brought to every scene a wondrous resonance.

Mayumi had left Japan in mid-June, taking the boys with her. They were staying at Green Gulch Farm in Marin County, California, on the winding road along the coast to Stinson Beach. The organic farm was owned and managed by the San Francisco Zen Center. They were there at the invitation of the Zen Center's American abbot, Richard Baker-roshi, who had become Mayumi's Zen master. I was fully engaged in my work but lonely for the family, forlorn.

The last entry in the journal I kept that year is dated August 8:

> Shirogane. The summer light is fading, the lizard the boys loved to tease is clinging to the lit glass of the ivy-covered panel in the large downstairs room. Alone. Cooler purring. Mayumi and the boys are long gone and I can never reach them by phone. This morning Mayumi called me to say with her voice tight that she was looking for a place to live near San Francisco. I wished to return home with my finished films triumphantly. What triumph can there be without a family to share it with! I am a fool to neglect—to push away—what is dearest to me.

Unraveling

At the end of August I left Haneda with pristine 16 mm prints of both films in custom-made carrying cases and flew to San Francisco to pick up the family. We spent two weeks together at Green Gulch, where Mayumi had been sitting *zazen* all summer. I felt very out of place among the Zen students who had made the pilgrimage here from their wealthy Jewish homes in Long Island to weed and irrigate the fields, meditate the nights away in the Dharma Hall, and achieve detachment from the neurotic tics in their privileged lives through intense communion—*dokusan*—with the abbot, Baker-*rōshi*. Her own Zen practice that summer seemed to have led Mayumi in the opposite direction of detachment to anger at me; I felt cowed in the searchlight of her critical regard. One day as we sat at a long table in the dining hall lunching on soup and veggie greens a young Zennie with a shaved head took a seat next to me and expressed admiration for my Mishima book. I felt Mayumi's attention pivot in my direction from across the table like a Gatling gun, watching to see if I would swell with the praise and become expansive, gesticulative, and, most offensive, loud. "No! No!" I murmured with a deprecating wave of my hand. "It was—an ego trip! I was trying to get myself some attention." The Zennie couldn't believe his ears and stared at me in bewilderment. Mayumi, satisfied, resumed her conversation with her neighbor. I would love to say I was being ironic or passive-aggressive, but I was actually feeling desperate to win Mayumi's approval and believed that abasing myself was the route to take.

By this time, Mayumi had been initiated into the inner-most circle of Baker-roshi's advisors and confidantes; we spent our evenings in the living room of his private residence, off-limits to ordinary students and all but the most enlightened monks. The abbot presided over a salon of new-age futurists: the entrepreneur Paul Hawken; Michael Murphy, the propri-

etor of Esalen and author of *The Inner Game of Golf*; Stewart
Brand, founder of *The Whole Earth Catalog*; and the architect Sim Van der Ryn, among others. Brand and Van der Ryn
had been appointed special advisors to the progressive governor of California in those days, Jerry Brown, who was also a
frequent visitor at Green Gulch. Brown was dating the singer
Linda Ronstadt; the first time we met I learned that Ronstadt's
Hardware in Tucson was her father's business. They would sit
together on the couch, cuddling beneath a blanket, while Baker-
rōshi discussed sustainability or gnosis or the nutrient value in
a placenta with his obsessively visionary cronies, his wife, Vir-
ginia, on his left hand and Mayumi on his right. I always felt
that my presence in the inner sanctum was tolerated because I
was Mayumi's consort and was never able to feel at ease with
Richard or his friends.

When it was time to fly home to Princeton, Baker-roshi drove
us to the airport in the white BMW that so many of the elders in
his *sangra* resented. As we were stepping on to the rampway to
the plane Mayumi turned back and, placing her hands together,
bowed deeply to the abbot, who returned her bow. It was a
perfervid gesture; I wondered uneasily whether the heat that
passed between them was entirely spiritual.

I screened the new films for the first time at the Japan Society of New York in early October. Fortunately, I began with
part 3 of the trilogy, *Farm Song*. In the middle of *The Blind
Swordsman*, my principal benefactor, Martha Wallace of the
Luce Foundation, stood up from her seat in the front row and
walked out.

The trilogy was televised nationally as a presentation of
Hawaii Public Television on three consecutive Sundays in
May at 8 p.m. and attracted large audiences. The Japanese
were becoming ferocious competitors and very much on the
American mind. The films won blue ribbons in a number

of documentary film festivals that year and were favorably reviewed.

That fall and winter I took the trilogy on the road and toured college campuses with them. The attention nationwide was the perfect escape from the desolate reality of my life at home; for weeks at a time I managed to disconnect from consciousness of what was happening in—slipping away from—my life. Mercifully, as a drunk is spared the vivid recollection of his behavior during a binge, I remember little of what happened stop by stop, but I do retain an impression that I sought relief from my unhappiness in profligacy.

I remember vividly the most distressing evening on my tour. It was at the Smithsonian. My distinguished friend Tatsuo Arima was the chief political officer in the Japanese Embassy in Washington that year and he and his wife, Fumiko, were in the audience. As the lights came up after *The Blind Swordsman* I saw them glowering at me, their hands still while others applauded. When I invited questions, Fumiko's hand shot up. What right did I have, she demanded to know, her voice taut with indignation, to call my trilogy *The Japanese*, as if to say that a crude, misogynist scoundrel like Shintarō Katsu was in any way representative of Japanese society? Shaken by Fumiko's animadversion I cracked wise, inquiring sarcastically if she would consider "The Scandinavians" a more suitable title. The Arimas and I got over this terrible moment, but it took years, and more than once along the way Tatsuo expressed his anger at me and his disappointment that I had chosen Katsu as a subject. I still feel there is merit in the Katsu portrait, "a ribald, perturbing adventure in personality," as *The Christian Science Monitor* described it, but I am aware there is too much homage and too little critique in the film.

■ ※ ■

Living Carelessly in Tokyo and Elsewhere

Thanksgiving 1978 was a bleak day. Instead of hosting a turkey dinner at our cherry table I took Zachary and Jeremiah to New York to watch the Macy's parade in a freezing rain and then to a double bill of kung-fu movies starring Sonny Chiba. Mayumi stayed alone on the farm in Princeton. I don't recall what we quarreled about, if indeed we had quarreled; perhaps we had just acknowledged glumly the emptiness between us. Early in the New Year, Mayumi decided she wanted to pursue her Buddhist practice with Richard Baker and told me her intention to move to California with the boys with or without me. I knew she was prepared to separate if I chose not to accompany her. I had no reason to feel sanguine about our future together, but I was feeling bored with my academic life at Princeton, just as Barney Rosset had predicted; it occurred to me that California was just the place to launch a new career for myself as a screenwriter and director. I decided to resign, even though the university had just promoted me to full professor. When I told the historian Marius Jansen, who had invited me to Princeton, he was angry. "You can't do this to Princeton," he said when he had collected himself. I explained that the move was largely an attempt to save my marriage. "Even so—" was all he had to say. It was the last thing he had to say to me for many years. Shortly before he died in December 2000, I returned to lecture at Princeton and at the reception afterward he approached to say he was proud of me. I felt forgiven, and it made me happy to feel so.

I have often looked back on this turning point in my life and wondered at my recklessness in abandoning a career I had devoted twenty years to building. It wasn't really about arrogance, for I was definitely nervous about jettisoning my credentials. I believe I was manifesting a refusal to acknowledge the degree to which I had wounded and alienated Mayumi with my carelessness and inconstancy and, as a consequence, imperiled the survival of my family. If I accompanied her to California—took the family with me to California, as I represented the move to myself—perhaps I could keep my place at the head of the table.

In midsummer of 1979 we moved into a rented house in Muir Beach, just down the hill from Green Gulch Farm. The abbot himself had gone to the trouble of locating it for us. It was a rambling single-story house in a hollow just off the beach, cold and damp in winter. A Zen student named Teresa Rivera and her ten-year-old son, David, lived in a room at the far end and we occupied the rest. There was room for a studio for Mayumi and a study for me in which I set to work on a screenplay based on high school experiences in Tucson. In the middle of the day, when the boys were over the hill at school in Mill Valley and Mayumi was at Green Gulch communing with Baker-roshi, I walked the road to Stinson Beach beneath the California sun and reflected uneasily that I was not only unemployed at the age of forty but, in the Japanese way of seeing things, unaffiliated and therefore without credentials.

Eight months after we arrived in California, with help from my friend, the actor Peter Coyote, who drove me and my belongings in his battered blue van, I moved out of the house into an apartment on Miller Avenue in downtown Mill Valley. It would take me years to allow myself to feel the pain of what had happened between Mayumi and me; I had left angrily, telling myself that the unrelieved tension between us was making it impossible to work creatively. I don't know if I considered that separating from Mayumi was a way of disconnecting my life from Japan, but I was aware that I wanted emancipation. I remembered Saul Bellow's devastating words to me seven years before, that I was "the best squaw man he had ever known." And I remembered something Katsu had said more recently, when he had demanded a performance fee as a condition of signing the broadcast release

PBS required. It was late at night and we were facing each other across a table in a hotel bar in Kyoto. "You understand us, and when you speak you sound just like we do," he rumbled, and then, switching to English, "But, John, *in Japan you cannot win*!" How right he was, I remember thinking that night, but for a different reason than he supposed. I took his words to mean that victory in Japan would never be a victory I had truly earned. For years I had been troubled by the possibility that I possessed the wherewithal to distinguish myself only as an exotic foreigner in an insular island country. I was determined to prove myself on home ground.

I finished my screenplay and it fell into the hands of a television agent, Eliot Webb, who found me my first Hollywood job on the strength of the writing. The producer Irwin Allen hired me to write a fantasy teleplay for an NBC prime-time series for children. The script was never produced, but my name appeared in a squib in *Variety*: "Irwin Allen to produce a 90 minute fantasy, untitled, for NBC's Project Peacock helmed by Edgar Scherick. Teleplay to be scribed by newcomer John Nathan" (emphasis mine). It made me proud to read my name in an industry magazine that had nothing to do with Japan. I cut out the page and taped it to the otherwise bare wall of my bachelor apartment.

PART 2

A More Jewish Neighborhood

Alone in my apartment on Miller Avenue in Mill Valley, or walking along Muir Beach beneath the autumn sunlight, the reality of what I had done walloped me. I had become an unaffiliated man, tossing away credentials—a reputation—it had taken me twenty years to acquire. As if that were not adequate disengagement, I had walked out on my family. I hadn't disappeared—the boys came to stay with me often—but I had broken the family vessel. I remember feeling acutely the deadness of the streets on Thanksgiving morning 1979. Christmas morning that year I drove over the hill to Mayumi's house in Muir Beach like a homeless Santa Claus with a bagful of presents for the boys but stayed only long enough for them to open them.

The screenplay I had begun before leaving Muir Beach was "The Gentlemen of Rhythm"; I took the script with me to my apartment and hammered at it for months, listening to Bartók's *Concerto for Orchestra* and Mendelssohn's *Italian* Symphony. (I intended the adolescent protagonist to conduct one or the other of these.) My story was about a high school boy who is uprooted by his parents from his star status at the cosseted Jewish world of Music and Art High School in New York City and transplanted to the violent Tucson desert. A misfit among the locals, he relies on his music to distinguish himself; he assembles a jazz band using blind musicians from the School for the Deaf and Blind, earns his classmates' admiration, and finally steals the Homecoming Queen from the letterman who has been among his tormentors. When I finished the script I sent it to my actor friend from Ninety-sixth Street, Paul Price, who was now earning a good living in Hollywood as a sitcom writer, and Paul passed it along to his agent, a small, aggressive man named Eliot Webb, who claimed to love the story and assured me he could sell it. He never did, but a number of the television producers who read it wanted meetings with me to discuss writing scripts for them. Presently I had three contracts for first drafts, each paying me the stunning sum of $30,000, two at NBC and one at CBS.

My first employer was Irwin Allen, five-foot-one in his elevator shoes, a giant of the industry whose films about catastrophes, *The Poseidon Adventure, Swarm* (killer bees), and *Towering Inferno* had earned him the sobriquet "Master of Disaster." Like all successful producers, Irwin had many irons in the fire, and what he wanted from me was a sixty-minute teleplay he intended to produce for a new NBC series of prime-time programming for children, Project Peacock. When I met him in the offices he maintained on the Columbia lot in Burbank, he was brief with me. "The Gentlemen" was unproduceable, too soft, but he had perceived talent in the writing and expected I could deliver Irwin Allen quality. He gave me a "one-line idea" that incorporated his signature pyromania: storybook characters (in the public domain!) journey from storybook land to Realworld (Los Angeles) to do battle against a king who has decreed that all books will be burned. He instructed me to contact him when I had a treatment thirty pages long and said I must be sure to ask him about any questions I might have in the course of the writing. He lifted two pencils from his immaculate desk and crossed them like the blades of a scissors. I prepared for what clearly was to be an object lesson: "You see how the distance between the pencils gets bigger as you move to the top." I nodded, trying to look as if I were beholding a miracle. "So that's you and me—if a writer of mine is going off the track I want to catch him down here. Before he strays too far. I don't care if you're William Faulkner!"

I splurged on an IBM Selectric typewriter, the one with the magical ball covered in raised letters and an erase key, and in two weeks finished a treatment that may be the best story I have ever written: the storybook heroes, led by Robin Hood, emerge into Realworld through their books on the shelves of the L.A. Public Library; King Gloom's men use ink-eradicator guns to turn the characters into life-size cardboard cutouts of themselves; Simple Simon leads the King into a trap ("Simple Simon says 'Follow me!'"); and finally, it is revealed, when the King is unable to read the boast on the sash across the Valiant Tailor's chest, that he wants books destroyed to conceal the fact that he cannot read.

I sent the manuscript to Irwin confidently. A few days later he called to inform me there was a problem—I'd better get down to Bel Air, a seven-hour drive from Mill Valley, right away. Irwin was waiting for me poolside. (A bright red London telephone booth, a prop from his 1959 film, *The Big Circus*, was installed incongruously at one end of the pool.) We sat down at a shaded table and my glass of lemonade arrived. My manuscript was on the table in front of him. "Something's wrong with the first page, John—I don't know what you're talking about here!" I had opened, cleverly I thought, with a father reading his son a bedtime story; as he reads from *Tom Sawyer*, the text changes and the illustration morphs into an animated scene of Robin Hood and Paul Bunyan searching for Tom in his cave. The camera moves through the illustration, and by the middle of page 2 the action is under way. "On page two," I began, and Irwin hushed me with a finger to his lips. "If page one is wrong, I don't read page two," he said. He produced the pencils again and scissored them in front of my face. "You remember what I told you?"

It was a smoldering day in August 1980. A beribboned miniature poodle leashed to the table was yapping at us in the quiet; a Mexican gardener was pruning lemon trees on the slope below. I pictured myself killing the gardener, then the poodle, then snapping Irwin as if he were one of his pencils and throwing his lifeless body into the pool. Instead, not quite ready to end my career in films before it had begun, I inhaled the affront.

With Irwin's bit between my teeth I made it through the treatment and a first draft. The day came when it was time for us to make the final pitch to the executive producer on the project, Edgar Scherick. Propped in the back seat of Irwin's Rolls Royce was a ghastly oil painting he had commissioned for the meeting: a comic-book frame on a canvas depicting Robin Hood and Little John confronting the gremlin in the Napoleon suit I had named King Gloom with a bosomy Rapunzel leering at the heroes. On the way he explained in an avuncular way that successful producing was about details, hand-delivering scripts, shtick like the painting, arriving at meetings just early enough but never too early. I confess I was excited and even proud to be riding along in his Rolls on the way to see another famous producer. Scherick had produced many television movies and miniseries and had a long list of film credits as well, including Woody Allen's *Take the Money and Run*, *Sleuth* with Lawrence Olivier, and Neil Simon's *The Heartbreak Kid*.

It was Scherick's birthday. There was a birthday cake on his desk, and when he had cut a piece for each of us he began to tear my script apart. I was caught off-guard by how heated he was and how abusive; he called me a show-off, deploring what he

204

called the "tricky logic" that had devised the ink-eradicator guns. Irwin jumped in to defend the script, which he had approved, and all of a sudden they were yelling at each other. Abruptly, I don't remember what incited him, Sherick threw a piece of birthday cake at me and screamed, "We're not paying you to get your Harvard balls off with your 180 IQ. This is *television*!" (Later I learned that Scherick himself was a Harvard man.)

My ego had been battered and I was mightily indignant, that much I knew, but I was unable to understand what had happened until I learned later that these men, both notorious "screamers," had been abusing each other in a heated rivalry for decades. I suppose I had had the misfortune of being caught in something that had little to do with me, although I couldn't help taking it personally. "The Fall and Rise of His Majesty King Gloom" was not produced; it became the third in a stack of my scripts that never reached the small or the large screen. If you have never created one of these you may not know that nothing in this world is quite so unappealing as an unproduced screenplay—not even your mother will read it.

Another of my employers that year was Don Ohlmeyer, a florid, garrulous former sportscaster who was establishing himself as a major television producer. Ohlmeyer had recently left NBC as executive producer of sports with options to produce several movies of the week; the story he wanted me to script was about a meltdown at a nuclear power plant and its effect on the community nearby. He wanted a "warm and harrowing" story, entitled (his choice) "Evacuate Now!" I never talked myself into taking Ohlmeyer's premise seriously, and the script I wrote reflected my attitude. Apart from the triteness of the material, working for Ohlmeyer came with its own humiliations. On several occasions he summoned me to nocturnal meetings in his weekend suite at the Pebble Beach Golf Resort. I would drive down from San Francisco at the designated hour, always after dinner, and find him in the company of his executive assistant, an attractive young woman named Avery, a fire laid in the hearth and wine chilling in the cooler. It was a transparent situation, and I always felt I was imposing during the thirty minutes he spent distractedly on business with me. The last time we met was the only time I was in his sunny hacienda in the Hollywood Hills above Sunset. As we sat in the living room discussing whether the female mayor I had concocted was too aggressive to be appealing, a black man staggered into the room with his brawny arms around a gigantic television set, a gift for his friend. Ohlmeyer introduced us and we shook hands. Years later I would recall the impression of savage power under tenuous control I received from O. J. Simpson as his shovel hand tightened around mine.

Working as a writer for hire in Los Angeles wasn't advancing me in the direction I hoped to go, nor was the San Francisco film scene offering me much opportunity. The kingpins were George Lucas, a spectral figure who secluded himself on his Skywalker Ranch in Marin, and the magisterial Francis Coppola, who was just completing *Apocalypse Now* at his American Zoetrope Studio on Market Street downtown. I had an introduction to Coppola early on, from Tom Luddy, who was working as director of the Pacific Film Archives, attached to UC Berkeley. Luddy had screened *The Japanese* at the Archive and had urged Francis to watch my portrait of Shintarō Katsu. The screening was scheduled for ten o'clock at night in the basement at Zoetrope. Coppola showed up an hour late with a date, plopped himself down in a seat in the front row, accepted a joint the girl rolled for him, and signaled the projectionist to begin. Halfway through my fifty-eight-minute film he stood up and left the screening room. I was glad of the darkness that concealed the chagrin that must have been written on my face. "That was beautiful," someone exclaimed when the film was over. "Francis saw himself in that little tyrant and couldn't bear it so he left!" I wasn't amused; I had earned admiration from Coppola's crew and alienated him.

Although Coppola and I never worked together and he always seemed puzzled when we encountered each other, as if he were struggling to remember who I was, I did receive invitations to parties and receptions at his manorial house in Pacific Heights on Broadway just off Divisadero Street. I hung around on the periphery when the German director Werner Herzog was staying with him—in those days Herzog was dressing in a sheriff's uniform, complete with badge and handcuffs—and I remember a resonant evening of chatting with a fragile, aging Michelangelo Antonioni about *Zabriskie Point* after a screening downstairs

The last time I visited Coppola's house was for a gala in honor of a visit to San Francisco by Akira Kurosawa, a director esteemed by both Coppola and Lucas as their master. The house was packed with an assortment of supernumeraries on the scene who were freeloading the liquor and food and posturing in loud voices while trying not to gawk through the large windows in Coppola's barn-size kitchen at the real action taking place in the garden just outside the kitchen door. Coppola and Lucas had taken Kurosawa into the privacy of the garden to present him with a gift, a video camera; now, inside the circle of a large sundial of Italian tile inlaid in the brick beneath the drooping elms, they were chatting— trying to chat through a haggard Japanese interpreter whose English was inadequate— with Kurosawa and the Italian actress Julietta Massina. Enclosing them in a semicircle around the circumference of the sundial with their backs to the house was an A list of Hollywood players who had been invited to join them for the presentation: Phillip Kaufman, Michael Ritchie, Paul and Leonard Schrader, the Belgian director Barbet Schroeder, Carroll Ballard, Irvin Ker-

shner, and one or two others I didn't recognize. I had a passing acquaintance with Phil Kaufman and the Schrader brothers,
and Michael Ritchie and I had been a year apart at Harvard and
had both lived in Adams House. But if Kershner hadn't been
there I don't think I would have taken the reckless, irretrievable
step I took. Irvin had directed a number of tasteful films in the
1970s, including in 1978 *The Eyes of Laura Mars*, a thriller
starring Faye Dunaway that had prompted Lucas to invite him
to direct *Star Wars* II, *The Empire Strikes Back*. At a screening
of *The Japanese* at Skywalker Ranch—Lucas was meant to be
there but never appeared—he had admired my films and we
had gone off for a drink and had discovered we shared interests in a number of subjects, including Mahler. Later he invited
me to listen with him over scotch to Mahler's Fifth Symphony,
our favorite, on a superior sound system he had installed in the
house he was renting in San Anselmo while he edited his movie.
I subsequently began visiting him regularly in the evening for a
meal, which he prepared, and some good conversation about
music and film. At some point I had shown him "The Gentlemen of Rhythm," and he had encouraged me to revise it once
again and offered to serve as executive producer on the project
to help me fund it.

The collective chutzpah packed into Coppola's kitchen that
night ought to have been sufficient to levitate the house sky-
ward into Zeus's face, yet no one had the nerve to do what I
now did: emboldened by Kershner's presence, I stepped into the
forbidden garden, a drink in my left hand, and closed the door
behind me. As I emerged, Kershner happened to look around
and our eyes met. Before I had time to register relief, he turned
away, presenting his back to me. And there I was, drink in hand,
aware of incredulous eyes on me from inside the kitchen, standing on the plank with no choice but to walk off it. Whereupon,
mercifully, I was delivered: Kurosawa, looking up, saw me and

beckoned me energetically to join the company. I had met him for the first time earlier in the evening and he must have enjoyed the respite of a conversation with me in Japanese. The whole gang turned welcoming smiles on me as I strode toward them. Ritchie, who had ignored me or brushed me off any number of times in Mill Valley and at the Harvard Club in New York, exclaimed that I was a sight for sore eyes after so many years, and Kershner shamelessly took my arm in a proprietary grip and whispered an urgent invitation to meet for lunch the following week.

Nothing came of the time I spent that evening in easy badinage with that celebrated company. More properly, I never turned it into an opportunity, as each of them might well have done. Was I afraid of failing in spite of efforts to succeed? Or was it success itself that caused me to withdraw whenever it was visibly close at hand? I suspect the latter was, continues to be, closer to my truth.

Fortunately, I had new friends to steady me during those unmoored years in California. Peter Coyote was a tangle of poses he had assembled into a magnetic persona that had carried him far afield of his heritage (farther than I ever traveled from my own): street-savvy renegade, activist visionary, impeccable Zen warrior. (He had changed his name from Cohon following a numinous encounter with a wild dog.) In those days, Peter was living in a small apartment across the street from the San Francisco Zen Center, where his wife, Marilyn, was a student of the abbot, Richard Baker-roshi. Peter was also sitting *zazen* regularly but had not committed to Richard as his formal teacher. Much of the time when he wasn't meditating he was fretting at the table against the window that looked down on the Center about the career he wanted as a movie actor. As I was doing a lot of fretting myself, and as we shared a Jewish inclination and a gift for the swift sardonic put-down of others and, less frequently, ourselves, we hit it off at once and spent hours sipping tea at his table and affirming each other as genuine artists. I loved hanging out with Coyote; he was better at taking himself seriously than I was, and his headlong comic riffs, cadenzas in Yiddish or British or a variety of other accents, put me on the floor laughing myself breathless.

Jeremy Larner often joined us at our weekly lunches in North Beach. Jeremy was a novelist, a poet, and a social essayist with a gift for elegant argument; tall and fit with Semitic good looks reminiscent of Philip Roth, he could be finicky and a whiner, but when he wasn't indulging his inner infant he stood his ground with gravitas that had its source in his talent.

To inspire me to write hard no matter how awful things seemed I also had Sam Shepard. Slouching around in his cowboy hat, twirling his lasso and rolling his own smokes, Sam played the Southern California yokel, but my eye was on the notepad he carried in the back pocket of his jeans, in which he jotted observations and lines of dialogue as they came to him, typing them out later on an old Remington at a table in the living room while his extended family whooped and hollered around him. I was in awe of Sam's commitment and discipline. One night as we stood outside the Sweetwater Bar in Mill Valley I confessed to him that I was beset by a fear of dying that had me too distracted to write. "That's when you do your best work," he drawled, "when you're runnin' scared!"

I was with my three friends the night I met Diane Siegelman for the first time in mid-January 1981. We were at the Magic Theater in San Francisco to see Martin Epstein's new play, *The Man Who Killed the Buddha*. Diane was there with her friend Martine Getty, an edgy, ambitious gamin just kinky enough to put me in mind of a Fassbinder film. I had seen Martine at

Coppola's house and knew her to say hello to, but she would never have approached from across the lobby with Diane in tow if I hadn't been standing there with Peter and Sam, who were celebrities at the Magic. Introductions were exchanged—Martine introduced me as "some kind of filmmaker, I think"—and then Sam pulled us away to a sawdust-on-the-floor bar where he liked to play pool. I went along reluctantly, unhappy about leaving Diane behind; her pale face framed in dark hair and her uncertain smile and knowing, wistful eyes stayed with me. I phoned Martine to ask for her number, and she surprised me by saying she thought Diane would be glad of a call from me. I reached her and we made a date for dinner. Hoping to make the afternoon pass more quickly that day I went to see *Raging Bull* but was too excited and nervous to sit still and left in the middle. On the way home I bought a bottle of champagne and some good scotch and, thinking to brighten a little the shabbiness of my tract house living room, a vase and some flowers. We drank the champagne, exchanged stories about ourselves with breathless eagerness, had dinner at an Italian restaurant just across the freeway in Strawberry, and, in the parking lot outside after coffee, kissed for the first time. I was in love before we left the table. Diane was an unornamented woman, sturdy and fit, fragrant in a wholesome way, like freshly baked bread. She was besides an acupuncturist who hoped she could help correct with her slender needles a variety of physical symptoms that were tormenting me. Her solicitude and tenderness felt like cooling lotion against my parched skin. As I had descended very low in my sky, I'm not sure what she saw in me at the time. Perhaps, as she said later reproachfully, she really had fallen in love with the man who had written my Mishima biography, a book I had made sure to put into her hands. Six weeks after we met, Diane moved in with me. My sons watched with their eyes wide as she unpacked from trunks in the garage relics from her adventurous past: pilot goggles and race car helmets, reflex bows, a .22 caliber rifle, underwater cameras and spear guns, a dressage saddle.

As our romance was blossoming, an Israeli producer named Zvi Dor-Ner called me out of the blue with a job offer. Dor-Ner was executive producing a season of business programs called *Enterprise* for the Boston PBS station, WGBH, thirteen thirty-minute documentaries shot all over the world. He had seen *The Japanese* and was inviting me to write and direct two install-ments in the series, one in Japan and the other in Hong Kong. Though I knew nothing about business and had no interest in it, I accepted the invitation on the condition that he would pay travel expenses for Diane. This was not a normal request, and it was uncharacteristic of me to assert myself so boldly; the pros-pect of showing Diane my Japan had swept me away. I had no idea at the time that Dor-Ner, who had grown up in the streets of Jerusalem and fought in the 1967 War, was a notori-ous *starker* who could not be pushed around. On this occasion, remarking brusquely that I drove a hard bargain, he acceded.

In May 1982 I went ahead to Tokyo to identify a business story, my first visit in nearly four years, and quickly made my way to Kentucky Fried Chicken's assault on the Japanese mar-ket. The Japanese operation was being run by an American named Loy Weston, a shrewd businessman and compulsive clown who managed his Japanese franchisees by bemusing them with antics. He would scud across a tatami floor on his knees at a formal banquet to pour a glass of beer for a Japanese guest and welcome him, bobbing his head in imitation of a Japanese bow, "*Ah-sō-desu-ka*-your-nose-looks-like-a-banana-*moshi-moshi-ano-ne.*" Weston was an outlandish character who was certain to appeal to the camera; I knew I had stumbled on a great story when I observed a pitch meeting from storyboards at the Hakuhōdō Agency for a new TV commercial campaign.

In the first sixty-second spot, Colonel Sanders is discovered as a boy of seven baking rye bread in the roomy kitchen of his "old Kentucky home." "A lifetime later," the narrator intoned, "this same tradition of excellence was transferred by the Colonel to his fried chicken." The preposterous selling point was KFC as traditional, aristocratic food from the American South. I couldn't imagine a more amusing example of an American advertiser playing to Japan's national obsession with American values and manners.

I have no memory of shooting *The Colonel Goes to Japan* because my attention was on Diane. I had prepared the curious International House staff for her arrival by introducing her as my fiancée; we stayed in the nicest room. At dawn every morning, as the crows began their summer yammering, we played tennis for an hour on the court attached to the Tōyō Eiwa Girls School just across the street (where I had taught ELEC English classes twenty years earlier). This was a blatant violation of Japanese propriety—we were trespassing!—and it would never have occurred to me to dare it on my own. Diane was amused by my timidity and coaxed me away from it until I began enjoying the game. How strange it was, how comforting, to feel that I was relinquishing myself to Diane in Japan, a country I presumably had mastered and which she was visiting for the first time. After breakfast downstairs in the I-House coffee shop, my NHK crew would pick me up in a van and take me to the location for the day's shooting. At the end of the day, which I cut as short as possible, I hurried back to pick up Diane and take her sightseeing. I have never been so happy in Tokyo as during those three weeks with her. Evenings we had dinner with Weston at the Playboy Club in Roppongi. One night he read Diane's palm and informed her gravely that there would be no children in her life. When we got back to I-House she threw herself down on the bed and burst into tears. Recalling her weeping I realize how young she was at thirty-four and how vulnerable despite her adventurousness.

From Tokyo we flew to Hong Kong, where Dor-Ner had been scouting the story he wanted, about an entrepreneur from Shanghai, S. T. King, who was getting rich manufacturing designer jeans for Sassoon and Calvin Klein and Sergio Valente. In spite of dreary accommodations and the withering heat, Diane and I had a fine time together. Every morning before sunup we took an hour run through a nearby park. When I wasn't shooting drab scenes at S. T.'s factory, we rode the ferry and watched people on the terrace of the Shangri-la Hotel in Repulse Bay and roamed the night bazaars eating seafood and dim-sum from open-air stands. I had never met anyone as good as Diane at sharing an adventure; I felt certain the excitement between us would last.

I edited *The Colonel* with a delightful fellow named Jay Miracle, a cinematic Jack-of-all-trades who had been working as an assistant sound editor on *Apocalypse Now* when I met him at Coppola's house the night I screened *The Blind Swordsman*. The film went together as easily as a children's jigsaw puzzle; in a month I had a KFC business story that critics called "a noir look" at Japanese society. In truth I was merely goofing on the self-seriousness that characterizes the Japanese approach to so many things. The program aired in October 1981; in April 1982 it won an Emmy for outstanding program in the News and Documentary category.

The Emmy had no effect on my professional life except to encourage me to a second assault on Hollywood. This time I decided to move to Los Angeles. I gave myself six months to accomplish my goal: to sell at least one original screenplay as a first step toward becoming a director of feature films.

I made the move alone. Diane and I had been renting a quirkish house above Stinson Beach with an atrium rock garden and a breathtaking view from the rear terrace of the sun settling into the ocean. And we had been talking about getting married. On a trip to New York we had looked at engagement rings along Forty-seventh Street, an excursion that led me to another program for Enterprise, *The Diamond Game.* One afternoon Diane had come home with her eyes sparkling and a borrowed dress she fancied being married in. I can still see that white dress hanging from our bedroom door, a daily admonition I was incapable of heeding, as the ease and intimacy between us began to erode. We had succumbed to a condition so very common it had a name, "Marin County syndrome." My first family was present in me, and Diane required a free man; our needs were at odds and we requited each other with resentment instead of generosity. For months we lived in gloom inside our beautiful house, and then I moved Diane into a basement apartment in Mill Valley and, shortly after, left for Los Angeles. Thus began the most desolate period of my life to that point.

I rented an apartment on Havenhurst just a block off Sunset. The building was done up to look like the prow of a ship, as if the occupants were on a voyage, but in truth we were becalmed: the neighborhood I had chosen as if by accident was a backwater. It wasn't a slum or even particularly seedy; it was more worn and faded, like the shag rug on my floor, and there was something else unpleasant in the air. When I learned that the neighborhood had been home to struggling screenwriters for decades I realized I was sensing a lingering pall of disappointment.

I began my day with early morning breakfast at Schwab's Pharmacy around the corner at Sunset and Crescent Heights. I arrived at seven as the doors opened. Two others showed up at the same time and sat down at separate tables in the coffee shop next to the soda fountain. One was the actor Roy Scheider, the other was a young woman who looked as if she had been up all night who turned out to be the corrosive comedian Sandra

Bernhardt, still working small comedy clubs along the strip in those days. For weeks we ate alone in silence, until one morning Scheider waved to me to join him, and a day or two later we invited Sandra to sit down with us. After that, breakfast together became a ritual. I suppose we provided one another momentary relief. I never saw either of them again after I left town, but I have wondered whether they continued having breakfast together until Schwab's was torn down.

The rest of the hot morning I sat out on the terrace above our parking lot scribbling story outlines for films on valise-size cards of heavy paper. I worked distractedly and largely without inspiration, driven by an urgent need to produce something salable. I had acquired a young agent at the ICM Agency, Rand Holston, who managed to arrange pitch meetings with producers around town. My pack of wares included a "Body Heat" film I called "Fool's Gold"; something more artsy, about a son in the shadow of his famous author father; and a trinket I hoped could be a TV movie of the week, "The Love Magnet," inspired by the Shaggy Man's magical device that could win anyone's heart. I pitched my stories vividly, uncomfortably aware there was nothing very special about them, and nothing happened. Since my agent was constantly at me to get racier and more violent, I wasn't surprised when he tried to dissuade me from wasting time on the one idea that excited me: a life of Beethoven. I disregarded his advice and worked hard on a treatment of the composer's life that opened with a piano duel at the home of a Viennese nobleman and ended with his listening without hearing it to a performance in his bedroom of his last string quartet. I knew I had the outline of a moving portrait, and I badgered Holston until he reluctantly arranged a meeting with a midlevel producer at Paramount. I pitched the film as an "overcoming adversity saga" that made *Rocky* look like "a walk in the park"; I described Beethoven howling at Heaven in the fury of a storm like King Lear, swearing to the God who had struck him deaf that he would realize his destiny nonetheless, to relieve the suffering of man with the magic of his music. By the time I was finished, the executive had covered his yellow pad with notes. "We're going upstairs to Jeffrey [Katzenberg] with this!" he said in a solemn voice that befitted the momentousness of his decision.

On the way upstairs a few days later, the executive warned me that his boss had a short attention span. I wondered how long he would give me to unfurl Beethoven's life. "Maybe five minutes," he replied with a nervous smile.

Katzenberg, in shirtsleeves and suspenders, sat at a white stem table empty save for a glass full of ice and a can of Diet Coke. As we sat down he turned to me unsmilingly and said, "Go!" I began my pitch. I was picking up steam when a phone behind him rang and he took the call, putting me on hold with his palm uplifted. Just what I needed: Eddie Murphy and Dan Akroyd were calling from a phone booth in New York. While Katzenberg gabbed with his stars I waited, willing myself to stay coiled. Beside me, the executive flashed me a covert thumbs up and whispered, "You're doing fantastic!" Katzenberg hung up and turned back to me and I resumed where I had left off. I wound up; he paused and said, "I can see it. One question: Who'll play Beethoven?"

I had anticipated the question. The day before, a Sunday, Paul Price had invited friends to his house for lunch, including, at my request, Robert Duvall. (Paul and Duvall, whom he called "Bobby," had begun their acting careers together at the Boston Repertory Theater.) I had cornered Duvall and had had little difficulty persuading him that Beethoven was a heroic part he was born to play. "Bob (!) Duvall would be perfect," I replied, "and he told me only yesterday that he's seriously interested in the role." For good measure I added that the German actor

Klaus Maria Brandauer would bring to the role his signature Teutonic fire. Katzenberg looked hard at me for a minute, considering. "Okay—we'll get back within twenty-four hours."

On the way downstairs the studio man jabbered with relief. He had rarely seen Katzenberg so responsive and wouldn't be surprised, though I shouldn't cash the check yet, if he wanted to make a deal. On the way back to Havenhurst I stopped for a carton of cigarettes and two dozen jelly doughnuts. I was very excited; I knew it was unreasonable to expect they would allow me to direct, and if a star like Duvall signed on there would be rewrites and very likely other writers on the job, but the credit would be mine, I had registered my treatment with the Writers Guild, and an original screenplay for a major motion picture would launch me on my way. For the rest of that long day, stuffing jelly donuts and chain-smoking, I stood vigil over my phone until finally, at nine that night, hunger drove me out to grab something to eat. When I got back half an hour later my message light was blinking. It was the studio man: "Just wanted to let you know, Jeffrey was on the fence but he decided to take a pass." That was it, nothing more, not even a "Better luck next time."

Four months into my self-imposed exile, missing my sons and increasingly lonely for Diane, I received a phone call that would shape the course of my professional life for the next ten years. It was from Sam Tyler, then director of corporate underwriting at WGBH; Sam had raised the funding for *Enterprise* and we had met at the Emmy Awards dinner in New York. He had resolved to go out on his own and was calling to ask if I would be interested in coproducing with him a ninety-minute film for Public Television based on Tom Peters's best-selling book, *In Search of Excellence.* As Sam conceived of the partnership, he would be responsible for managing the business end of the project and I would write and direct and narrate the documentary. Sitting where I was, in my dreary apartment with no prospects to sustain me, his proposal was appealing.

I bought a copy of *In Search of Excellence* and knew when I had read it through in a single sitting that I could turn it into an engaging documentary. Peters and his coauthor, Bob Waterman, had traveled across the American corporate map documenting examples of business excellence in Fortune 50 giants like 3M and IBM and small businesses like Stew Leonard's Dairy, a family-run grocery emporium in Norwalk, Connecticut, that drew shoppers from a hundred miles away. Written in 1982, when Japan was stealing markets that had belonged to the United States, the book celebrated American business superiority, insisting that apple pie was better than sushi. Business readers sunk in gloom found its hysterical exuberance uplifting; by the time Tyler called, *Excellence* was setting new sales records for a business book.

Sam flew to L.A. for a meeting and we shook hands on our partnership and agreed to call our production company Nathan/Tyler. Before we could begin to look for funding we had to secure film rights to the book. In September we met Tom Peters for the first time at his offices in Palo Alto. In those days he was careening across the country giving corporate speeches for ever higher fees, dictating new books on the move, flushed and wild-eyed with his escalating success, the Jimmy Swaggart of the business revolution. We weren't the only producers courting him, and he was a hard sell. But Tyler and I were an effective, if unlikely, team. Sam was as straight as a ruler, a good ol' boy from Princeton whose father had been assistant rector at Boston's Trinity Church; easygoing and clean-cut, he was eminently respectable in a familiar, comfortable way and radiated balance and sound judgment. I was Peters's match in voltage and volubility, using words like strings of Chinese firecrackers to vivify my approach to filming his book. At the end of our meeting we had a deal that gave us creative control of a ninety-minute documentary based on his book. We had no trouble raising from Merrill Lynch the $550,000 we needed to fund the project.

I drove north to Mill Valley to share my good fortune with Diane. In her presence I felt her tenderness and how keenly I had missed it, and I asked her to marry me. She agreed. Shortly after we had moved into a small rented house on Morning Sun Avenue, I left on a tour of companies looking for stories I needed for my film.

In February 1984 I went on the road with a film crew of the best freelancers in San Francisco on the first of several sweeps across the country to film episodes at eight companies. Overall, let me admit this and have done with it: *In Search of Excellence: The Film* was as jingoistic about business as the book, created with an eye to extolling corporate virtues even when there were none, full of claptrap devised by me, uncritical to a fault. Even so, I would be lying if I didn't tell you that I had a grand time working on it and am still proud of how well it is made.

On April 8, 1984, in the middle of production, Diane and I got married in New York in the Fifth Avenue apartment of our diamond dealer friend, William Goldberg. Before decamping for Los Angeles I had made a film about Goldberg for *Enterprise, The Diamond Game.* I had begun looking for someone to film after an afternoon on Forty-seventh Street shopping with Diane for an engagement ring. My search for an appealing character had led me first to Nachum Stein, the junior proprietor of the diamond firm Hasenfeld and Stein. Handsome and tightly coiled, with eyes that gleamed with ambition, Nachum was a blessed man: Jacob Hasenfeld had been looking for a Yeshiva student to become his son-in-law and heir, and Nachum's brilliance had distinguished him. Now at forty-two he was wealthy and married with six little girls.

Diane and I joined Nachum and his family for a Sabbath in their home in Crown Heights, Brooklyn, a district occupied by Hasid families. Sitting at Nachum's table Friday night with Diane and his wife, Feigey, and their six daughters, I felt comfortable in the gray fedora Nachum had given me to wear at table for Shabat prayers and dinner, and I was moved, as though I had made contact with an essential part of myself that had been unattended until that moment. When Nachum said "You make a good Jew!" I felt that I was being commended for something genuine in myself.

Saturday morning, Diane stayed at home with Feigey, and I accompanied Nachum on foot to the neighborhood synagogue. I stood there with my head bowed while Nachum and his neighbors raced through the prayers by heart in half whispers and rocked back and forth in the gloom. I can still see the pale, winsome face of the Hasidic boy who happened to be standing alongside me—he must have been about bar-mitzvah age—and his surprise as he realized, observing me, that I was staring blankly at the floor with my lips still. He smiled quizzically and I smiled back. Then, "You don't know how to pray?" I shook my head apologetically. "Your father didn't teach you?" he asked wonderingly. Again I shook my head. I could see him wrestling with this impossibility. "Where do you live?" he inquired. I told him that I lived in San Francisco. He reflected again a moment, then stepped closer to me and said sweetly, sympathetically, "Maybe you should move to a more Jewish neighborhood."

Nachum was a charming fellow in his intense way, but I stopped thinking about featuring him in the film the minute I met William Goldberg, president of the Diamond Dealers' Club in those days and widely acknowledged among his brethren as "the king of diamond street." Goldberg had begun life as a Yeshiva boy studying to become a rabbi, but had abandoned his calling to become a diamond cutter and subsequently, discovering he lacked the hands for the job, a middleman peddling stones for commission. By the time we met him he was specializing in extraordinary goods, "D" flawless treasures that he sold for millions of dollars to a loyal clientele that included Jews and Arabs in equal number.

Goldberg—Willy to his friends—was the sort of subject that lights up a filmmaker's dreams. Everything about him was imposing, including his appearance, which, because of his bald pate and the mane of silver hair he wore long to his shoulders, always put me in mind of the fearsome convict Magwitch in David Lean's *Great Expectations*. On the street, heading for Harry Winston's around the corner to cut a deal, Goldberg wore his expensive Italian suits with élan; in his tenth-floor suite of offices, padding around in his socks and suspenders and monogrammed shirts that looked as though they had been spun from heavy cream, he was a bear with hauteur. Unlike the other dealers we met, who tended to be self-contained and watchful, Goldberg was expansive and massively charismatic. He was also a pontificator with a hot temper, which made him difficult to handle. But we hit it off right away—perhaps my predilection for grandiloquence matched his own—and before long he was allowing me to interrupt him when he was blowing hot air or to chide him for a temper tantrum.

One night after work we were sitting alone in the dining room in his office, where the entire family ate lunch every day. His kosher cook, a Chinese sphinx named Mr. Han, had served us a dairy meal and gone home for the day. Goldberg poured us some brandy, lighted one of his Cuban cigars, and inquired whether I planned to marry Diane. When I replied indefinitely that we had been discussing marriage, he made me promise to allow him when the time came to arrange "a proper Jewish wedding" for us.

A More Jewish Neighborhood

A year and a half later I made good on my promise and he made good on his. I called to tell him our news and he asked me to send him a date and a guest list and to leave everything else to him. Preoccupied with *Excellence,* I accepted gratefully, a careless thing to do. We had been legally married at the Marin County Courthouse a month before. I had showed up in a suit with a bouquet of roses for my bride. After signing the papers we had gone out for champagne and then home to our house on Morning Sun. As we stepped inside Diane had burst into tears. Why hadn't I carried her across the threshold? she asked me reproachfully, and why had I allowed her wedding, her first and only wedding, to feel so happenstantial? I was horrified at having hurt her and cursed myself for a profane man. I swore never again to be so careless. Then I turned around and handed the keys to our wedding ceremony to Willy Goldberg.

The day before the wedding Diane flew to New York from California and I hitched a ride in a Falcon jet with Roger Milliken from our shooting location at Milliken Textiles in South Carolina. The following afternoon, in his sumptuous apartment facing the park, Goldberg laid on a lavish orthodox wedding, including a klezmer band, a renowned cantor from Morocco, fine champagne, and platters of lamb chops. I had only my parents to represent me; Diane's relatives, her mother's many brothers and their wives, filled one of the tables that had been set up in the large living room. I think we also invited about fifteen friends from various chapters in our lives. Together Diane and I dutifully went through the steps of the ritual, following instructions, largely ignorant of the symbolic significance of any of it. It wasn't that the wedding canopy or the smashing of the glass or the wedding songs and dances were unfamiliar—we had both seen Neil Diamond in *The Jazz Singer.* But growing up in our unobservant families—unobservant in every sense of the word—we had never experienced religious Jewish life and had no personal connection to any of its tenets or traditions. As a consequence, we attended rather than partaking of our wedding, uneasy and even embarrassed. The moment I recall most vividly occurred when Goldberg rose to say a few words. "John is a great man," he began promisingly, then, veering, "but his father chose not to give him a proper Jewish education. Each man has his own reasons, and so I feel honored to be standing in for his father in offering him and his beautiful bride a proper wedding for our Jewish faith." Goldberg wasn't being malicious; his own largesse as my surrogate father had filled him with helium and borne him aloft. Mercifully, my true sire was even then moving toward deafness; straining to hear, his head cocked to one side and his eyes narrowed, he was aware that Goldberg was talking about him, but I don't think he realized how presumptuous and insulting his words would have been had they been audible. It might have been comic if it hadn't been so very awkward.

Married now under California and Jewish law, Diane and I left the next morning for a honeymoon on the Caribbean island of St. Barts. After a week of taking refuge in whatever shade we could find, we returned to Mill Valley to begin married life.

11

Mercantile Years

My editor, Jay Tannenbaum, and I screened a rough cut of *Excellence* for Tom Peters and Sam Tyler, and they were overwhelmed. Tyler was so impressed that he borrowed additional money and used it to prepare videocassette copies of the film in advance of the broadcast. He also persuaded the presenting station, WETA Washington, to allow a card after the closing credits notifying the audience that copies were available for $450. Common practice today, this was an innovative move at the time.

In Search of Excellence aired on PBS at 9 p.m. on Wednesday, January 16, 1985. The program attracted the largest audience for a business program in PBS history (a record it still holds). I was sick in bed with the flu, but I remember Diane waking me up at around midnight to take a call from Tyler in Boston. He was babbling with excitement: phone lines at PBS stations across the country were jammed with people placing orders—we were going to be rich!

Excellence sold robustly in the first year after it aired, with spikes in sales after each of three rebroadcasts, and sold steadily if more moderately for years after that, thousands of cassettes at an average price of $400. In the first year, before we made the mistake of becoming a company, the lion's share of revenue flowed directly into our pockets. It was an exciting time for us. We had purchased our first house at 4 Blythedale Terrace, a brown shingle two-story halfway up a hill that opened on a sunlit terrace. And Diane was pregnant. On our daily walk down the Tennessee Valley Road to the little beach beneath the Marin headlands, we discussed plans for the future. Our goal was to avoid slipping into the roles that seemed preordained by our dismayingly similar families. Both our fathers had been raised by women, a bitter, abandoned wife and, on my side, two spinster half-sisters who worked in the needle trade. Victims of a similar deprivation as they grew up, our fathers had never known how to offer nourishment to the women they married: withdrawn, hapless fathers with no authority to assert in our direction; emotionally neglected, resentful mothers. Sitting on the beach in the late afternoons we pledged to stay open to each other always and never to retreat into the hostile separateness that we knew so well in our own homes. I promised to be the kind of father I had never had; I would install a rocking horse on the set wherever I was working in case one of my babies showed up.

Our daughter Emily was born on June 21, 1985, the summer solstice. We called her the baby who glowed in the dark, and today she retains the incandescence that accompanied her into the world. Mayumi created a silkscreen print in Emily's honor, a robust nude beauty with a mermaid's lower body riding the churn beneath a Hokusai wave that lifts to the hint of a rainbow in the blue sky. It was titled *Mamala, the Surf-rider*, and she inscribed the artist's proof she presented to us, "To our family baby girl—hope that you will be the great surf-rider of life. With my love, Mayumi."

By that time, things were better again between Mayumi and me, and as time has passed we have grown closer. For twenty years she lived and worked in the house in Muir Beach that we had briefly shared. In 2000, she bought an untended five-acre farm on a cliff above the sea just south of Kona on the island of Hawaii, and now makes her permanent home there. She is still an artist, and she has also become an environmental activist, a spiritual teacher, and a Buddhist gardener. When she isn't lecturing and giving workshops in Japan or on the mainland, she works in her "mandala garden," an acre and a half of organic fruits and vegetables planted in concentric circles, from sunup to dark. Guests in the house are expected to put in their time. Returning to L.A. from an exhausting visit, our elder son, Zachary, said to me wryly, "The place isn't designed for recreation. She never stops moving and she wants you to keep up, but you can't. Out of the question."

There have been significant men in Mayumi's life, but she has never remarried. Recently she told me she had no more need of men. "But I've learned something about life I treasure from every man I've known," she said. With trepidation I asked if she had learned anything valuable from me. "You taught me scale, John," she replied, "to see how large life could be." I wasn't sure what she meant, but I felt relieved.

By the time Emily was born I was already at work on *Entrepreneurs*, a second ninety-minute documentary special for PBS. I had chosen entrepreneurship on the advice of a friend of Tyler's named Bill Sahlman, a professor at Harvard Business School who assured us we were entering the age of the entrepreneurial revolution. Merrill Lynch was delighted with *Excellence* and funded the new project without even seeing a proposal.

In the new film I tracked episodes in the business lives of five entrepreneurs who had founded spectacularly successful companies: Steve Jobs of Apple, Mitch Kapor of Lotus, Doug Tompkins of Esprit, Lane Nemeth of Discovery Toys, and the Memphis fox, Fred Smith of Federal Express. The most memorable sequence was Steve Jobs laying the foundations for his new company, NeXT, Inc., at a series of secret retreats at the Pebble Beach Lodge outside Carmel. When I was filming the Macintosh story at Apple the year before, Jobs had outdone himself, dropping disparaging remarks about my crew and marring the spontaneity of the sequence by stepping in and out of it like the willful saboteur that he was. For his own reasons, he granted me unlimited access this time; the result was the most intimate and exciting business footage I have ever filmed.

Entrepreneurs aired at 9 p.m. on Wednesday, November 5, 1986. It was a commercial failure. Whereas *Excellence* had earned a 9 rating (equivalent to 900,000 households), *Entrepreneurs* was in the 1s and 2s. To be ready for the sales activity we hoped for on the day following the broadcast, Sam Tyler had installed ten additional phone lines in our office in Waltham near Boston; we received two hundred calls that day but sold only ten videocassettes. At the end of the first week, we had managed to sell only four more.

It is clear to me now that the moment had arrived when I should have changed direction while I was still ahead. With the money I had earned from *Excellence* I could have bought a year and used it to write a new screenplay. Or I might have leveraged my reputation as a documentary filmmaker to help me develop a documentary project with some social relevance or a focus on people and feelings in the manner of Fred Wiseman's probing life studies.

While I worried about the direction I ought to take, Nathan/Tyler was transforming by imperceptible degrees into a business with a maw that needed feeding. In Mill Valley I was renting a curious four-story building that reminded me of the shoe in the nursery rhyme about the old woman, and employing a secretary, a producer, and a full-time editor, Tyler was handling sales and service with a full-time staff of four youngsters from

WGBH in a rented space in Waltham, our "East Coast office." *In Search of Excellence* was still selling, but not well enough to support Tyler and me while covering expenses and funding growth. We had unwittingly created a situation that left me no choice—appeared to leave me no choice—but to produce more Nathan/Tyler products. We contracted with a modestly successful business consultant named Ron Zemke to produce a series of three video workshops on his specialty, customer service. These had me running around the country again through much of 1987 to Marriott hotels in Bethesda and FedEx delivery stations in Colorado and a Cadillac dealer in Dallas. By this time we were no longer producers of documentary films about business for television; we were in the very prosaic training business.

In the fall of 1987, having failed to produce a hit since *In Search of Excellence*, we decided to focus on senior executives, the decision makers in the Fortune 500 companies. From there logic turned us toward the country's richest stable of talent with names that would sell a program in that market: the Harvard Business School. For our first raid we chose the school's brightest star, Michael E. Porter, still a wunderkind at age forty, a PhD in economics who had become a management guru specializing in the science of competitive advantage. Porter agreed to the deal Sam Tyler proposed: Nathan/Tyler would finance the production; Porter committed to giving us twenty full days, not including travel time, when and where we wanted him; he would also receive a heavily discounted day rate of $1,500 for the time he put in.

Before we were under way, the dean of the Business School, John McArthur, intervened. McArthur ran the school with a heavy hand; he made it clear to us that Porter wasn't going public in a video as an HBS professor unless the school was a partner in the enterprise: Harvard would invest and take a share of revenue. Porter pouted a while and inevitably acceded to his dean's demands, giving up some of his percentage to the school. We were also required to diminish our position to somewhere around 40 percent. It was hard to complain, since HBS would share the burden of financing. The best thing about McArthur's intervention was his insistence on a series of videos instead of one; when the meeting he had summoned us to was over we had a three-picture deal. Henceforth, in partnership with the school, Nathan/Tyler would be producing the Harvard Business School Video Series.

Between January and May 1988 I was on the road shooting scenes for *Michael Porter on Competitive Strategy*. Traveling with Porter for weeks at a time I grew fond of him almost in spite of myself. His accomplishments were dazzling, and there was something eerily perfect about him: scratch golfer, scholar, theorist, entrepreneur. But if he was unremittingly self-serious, an elitist whose blue, unblinking eyes behind his eyeglasses reminded me of the children in *Village of the Damned*, he was also naive and eager and affectionate in a boyish way. When expounding on his favorite subject, the dynamics of competitive advantage, he was elegant and unfaltering, but he confessed sheepishly that he had trouble appreciating books and movies, which we sometimes discussed, because by his own account he found feelings confusing. As far as I could tell, his only indulgence was Diet Coke—we had to carry cases of it on ice wherever we went—and a gummy mixture of M&Ms dissolved in Diet Coke that he liked to sip when he was writing. Since the days I am recalling, Porter has climbed to ever higher altitudes; today he is a university professor, the highest rank Harvard bestows on faculty, director of an institute the Business School endowed for him, special consultant to the Boston Red Sox, and on and on. But I like to picture him at a farewell dinner for our crew at a barbecue restaurant in Heber Springs,

Arkansas, on a late Sunday afternoon. Sitting at my side at the head of the table, Porter lifted his glass to toast "the best crew in the world" and then, turning to me, with a twinkle in his eye and an uncharacteristic giggle, "and to the worst—the worst director in the world!"

Working with Porter should have been a full-time job, but during those same early months in 1988 I was also moonlighting as a director of television commercials. Like so many other opportunities in my life it arrived at my doorstep unexpectedly, like a benefaction, and I had only to accept it. In November 1987 I received a call from Ray Lofaro. Though I had never heard of him, Lofaro was a fabled character in the New York ad agency and production world. A crafty, oleaginous Italian with a gimp leg and a walking stick with an ivory handle and silver ferrule, he had been a high-end commercial producer in his heyday and was now a directors' rep who specialized in bringing outsiders into the commercial business; when I knew him he was managing careers for people like John Milius, Peter Max, James Ivory, and David Fincher. In our first phone conversation, he told me something I didn't know: that agency producers were using clips from my business films to add color and spice to their pitches to clients. This gave me a certain cachet, and the perfect moment to act on it had arrived. AT&T was preparing to launch a national TV campaign aimed at businesses and was calling for a competitive shootout among its three principal ad agencies to compete for the lead position. Ray had taken the liberty of mentioning me to his friend John Doig, the creative director at Ogilvy and Mather, and Doig wanted a meeting.

We met in New York at Ogilvy's offices on the tenth and eleventh floors of a terraced building on Forty-eighth Street between Fifth and Madison Avenues. (On Father's Day 2006 the block was designated "William Goldberg Way.") Doig was a fiery New Zealander, cockily self-assured, foul-mouthed and irreverent about everything except advertising, a subject that became a source of contention between us. He was looking for a new angle on business-to-business advertising to propose to AT&T; I observed that the business environment was always portrayed as upbeat and benevolent when in fact employees lived in fear of their managers. Doig bit hard; he asked me to write and direct a test commercial for a hypothetical "grim reality" campaign. Working with one of Ogilvy's copywriters I devised a scene in which a large order is lost as a result of a phone message ending up on an unused extension, a costly gaffe with unpromising consequences for the salesman who was responsible that would not have happened on an AT&T phone system. I picked the six actors I needed to play out the scene around a table at a casting session the following day and directed it in a conference room at Ogilvy, shooting on grainy 16 mm film to enhance the "grim reality" of the moment. Submitting a finished commercial in place of the standard storyboard presentation was a bold stroke; though the production was crude it must have cost Doig at least $50,000. I received $8,000 for my three days' work.

Lofaro reached me on a sound stage in Boston, where I was shooting Porter. O&M had won the competition, and that wasn't all: AT&T had stipulated that I was to direct all the commercials in the new campaign, not only at Ogilvy but also at the other two agencies, McCann-Erickson and Young and Rubicam. Lofaro assured me this was unprecedented in his thirty years in the business.

From January to mid-April 1988, between locations for the Porter show, I shot fourteen sixty-second AT&T commercials and fourteen thirty-second versions at three ad agencies. Fourteen minutes of work in four months may not sound like much if you don't know what is involved in the making of a single commercial, but this was a huge job. I worked in Los Angeles and New York; frequently I wrapped a job in one city and flew a red-eye across the country to the other, where sets for the following days' work had already been constructed for me to approve when I arrived.

Each of the commercials delivered the same cautionary message: choosing office phone systems other than AT&T's may be hazardous to your career. To enhance the feeling of "grim reality" I filmed each of them in a single, unedited shot and positioned the characters apart from one another so that the camera had to rake back and forth across the frame to find the speaker, as if it were an unprepared observer. I began the day rehearsing my ensemble of two or three and sometimes as many as six players and choreographing the camera's moves as it followed the story. My cameraman worked in a wheelchair that allowed him to dolly in and out and swivel (a steady-cam would have been too smooth for the effect we wanted). When the scene was ready we began shooting it over and over again in single takes. I fine-tuned performances and adjusted camera moves as we went until takes began timing out at exactly forty-five seconds as required; the last fifteen seconds delivered the pitch, the warning, on four cards, white letters on a black field with ominous music in the background. We worked all afternoon until we had ten or a dozen perfect takes in the can. Editing the next day was a simple matter of choosing the best single take.

Directing a television commercial can be a nerve-wracking experience, but the work came naturally to me and I reveled in it, partly, I suppose, because I was unable to take it seriously. I beguiled my temperamental crews with the blend of humor and sternness that I had learned from Shintarō Katsu; I made the anxious, tight-lipped clients feel that they were being heard when they violated the taboo about speaking to me directly and asked for a smile from an actor that was "confident but uncertain, gentle but a little cruel, amused but grieving." And I cajoled, scolded, and threatened good performances from my actors again and again, walking them around the block when they froze up or, in moments of crisis, with the expensive clock ticking, modeling their lines and commanding them to imitate me word for word until they regained themselves. Commercial directors tend to specialize: there are the graphic Mondrians, the table-top lighters who make a glass of foaming beer look like ambrosia, the automobile wizards, and the shampoo men who capture the cascading, slow-motion beauty of a hair toss. Word got around that I was about performance, an actor's director. Jounalists began visiting my set to watch me work. Ray Lofaro paid regular visits and nodded approvingly. (I was paying him 10 percent of what I earned.) Ridley Scott came and later invited me to sign on as a staff director in his TV production company, RSC. I declined; I was already being paid a class-A director's rate of $10,000 a day. I was, moreover, producing the commercials through a company I had incorporated for that purpose, Giant Step Productions, and was receiving, in addition to my fee, a 20 percent production markup with no fixed overhead to support. What I should have considered was that affiliation with Ridley Scott would have helped me get work after the AT&T campaign. But building for the future is something I have never done well. Meanwhile, money was pouring into our pockets and I was having a grand time into the bargain.

Our son, Tobias, was born on November, 8, 1987, the very day Lofaro called for the first time. When I was shooting in Los Angeles for more than a day, though I didn't go so far as to install a rocking horse in the studio, I brought Diane and our babies down and installed the family in the Hotel Bel Age. Diane's mother, Linda, flew out from Florida to join us at the hotel more than once, releasing Diane to accompany me to the dinners with Doig and his counterparts at the other agencies I was expected to host in my capacity as producer.

I hadn't bothered to inform Sam Tyler that I was working

on commercials because I knew he would object. In truth, I had arranged to have his calls to me in Mill Valley, where he assumed I would be, forwarded to Los Angeles or New York without his knowledge. Then, in February 1988 the ad industry magazine *Adweek* reported that I had emerged "from nowhere"—to people in the business only advertising was somewhere—to bring to AT&T's newest campaign a brand new look. Inevitably, someone saw the article, which was followed by another in *Backstage*, and the word spread among our investors that I was not only moonlighting but attracting national media attention. The timing couldn't have been worse: Bill Sahlman was just embarking on a second round of fund-raising on our behalf, actively recruiting new limited partners. He had led the first round, buying in himself and inducing his wealthy friends and business associates to follow suit. Now someone was waving *Adweek* in his face. The next thing I knew I received a letter from the venerable Boston law firm of Hill & Barlow threatening to sue me for breach of my employment contract with Nathan/Tyler. I have always been fearful of anything that smacked of the law; the letter, dispatched by people who had always led me to believe they supported me, was a shock. In the end, after a nasty confrontation with Sahlman and Tyler in Boston, I agreed to limit my time away from the company to a designated number of days a year, and we resolved our dispute without a lawsuit. Upsetting as it was at the time, this contretemps turned out to be trivial compared to the debacle to come.

Early in March, on the road with Porter between back-to-back commercials in Los Angeles and New York, another opportunity presented itself. An old friend from Princeton, Yoshi Shimizu, had been appointed guest curator of an exhibition at the National Gallery of Art in Washington: *Japan, the Shaping of Daimyō Culture, 1200–1800*. The gallery was planning to produce a film to be screened daily as an adjunct to

Living Carelessly in Tokyo and Elsewhere

the show and to be broadcast on PBS. In his capacity as guest curator, Yoshi was asking me to submit a proposal. I jumped at this and was awarded the job. The gallery also approved the substantial budget I submitted: $400,000 to cover a week of preparation and two weeks of filming across Japan. (Each of the AT&T commercials cost at least this much.) Lofaro advised me not to go: I was just beginning to establish myself on the commercial scene—AT&T had launched the campaign with three of my spots on the Superbowl at the end of January and was proclaiming an upturn in business phone sales—and new job inquiries were coming in. This is a fickle business, he warned, with an impossibly short memory; if I disappeared for a month now I could count on being yesterday's lunch when I returned. Lofaro was emphatic, but I don't think I believed him. Besides, I didn't care. What was working in advertising compared to making a film for the National Gallery of Art!

On May 8, 1988, having turned down an American Express commercial with Henry Kissinger that was offered to me without an audition, I left for three weeks in Japan with Diane and the children and my mother-in-law, Linda. My friend and lighting man, Jon Fontana, and the cameraman I had used on AT&T, John LeBlanc, joined us and my Japanese crew in Tokyo. We were on the road for two weeks, west from Tokyo to the ancient castle town of Kumamoto in Kyushu and back through Kyoto. I often carried Toby, just six months old, on my back, attracting stares and giggles; Emily skipped along at my side infiltrating scenes, asking questions in stage whispers that made their way onto our sound track, or jumping into my lap in the middle of an interview on camera.

I had decided to focus the film on the ideal known as the "dual way of the pen and the sword," the blending of fierceness and delicacy which had been the lifelong goal of feudal Japan's warrior-poets, the samurai. (The *Daimyō* in "*Daimyō* culture"

236

referred to the warrior aristocracy, the heads of the feudal families to whom fealty was owed by samurai retainers.) The gallery had used its prestige to enroll the normally recalcitrant Agency for Cultural Affairs; the bureaucrats had put me in touch with the artists and performers I needed for the film. The time I spent with *kendō* swordsmen and mounted archers, tea masters, a family of Noh actors, and a renowned calligrapher felt like a homecoming and was full of joy for me. I hadn't felt so excited about capturing scenes on film since *Farm Song*.

The last day of the shoot we filmed the eighty-one-year-old calligrapher Shinzan Kamijō at work. Shinzan inked his characters with slashes of a large brush, thick, bold strokes that recalled the calligraphy of medieval warrior-artists (the style emulated by Robert Motherwell). I had asked him to write the four characters that I was translating "the dual way of the pen and the sword"—*text-martial-both-roads*—but he chose a two-character compound; perhaps my request would have been too much work. The first character, *gan*, means to contain, include, subsume. The second, *kō*, means light or radiance. Together they were the name of a mythical sword from ancient China; the compound also signified the light contained and radiated by the right action of a Confucian gentleman.

A masterpiece of calligraphy, a singular art, can be created in a few seconds of intensely focused activity. Watching Shinzan work was breathtaking: he gathered himself, eyes closed, lifted his heavy brush from the stone inkwell, and, in a single motion of unbroken, unerring strokes, inscribed the two characters on the three-foot sheet of rice paper on the floor in front of him. Because we needed coverage to edit the sequence together, footage of the process filmed from different angles, I had to ask him to begin and complete the same scroll a number of times, and he obliged me. The intensity of his energy never flagged, and he completed each version by signing it "Shinzan" with a smaller brush. In the end he had created nine identical signed scrolls, each one a valuable work of art. I was seized with a desire to own one and dropped hints as we went along, imagining aloud how very fortunate a man would be to hang such a scroll in the place of honor in his house so he might enjoy it day and night. No one seemed to be listening; as the master completed a scroll his apprentices rolled it carefully and packed it away in a lacquered tube. At the end of the morning I thanked Shinzan, bowed deeply to him, and watched him and his retinue drive away with his precious morning's work. A year later, shortly before the calligrapher died, a mailing tube arrived at our house in Mill Valley. It was one of the *gankō* scrolls. We had it beautifully faced and mounted in a heavy black and silver frame and it hangs even now in our living room, in the place of honor.

In Japan for the first time in four years, I made no attempt to contact any of the people who had been so important to me in the past. To be sure, I was working or on the move most of the time, but a busy schedule shouldn't have stopped me from reaching out to friends so close and dear in the past, Ōe and Kōbō Abe, for example, who were both in Tokyo that spring. Truth was, I had already let important connections unravel through inattention, and that predilection for carelessness has been a bane to me all my life.

I did make one new friend during that shoot, a remarkable Noh actor named Otoshige Sakai. The son of an actor in the Kanze School, Sakai liked to say he had begun preparing for the stage in his mother's womb: he first appeared on the stage at three and performed his first role as a protagonist at the age of eight. Despite his relative youth, by the time I met him, at forty-nine, he had been designated a Bearer of Important Intangible Cultural Assets, Japan's equivalent of knighthood, and his three sons, ten, twelve, and thirteen, had been apprentice performers for years, training with their father on the Noh stage

238

in his house. There is nothing unusual about screening rooms at home, even luxurious ones with Italian sofas for seating, but a Noh stage with runway entrance and spring-loaded floor of aged Japanese cypress is another matter; when an assistant ushered me into the theater on my first visit to Sakai's house I was overwhelmed.

Our meeting began badly. I sat facing the stage at a low table on the tatami floor; two editors from the *Yomiuri Shimbun*, Sakai's sponsor in some capacity, and several bureaucrats from the Agency for Cultural Affairs were already seated stiffly at the table. Sakai made his entrance in formal kimono and *hakama*, gliding across the floor with feline litheness, and sat opposite me, his back to the stage. He bowed and welcomed me to his home; I thanked him for his graciousness in consenting to see me at such a busy time. Attendants appeared with green tea and placed a cup in front of each of us. "Now then," Sakai began unsmilingly, "what's all this about *Atsumori*?" He was referring to a fifteenth-century Noh play I was proposing to film. The warrior Kumagae no Naozane discovers Atsumori swimming toward the fleeing ships of his defeated clan and challenges him on his honor to return to shore and fight. They grapple on the beach; Kumagae overwhelms the younger man and pulls off his helmet, thinking to behead him. He is struck by Atsumori's youth and beauty; he appears to be just the age of his own son. Kumagae fain would spare him, but he is aware of his comrades galloping toward them. Preferring that the boy die at his own hands so that he can offer prayers for him in the afterlife, he strikes off his head, weeping. Then, in a brocade bag at the youth's side, he discovers a flute and realizes that it was Atsumori who played poignantly each night from the battlements of his besieged castle. Kumagae is so moved by this encounter that he renounces the world and becomes a Buddhist monk.

I had requested a performance of *Atsumori* because the play evoked beautifully the ideal of the "dual way," and that was what I tried explaining to Master Sakai as he sat listening to me impassively. I realized he was putting me on the spot intentionally and he allowed me to feel that he was not inclined to take me seriously. It had been years since I had been required to express myself subtly in Japanese, but the language has always come to my aid at moments of crisis, and as I held forth I could sense fluency returning to me. When I finished, Sakai looked hard at me for a moment, then smiled for the first time, a broad grin of a smile, and clapped his hands sharply twice, at which signal *shōji* doors to one side of the hall slid open and attendants appeared again, this time with sumptuous lunches for all of us in gold lacquer *o-bentō* boxes inscribed with Sakai's insignia in gold leaf. How can I expect you to believe the transformation in his mien and behavior toward me from that moment forward? Aloof, condescending, icy until just a minute ago, he now became gentle and solicitous, full of mischief and even flirtatious in a slightly effeminate way, inquiring with a smirk and a giggle what kind of a drunk I was and whether I knew how to comport myself on the town at night at geisha parties, an art he promised to teach me. I can't account for the change, except to imagine that he was inclined to like me from the onset and needed only to reassure himself that I was in earnest. I didn't film *Atsumori*— Sakai chided me for expecting naïvely that a performance would be staged to accommodate me—but I did film him performing a passage from *Funa Benkei* (Benkei in the Boat), in which the frenzied ghost of a warrior seeking to avenge his drowned clan rises from the sea to assail Yoshitsune, performed by a child actor to represent that noble lord's purity. I also began under his tutelage my study of the geisha "world of flowers and willows." If Sakai possessed an encyclopedic command of Noh—the difficult texts and performance traditions of course, but also masks and costumes and music—he was equally a connoisseur of the

arcane world of the geisha and a familiar figure at exclusive geisha establishments in Tokyo and Kyoto. Frequently he took his
wife along with him, a measure of how at home he felt and, I
suppose, of his ease with Mrs. Sakai. Bringing one's spouse into
the inherently suggestive if not explicitly lascivious atmosphere
of a geisha house was an unheard of thing to do, and I have never
known anyone else to do it. I know nothing of Mrs. Sakai's background, but clearly she was comfortable in the company of geisha and they seemed to enjoy her presence as well. Chiefly they
were delighted to be entertaining Sakai himself, who basked in
their attention, smoked cigarillos from a mother-of-pearl case
he carried in the sleeve of his kimono, drank heavily of scotch
and brandy and, on occasion, sake served cold, played exuberantly their parlor games full of innuendo, and, with increasing
frequency as an evening wore on, responded to pleas from the
table to sing and joined the troubadours who circulated among
the establishments like Mariachi bands to croon a ballad in the
old Japanese style. There was a dramatic, a marvelous incongru-
ity about these moments—imagine Placido Domingo singing at
a karaoke party.

In the 1990s, when I was returning frequently to Tokyo once
again, I spent many evenings on the town with Sakai. Often he
would inquire before picking me up in his chauffeured Daimler
what kind of food I would prefer, offering me an opportunity to
reply, as I invariably did, "Japanese." Japanese haute cuisine, a
suite of one ineffable surprise after another, is an extravagance
that has always been beyond my means. But clearly the expense
meant nothing to Sakai; over time I came to understand that
his exorbitant lifestyle was supported by patrons in thrall to
his art, wealthy women mainly, who formed a sort of women's
auxiliary attached to him exclusively. I had observed this sort of
patronage in the Bunraku puppet theater years before, but not
on the kingly scale that Sakai enjoyed.

Living Carelessly in Tokyo and Elsewhere

* * *

Ray Lofaro's prediction about my TV commercial career proved accurate. Returning to Mill Valley, I discovered that the qualities that had attracted positive attention to the AT&T campaign, the grainy look and restless camera and flat "refrigerator lighting" as one producer described it disparagingly, were now liabilities. I continued to work occasionally but only on tiresome or trying jobs that were a far cry from AT&T. Late in August I went to Miami to direct a campaign for Florida Light and Power that began with an intrepid meter-reader lady being chased around by a customer's attack goose. Blind with sweat in the sweltering heat I tried to coerce the goose at the end of a slender wire to advance menacingly into the camera, take after take, and ultimately failed. At Thanksgiving I landed another job in New York that took ten dreary days, a dozen weepy convalescents in wheelchairs or hospital beds thanking Charter Medical for the hospital care they had received. There was a series of static dialogues across a table in a diner on a set in Los Angeles; I don't even remember who the client was. Finally, in Atlanta the week of January 17, 1991, just as Desert Storm began, this time for Georgia Power and Light, I traipsed around the twilit hills outside the city following a Promethean caveman discovering that a firebrand could light the gloominess of his cave after dark.

I was a TV commercial flash in the pan, a has-been by the time I returned to California, but I was too excited about *Daimyō* to care. That summer my full-time editor, Jay Tannenbaum, and I moved back and forth between two of the narrow floors of our lopsided building, editing Michael Porter on one floor and *Daimyō* on the other. My composer friend Andy Kulberg found Japanese musicians in Los Angeles, *biwa* and *shakuhachi* players, and produced a score with a genuine Japanese feeling. In September, for the opening of the exhibition,

242

Sakai brought a troupe of Kanze School chanters and musicians to Washington and performed on a raised stage in the National Gallery courtyard the frenzied scene from *Funa Benkei* I had included in the film, which also premiered that night in the gallery auditorium.

Michael Porter on Competitive Strategy was a hit that fall, our first bonanza since *In Search of Excellence*. It came in a thick 9" by 12" box that included two videocassettes, a user's manual, a viewer's guide summarizing the lessons in the program, relevant articles from the *Harvard Business Review*, and a case study on the Skil Corporation. It was priced at $1,500. When we determined that the response rate to our direct mailing was an astounding 10 percent, the marketing mavens at the school who had set the price acknowledged they had blundered on the low side, leaving money "on the table." Perhaps, but all parties had reason to be pleased even so: in its first year on the market *Competitive Strategy* generated gross revenue of $2.6 million. Porter took home wheelbarrows of money, and the school and Nathan/Tyler divvied up the rest. It was a very different experience from the early days, when Sam Tyler and I pocketed 80 cents of every dollar generated by *Excellence*. Now we had production costs to finance and mounting overhead; still, after *Porter* we took substantial raises and felt very well off.

I have at hand the Nathan/Tyler product catalogue for spring 1993, our last catalogue. An expensive affair for a mailing piece, sixteen pages of graphics and photos in five-colors, it offers clients twelve executive video seminars priced from $2,000 to $10,000. Each of the seminars we peddled cost me weeks and months away from the family on the road. Perusing the catalogue that is now a relic, I recall countless CEO interviews, scenes in boardrooms, showrooms, and on factory floors, marathon taping sessions on sound stages in Boston, where I managed my uppity presenters with a mixture of ingratiation and fluency and arrogance that outmatched their own, and endless days and nights in editing rooms. I was troubled all along by the sense that I was selling myself short, even during the brief period when Nathan/Tyler was flourishing, and noted my uneasiness often in the diary I kept for Emily and Toby during these years.

> June 2, 1990
> This morning I flew to Memphis, Tennessee to set up some scenes inside Federal Express. I am very skilled at visiting a giant corporation and in one day of conversations figuring out where to aim my cameras to capture the illustrations of a point I need in a unique and dramatic way. But this is draining work, and even as I write these lines to you I feel a bit sad, depressed, that I am still harnessing my talent to this business video claptrap instead of somehow breaking into feature films.

I wasn't always berating myself. Sometimes I effused about the company I was in charge of creatively, "the Rolls Royce purveyor" of this and that, as I called it to anyone who would listen. I enjoyed my large corner office on the tenth floor of a building in Copley Square, and my two executive secretaries, and I enjoyed enriching the look of our shows, spending money on increasingly lavish sets and dramatic lighting effects. At some point we acquired a model of an elegant T'ang Dynasty horse that I installed somewhere in view on the principal set of every program we produced, a migrating symbol of Nathan/Tyler quality.

Mercantile Years

In the summer of 1989 I moved the family from California back to Massachusetts, where I was spending most of my time. Diane didn't want to go; her acupuncture practice and her friends were in Marin County. But she was willing to accommodate the vagaries of my career and threw herself into the move. I had brightened the picture I painted of life in Massachusetts with an empty promise of stimulating evenings with old friends on the Harvard faculty.

On a reconnaissance trip in May I had been ensorcelled—no other word will do—by a house in Essex, a small town thirty-two miles northeast of Boston on Cape Ann. The house had been built in 1907 as a wedding gift for a young couple from Boston. It had been intended as a spring residence—the Beacon Hill aristocracy maintained both spring and summer homes out of town—and was landscaped to present itself most gorgeously at just the moment it took my breath away: apple trees in blossom, clover in the lawns, flowerbeds on fire. It was a three-story brick Georgian at the top of a hill on seventeen acres of meadows and woods. There was a stone tower with a rickety spiral staircase that ascended to a lookout room, and a large barn. On one side of the house was a swimming pool on the site of what originally had been the ballroom. The shade trees and expansive lawn in front felt like a park, and at the back three acres of fenced meadow sloped down to a tree line of tall pines and, just beyond the pines, Cape Ann Bay. From the balcony of the master bedroom on the second floor we could see beyond the beach the estate that had been home to Jack Nicholson in his role as the devil in *The Witches of Eastwick*. John Updike lived just down the road and was often to be seen running errands in his corduroy slacks and fraying sweaters.

The minute I saw the place, I wanted it unreasoningly. I called Diane and asked her to fly east the next day; I drove her straight to Essex from Logan Airport and the house bewitched her as it

245

had me. We bought it from a bond trader who was in financial trouble and desperate to sell. As we walked the grounds the day before the escrow closed, he confessed he was heartbroken to lose the place, which his wife and three children loved. I remember feeling bad for him as we returned to the house across the sweeping lawn, and fortunate for myself. The prospect of living like a country squire had me dizzy.

We moved in on July 7, 1989. There is something fervent about my entry that morning in the diary I was keeping for the children:

> 7 a.m. You are all asleep in our motel room, Toby is in a crib. We are in Essex, Mass., 32 miles northeast of Boston. Today we will complete the purchase of our new home here, Rocky Hill Farm!
>
> Now at last we have found a wonderful old home on 17 acres of lawns, and we shall indeed have a dog and pony for you and Toby, and who knows what else. I do confidently believe this is—and will continue to be!—our true home. I believe that you, Emily, will first read these pages here at Rocky Hill, in your bedroom here as a young lady of twelve or thirteen. I feel certain I am right about this. But only time will tell. . . .

Though it seems clear enough now, I don't think I realized that Rocky Hill Farm was an extension of the fantasy I had once projected more modestly on my cherry dining table at Princeton. Moreover, that huge white elephant of a house served me for a passing moment as tangible evidence of the substantial self that continued to elude me.

Life on our estate was very different from my grandiose projection of what it would be. I had forgotten about sultry New

England summers and about the mosquitoes, which attacked the children every time they ventured outside and sent them screaming back into the house. Emily picked at the bites until they bled, and they added to her distress at being uprooted from her home and friends in cool, bug-free Mill Valley; clomping down the stairs in Diane's shoes and a sequined pale yellow gown she insisted on wearing daily, her legs and neck dripping blood, her eyes wild and her curly hair standing straight up, she was like a tiny Madwoman of Chaillot.

Toby, just under two when we moved in, seemed unfazed. Perhaps more than any of us he reveled in the house, climbing and descending the endless flights of stairs in his Superman costume and pilfered sunglasses and invading my third-floor office just long enough to scramble my computer while I was on the phone before setting off on another careening, wobbly round of discovery.

Diane was struggling to wrestle the house into submission even as she undertook to remodel it. Every day local workmen arrived at sunup to hammer and plaster and to grind and polish on their knees the pine boards in the floors and the long halls. Diane sat at her telephone in the brick room off the kitchen, giving instructions and paying bills. Weekends we drove to Cambridge to look for lighting fixtures and antique sconces and tiles to haul home. Her first project was the third floor, which she converted to a suite of Nathan/Tyler offices; there was a large office for me, a smaller one next door in which I installed a secretary, two editing rooms, and a conference room.

My spacious office overlooking the lawn allowed me to work at home when I wasn't on the road. But maintaining the house proved to be costly beyond our means, not to mention the toll it was taking on Diane. After moving in we discovered there were no storm windows on the twenty-seven sets of French doors on the first floor; the furnace system burned a fortune in oil all winter; an entire wall sweated beads of moisture for reasons no one could determine and kept the dining room dank as a greenhouse. That fall I brought home a video of *The Money Pit* and Diane cried all the way through it.

Living at Rocky Hill Farm had its lovely moments. At apple picking time we went to an orchard just down our road, Apple Road, where visitors could pick a bushel of apples for a few dollars. At Christmas we cut a tree in our own woods. (My friends in elementary school had come to our apartment to gawk at our Christmas tree, the only one in the neighborhood.) We kept chickens and an entire petting zoo, including a miniature horse and a llama named Skipper.

But we felt isolated. The locals in Essex and nearby Manchester and Gloucester were laborers and fishermen, many of them descended from Portuguese whaling men. The estates were occupied by Boston Brahmins who were remote. I happened to know one of them because he was a friend of Sam Tyler's. A Boston real estate mogul, his name was Ferdinand Colloredo-Mansfeld, but he was known to his friends as "Moose." Moose took a personal interest in what I was up to because Sam had recruited him as an investor in Nathan/Tyler—I think Moose suspected me of extravagance and disapproved—and he invited us to dinner at his nearby farm and allowed Diane to ride one of the horses in his stable once or twice. It was Moose who counseled me not to take offense if my other neighbors seemed unfriendly. In this neck of the woods, he explained, it took people five years at least to accept newcomers.

One day in April 1990 I came home from a Harvard shoot in Sudbury and was surprised to hear a song coming from our living room, four or five male voices singing out of tune, and someone who could scarcely play accompanying them on my Yamaha baby grand. (I had no idea at the time that any teenage girl in America would have assigned her soul to the Devil

for the opportunity of being there.) I found Diane in the sun-
room and she told me excitedly that a "famous rock band" had
showed up at the door with a real estate agent and was considering making us an offer. I was surprised but far from dismayed.
Our mortgage was $9,300 a month, and though I was draw-
ing a hefty salary from Nathan/Tyler and we were charging the
third floor to the company, the property was straining us finan-
cially and it had occurred to me that a downturn in the business
would leave us with an albatross around our necks. Diane had
ample reasons of her own for wishing to be emancipated. If we
hadn't discussed selling the house it was because we were certain that it was a white elephant that no one would be foolish
enough to buy.

How could we have dreamed that our deus ex machina
would appear in the form of juvenile rock stars! The band
turned out to be New Kids on the Block, a boy band that was
the synthetic product of a marketing strategy that had little to
do with music, as we knew from what we had heard in our living room. Two of the members, Jonathan and Jordan Knight,
had decided they wanted the seclusion of Rocky Hill for themselves and their mother and three grown sisters. At the time they
were the highest paid performers in America, above Michael
Jackson and Madonna, and they quickly accepted the price
we proposed. But there was a contingency: if the word got out
that the Knight brothers were moving in, the deal was off. We
were on tenterhooks during the six weeks until the closing, and
there was at least one leak. We found a note scrawled in pencil
form the cleaning lady's thirteen-year-old daughter: if we would
allow her to sneak one look at the Knight brothers she pledged
to wash our dishes for the rest of our lives. As far as we knew,
the single breach in security didn't envelop the town in hysterical anticipation.

Closing day I found myself walking the grounds with Jonathan Knight, just as the bond trader had walked with me. It was June 14, 1990, a month short of a year since we had moved in. I wasn't heartbroken for the family: it had been a traumatic year for Diane and the children. For myself I felt relieved and sad. I still loved the place, and our move after such a brief time there confronted me with the instability that seemed to plague us (our new furniture had just arrived and was sitting in the living room in unopened crates). Had I known how much longer continuity would continue to elude us I would have felt lower.

Jonathan Knight had two pressing questions on his young mind. What did I think, he wanted to know, about putting in a *koi* pond? The teenage singer Tiffany had one at her place and seemed to enjoy it. I said a *koi* pond sounded like a capital idea. And how about a helipad? The notion amused me. When we moved in I had watched our blue-blood real estate agent go pale when I told him I intended to hang a neon Star of David from the top of our stone tower. I confess it pleased me now to picture the neighbors when they learned that we had left the property in the hands of teenage rockers intending to fly in and out by helicopter.

12

Stockholm

We had left Rocky Hill Farm, but I never abandoned my dream of the paterfamilias installed at the center of an abiding family homestead. Nevertheless, I count eleven houses we have moved in and out of since then, a few rented but most purchased, first in Massachusetts and then back in California.

For the remainder of that summer we rented a light, airy house on the dunes at Singing Beach in Manchester, just down the road from Essex. It was a carefree summer. We had money in the bank, and Diane was relieved to be released from battle with Rocky Hill. I was enjoying what turned out to be short-lived relief of my own after hiring someone to manage the business. Scott Rossborough had come from a first career in sales at an ad agency; he was a pasty-faced, humorless, would-be executive, with monogrammed shirts and a shiny briefcase. At the end of the day before he left his office he untangled his telephone cord and arranged it neatly on top of his desk. He claimed to read spreadsheets fluently, and when he looked at ours he vowed to move us toward our terrific potential by cutting costs and increasing sales. I hired him as president of Nathan/Tyler at a salary that was more than we could afford, even though I was never comfortable in his alien presence. I suppose I assumed that because he was so unlike me he was bound to do well what I had neither gift for nor patience to do. That faulty logic would cost me dearly.

We spent the long, dark winter that year in a drafty rental half a mile down the road on Manchester Harbor. We had been obliged to take it at the last minute because I had neglected to spend the time needed to find us a nice house to rent in Cambridge. At the end of March we moved again, this time into an elaborately remodeled Victorian with lawns that sloped down to an ocean cove and a view of Bakers' and Misery Islands that reminded me of the Inland Sea. We rented the house for a year from a wealthy entrepreneur named Tom Gerrity, a friend of Mike Porter's, who was moving to Philadelphia with his family to become dean of the Wharton School. There was an exercise room and a sauna and a paneled office on the third floor, and a children's room with wall frescoes of Disney characters.

I commuted to our office in downtown Boston and was as always away on location for weeks at a time. Midway through 1992 we went into production of what was to be our last hurrah, an ill-considered attempt to adapt to video Michael Porter's massive analysis, *The Competitive Advantage of Nations*. We taped Porter introducing his model on a set and again in front of an audience of young entrepreneurs, then took our traveling circus on the road to the Amsterdam flower market, Miele Appliances in Hamburg, Ferragamo in Florence, Honda and Canon Camera in Tokyo, and NEC in Singapore. At these and other locations Porter did more talking into the camera and conducted interviews with CEOs and government big shots. When we were finished months later, we had five hours of talk and graphics on four videocassettes in two versions, one for corporate and one for government clients. At just over $1 million, this may have been the most expensive video ever produced at the time; fortunately, according to the terms of our new agreement, Harvard Business School put up all the money and we were paid a production fee for our services and a modest royalty. But there were no royalties: only a handful of customers were willing to pay $3,950 to watch Mike Porter in endless stand-ups around the world. This time we had gone too far.

I was still on the road with Porter when we bought a house Diane had found in Mill Valley and remodeled long distance. Now I was commuting to the East Coast again and even less frequently at home. We bought a one-bedroom condo on Beacon Street in the Back Bay, a five-minute walk from Nathan/Tyler, where I stayed when I was in Boston; Diane found the place and went to a lot of trouble furnishing it for me but never spent a night there.

One morning in August 1993 my executive producer, Maureen Ryan, came into my office at Nathan/Tyler with a disturbed look on her face and reported that we were unable to complete our three programs in production because we had run out of money. She didn't know how this had been allowed to happen; her job as head producer was managing production costs and had nothing to do with profit and loss. Funding should have been my responsibility; I was chairman of the company and principal stockholder. But I had never paid much attention to running the business, especially not since hiring Rossborough. Every so often, when I remembered, I had asked him dutifully the one question I knew to frame pertaining to the business, whether we were making more money than we were spending, and had been told condescendingly that there was no simple answer. As it turned out there was a simple answer and it was emphatically No! I have mentioned the pleasure I took in lavishing money on our productions in the name of Nathan/Tyler quality; as it turned out, our marketing campaigns had been similarly extravagant, costing us more than the revenue they generated. Maureen was alarmed at having discovered that our production funds were gone, but I don't think she realized she was telling me that we were going out of business. At that moment I'm not sure I realized it myself.

I knew enough to know that we were in big trouble. At the time we had three partners, the Harvard Business School, *Fortune* magazine and the American Institute for Managing Diversity. Our coproducers had paid in their half-share of production costs, $200,000 to $250,000 each, and we had used their money to launch the productions. Now we were obliged to complete them with our half-share of the investment and Maureen was telling me we didn't have the funds to spend. That meant that we were in breach of contract.

There was something else dismaying to me. Four months earlier, Rossborough had informed me matter-of-factly that we needed an immediate cash transfusion due to the fact that his sales projections had been off. A minor glitch he said, a "cash flow problem." Cash flow is among the most dangerous euphemisms in business parlance; it means the business isn't making enough money to sustain itself. In July 1991 Diane and I had already loaned the company $155,000 to help with cash flow; our promissory note, due in May 1992, had not been paid. This time, covering my desk with spreadsheets, Rossborough assured me that just the other side of this last steep pass lay an alpine meadow of profitability. Unfortunately, we had money in the bank from the sale of our house. Without hesitating, and with assurances to Diane that there was no risk involved, I loaned Nathan/Tyler $630,000. Now it seemed that our loan had disappeared down the gullet of runaway expenses. The sum of my two loans to Nathan/Tyler, plus money I had paid Tyler for his interest in the company the year before, came to $930,000.

In September I met with *Fortune*'s man in charge of our video partnership, a youngster on the fast track named John

Needham. At a nasty lunch in the saloon across from the Time-Life Building on the corner of Fiftieth Street and Sixth Avenue, I hinted that we were having financial trouble completing the next video for the Fortune Video Series, a program about Jack Welch's management revolution at General Electric. Needham got hot under the collar, promising to take serious measures if we failed to deliver the program. (Within weeks *Fortune*'s lawyers advised us that we were in default and demanded the return of all rights to the Fortune Video Series.) I called Boston thinking to discuss a *Fortune* strategy with Rossborough and was told that he had resigned during my absence and cleared out. I suppose he had seen what was coming and wanted no part of it; he had been careful to construct his employment contract so that he had no fiduciary responsibility—liability was all on me. In the terrible months that followed I never heard from him. I had managed to procure a ticket to the Met that night for *La Bohéme*; halfway through I walked out, no longer able to numb myself against the presentiment of the horror that was on the way.

From August to the end of that year I went home only once for a week. Each morning I walked to work from my Back Bay apartment and sat in the empty Nathan/Tyler offices—I had laid off the staff of twenty young people in September—struggling to bring the business down for a crash landing without going into bankruptcy. All day long I took phone calls from creditors and tried to persuade them to accept a nickel or a dime on every dollar they were owed. Between calls I opened the mail and read daily letters from in-house lawyers informing me they were preparing to file suit.

I took a lot of abuse. Our creditors were angry, Harvard Business School and *Fortune* and the Institute for Managing Diversity in Atlanta, Georgia, were angry. Our limited partners, who had never received a dividend, were very angry. (Tyler's friend Bill Sahlman congratulated me for "wresting defeat from the jaws of victory.") Only the bankers didn't seem angry at all; over coffee and doughnuts in our conference room one morning they informed me affably that the bank was calling our loans and expected full repayment in seven days or they would place me in bankruptcy. Fortunately we still had an advance payment of royalties coming from Harvard that enabled me to pay off the bank.

I was stunned by how abruptly the business had collapsed on me and by its crushing weight when it did collapse. I had been playing at business as one plays house, but now I was being given to understand that business was no trifling matter and that the distinction I had maintained between myself and real businessmen, whom I had always belittled, was an irony I could no longer afford. Day after day I was also flabbergasted all over again, naïvely enough, by people's coldness when it came to money. Moose's response was typical. When he got wind that the business was failing he demanded immediate payback of his investment of $120,000, due on September 30, 1993. On November 3, I wrote to ask him for an extension, explaining the personal losses I had sustained and that I had been working without salary since July. Moose replied on November 9: "Thank you for your letter of November 3, 1993 explaining your complicated financial situation. . . . I am herewith turning over the entire matter of collection of my note to my attorneys at the firm of Hill and Barlow." Businessmen reading this exchange will smile at its predictability. Translators of Japanese literature who have no business meddling in business may be as horrified as I was.

With guidance from a brilliant lawyer named Stuart Cable, who took me on despite the fact that Nathan/Tyler was the size of a corner candy store from his perspective, I managed to avoid bankruptcy. On the last day of 1993 I sold off our best-known films and programs for a fraction of their value to a bumptious video peddler in Chicago. I was supposed to receive royalties "in perpetuity" of 5 percent on subsequent sales of the programs, but, as my lawyer had predicted, payments dwindled during the first year and had stopped entirely by the second. Later I pursued the money half-heartedly, but the company was in receivership by the time I made inquiries, and the properties had already passed on to somebody else. I have no idea where they landed.

During those lonely months as I closed the company down I managed to insulate myself against feelings of loss. I achieved this in my usual way, transmuting the experience into a tall tale that told well to myself and any audience I could find. The gods on high in their council chamber had observed me disporting myself with careless arrogance and infidelity; let's watch how mountainously a man of heroic stature can fall, they agreed, and, pulling the thick carpet from beneath my feet, laughed to see me tumble backward head over heels and fall heavily to the ground. Such a fall, I told myself, no ordinary man could have survived: had I been burdened by material attachments, why then the loss of my business and life's savings would have killed me. Thus I brashly transformed my failure into tinsel victory. I wasn't exactly insouciant; I had my moments of bleakness during the process and was aware of a pressure against my chest as though a heart attack were building. But I don't remember any stabs of regret. While it was still in the present I receded the demise of Nathan/Tyler into the past.

Diane was devastated. Looking back on this destructive moment in our life together, I see that I was unable to perceive what had happened as she saw it and, failing to experience what she was feeling, how unredeemably I betrayed her. From her vantage, I had carelessly thrown away something as much hers as mine. Since the filming of *In Search of Excellence* in 1984,

Living Carelessly in Tokyo and Elsewhere

I had been spending months of every year away from home. Diane had followed me to Boston because that was part of my job, pulling up her roots in California and leaving her friends behind; she had lived with the tension that the ups and downs of the business and my road fatigue produced in me. These sacrifices she had made for years in anticipation of the reward that had seemed to be moving closer, the eventual sale of the business that would earn us—should have earned us—enough money to live as we pleased, traveling the world as a family when I wasn't writing, and playing with the children at home. That harvest had seemed almost at hand, and then I informed her matter-of-factly that we had lost everything, including the huge sum of money we had just loaned the business. Ten years lost, as she saw it, along with all our savings. Perhaps worst of all from her point of view, she felt certain that I had created the catastrophe with my arrogance and carelessness (and to be sure, my carrying on). She was of course right, but I was a long way from being able to acknowledge the truth of what she perceived. She needed and deserved acknowledgment and what she got from me was resentment: her bitterness affronted me and I closed down against it. How I regret my failure to join her in grief about what had happened!

There was one aspect of my reality that even I was not able to deny: at age fifty-three, with little to show for the fourteen years that had passed since I left Princeton, I had a family to support but no income or savings to speak of. I needed a real job with a salary and benefits that included health insurance. Surveying the rubble, I recalled what came to mind at that moment as the tranquil security of university life. I made some calls to former students and friends who were now professors at premier schools and was told by someone, possibly Norma Field at the University of Chicago, that the University of California at Santa Barbara had a newly endowed chair in Japanese cultural studies and was in the middle of a national search for someone to fill it. The chair had been endowed by the third-generation owner of a small steel manufacturer based in Osaka, Seichirō Takashima, who had inscribed his name in the halls of American academe two years earlier with an identical chair at Harvard that had cost him $3.5 million. He had been wooed and won for Harvard by Haruko Iwasaki, a scholar of premodern Japanese literature. When Harvard cold-bloodedly declined to grant Haruko tenure in the same year that the money had been received from Takashima, she moved to UCSB and persuaded him to endow a second chair, this time at a bargain-basement price of $500,000.

It was a stroke of luck for me that Haruko was responsible for the endowment; I had known her at Princeton, where she had worked as a Japanese-language instructor, and she seemed to remember me fondly. She encouraged me to compete for the appointment and promoted me to her colleagues. I solicited letters of recommendation from old, distinguished friends—Henry Rosovsky, Carol Gluck, and Donald Richie, among others. In mid-March, the department invited me and Diane to visit Santa Barbara for a job interview that was to include a lecture and a screening of *Farm Song*.

I worked hard on the lecture for two weeks, ransacking cobwebbed boxes of lecture notes I had lugged back and forth across the continent and cobbling together observations on Meiji writers, Yukio Mishima and the postwar identity crisis, Tōru Takemitsu and Alfred Schnittke, Jūzō Itami the director, Banana Yoshimoto, the sociology of business, and anything else I could make fit. Though I had been away from classrooms for fourteen years I hadn't lost my fluency; if anything, I was a smoother talker than before, the fruit of years of managing the gurus at HBS and disarming CEOs of major corporations. Still, my presentation must have sounded antique: I had never heard of postmodernism and was not aware that talking about culture was a felony. When I was finished someone asked whether deconstructionism could be applied to Japanese texts, and I confessed that I was ignorant of the theory and added that I had a lot of catch-up reading to do, like the Rip Van Winkle of the field, that would probably take me a number of months. My allusion to the somnolent Dutchman was an unfortunate choice inasmuch as, I learned later, my detractors in the audience were arguing against employing a man who had been sound asleep for years. Those same malcontents were also offended by my cavalier attitude about the time I would require to reeducate myself.

Over the objection of some, I received the appointment and became the first Takashima professor of Japanese cultural studies at UCSB. The appointment came with tenure and full benefits for the family and a Takashima Fund that would reimburse me for some research expenses.

Our life in Santa Barbara got off to a bad start. The house we had rented long distance was in need of repair and located just fifty feet from the open terrace of a clamorous Italian restaurant. Our first and only night there we slept huddled on the floor downstairs with pillows around our heads to muffle the noise from next door. Diane cried herself to sleep. I was aware of how dismal she was feeling. For the second time in five years she had uprooted herself to accompany me.

The moving trucks arrived the next morning and we directed them to unload our belongings in storage while we searched for a suitable house. We were living in motels, hiding our golden retriever, Sherlock, until he gave himself away with a bark and we were asked to move on, when an old friend, Peter Grilli, contacted me through the university with an urgent message to call him in New York. "Where have you been?" he asked excitedly when I reached him from a phone booth. "Do you know that Ōe won the Nobel Prize yesterday? People are looking for you!"

Peter gave me numbers of reporters at newspapers and national magazines who wanted to talk to me, and I spent the next several days on the phone giving interviews about Ōe and his writing and the process of translating him. Suddenly, unexpectedly, I had my credentials in hand again and felt legitimate for the first time in years. I couldn't help taking the timing of the prize personally, as if it were also a signal to me, endorsing my decision to return to university life and, as a corollary, to Japan. At the time, except for a brief meeting in New York a year earlier, I hadn't seen Ōe or been in touch with him for ten years. My letter of congratulations was dated October 17, 1994:

> Dear Ōe-*san*:
> Please accept my jubilant congratulations on this wonderful occasion! I feel fiercely proud of you and very happy for you and your family. I confess that I also feel happy for myself. Partly, I suppose, because I like to think my translations, inadequate as they are, have allowed readers at least a glimpse of your vision. And partly because I can't help responding to the timing of your award as an *indication* (!?) that my decision to return to university life and studying Japanese literature after an hiatus of fourteen years was correct and will lead me in the direction of the "extraordinary mildness" we used to talk about. And so, if you will permit, certainly for you, and even for myself, I *rejoice!*

"Rejoice," in English, was the last word in the concluding volume of Ōe's trilogy, *The Flaming Green Tree*. The previous

261

year, completing the final page of the manuscript on camera—
a film crew from NHK was making a documentary about Ōe
and his son, Hikari—he had misspelled the word "Rejoyce!"
When the documentary aired later in the year the last scene had
sent Japanese Joyce scholars to their books to ponder an allusion they couldn't identify. "An extraordinary mildness" was
from a line in W. H. Auden's "Herman Melville," a poem I had
read for the first time when Ōe brought it to one of our English-
conversation sessions shortly after we met:

> *Towards the end he sailed into an extraordinary mildness.*
> *And anchored in his home and reached his wife*
> *And rode within the harbour of her hand.*

Ōe found Auden's phrase appealing and spoke about it excitedly. I didn't realize at the time how important the words would
become to me, growing in allure as they beckoned me toward
a state of existence that has continued to evade me in my own
life.

My letter continued, asking Ōe for permission, for myself
and for Barney Rosset, to translate and publish one or more of
his novels:

> Grove/Atlantic has offered to share publication
> with Barney of any new Ōe literature he can make
> available in English. Barney phoned to ask me if I
> were interested in being the translator. Truth is, I had
> already proposed to the University of California that
> one of the projects I intended to begin upon receiving
> my endowed chair here last month was the translation
> of an Ōe novel (here again, profane as I am, the tim-
> ing of your Nobel Prize award presents itself to me as
> some kind of augury). Needless to say I am more than

interested in being the translator: I am determined to do whatever I can to allow Western readers access to your writing.

Ōe replied two weeks later:

October 31, 1994

Thank you for your gracious letter. This all began with your translation of *A Personal Matter*. I shall always be deeply grateful to you.

Nothing could make me happier than to have you and Barney Rosset translating and publishing my work as a team again. I am hoping most eagerly for a translation of my trilogy, *The Flaming Green Tree*; the complete three volume edition will be published (by Shinchōsha) in March of the coming year. I believe you know my agent in Tokyo, Tatemi Sakai at Orion.

I am looking forward to seeing you again. Thank you for your comments in the press.

Kenzaburō Ōe

By 1994 when the prize was announced, Barney Rosset, having lost Grove Press in the mid-1980s, was living impecuniously with his companion, Astrid Myers, on the top floor of a four-story walkup on lower Fourth Avenue just above Union Square. Understandably, Rosset leaped at the opportunity that now presented itself. Within a week, he had sent to Grove/Atlantic an outline of a proposed contract that would pay Ōe a $10,000 advance for each of five titles against a 7 percent royalty. I would receive an amount equal to 25 percent of Ōe's deal, "paid out somewhat differently." For himself, he suggested a fee of 25 percent to be paid in advance. He followed this with letters to both Ōe and his agent at Orion, Tatemi Sakai, asking for control of all of Ōe's contracts in the United States.

We arrived in Stockholm on December 6 with nothing resolved and checked into the Grand Hotel on the harbor, home to the Nobel festivities for decades. Grove had paid for our airfare, but other expenses that week were on us; Rosset's friend, the Swedish director Vilgot Sjoman, had arranged a room for him and Astrid at a more modest hotel a few blocks away, the Esplanade. I first laid eyes on Ōe late the following afternoon, hours after the sun had dropped, when he delivered his laureate address at the Swedish Academy of Arts and Sciences. The Grand Hall was packed. Ōe began a solemn reading of his address in English. Nervous that evening, he was mispronouncing so woefully that his words must have been scarcely comprehensible to the largely European audience. The title of his lecture, "Japan, the Ambiguous, and Myself," was an ironic allusion to Yasunari Kawabata's Nobel lecture in 1968, "Japan, the Beautiful, and Myself." Sitting in the Hall, I recalled with a twinge of envy that Kawabata's translator, Edward Seidensticker, had been at his side at the podium, reading his translation of Kawabata's address. Kawabata had chosen to mystify his Western audience with a reverie on "emptiness" as expressed in two Zen Buddhist poems from the Medieval Period. Under cover of admiration for his "bravery," Ōe conveyed disapproval of the curtain of orientalism Kawabata had drawn between himself and his Western audience. In his own lecture he alluded to Mark Twain, Rabelais, Kundera, Flannery O'Connor, James Orwell, and Mikhail Bakhtin, quoted lines from Blake and Auden, and declared he felt "more spiritual affinity" with his Nobel predecessor William Butler Yeats than with Kawabata.

But the big surprise was his opening, in which he claimed to have read *The Wonderful Adventures of Nils Holgersson across Sweden* as a boy and avowed its formative effect on his writer's imagination. Written in 1906, *Nils* is a saga about a schoolboy who traverses Sweden on the back of a magic goose. Over time it became mandatory reading as a geography primer in Swedish primary schools and is remembered by many Swedes with the same distaste that *Silas Marner* evokes in Americans who labored through it in the ninth grade. The author, Selma Lagerlöf, was herself awarded the Nobel Prize for literature in 1909, two years after Kipling. In his lecture, Ōe read the lines from the book that had moved him most deeply, quoting them, inexplicably, in French, as if he had first read the book in the French version at the age of eight: "*Maman, Papa! Je suis grand, je suis de nouveau un homme!*"—I'm a human being again! Ōe continued: "As I grew up, I was continually to suffer hardships in different realms of life. . . . I have survived by representing these sufferings of mine in the form of the novel. In that process I have found myself repeating, almost sighing, *Je suis de nouveau un homme!*"

Although for many years I'd heard Ōe speak of Western writers who had influenced him, this was the first time I had ever heard mention of *Nils,* and I couldn't help wondering if Ōe might be flattering his hosts. The Swedes were beguiled and thrilled: day after day the press informed readers of Ōe's love for *Nils;* the front page of the culture section of the *Svenska Dagbladet* on December 13 carried a full-column picture of him standing in front of a portrait of Lagerlöf, a white-haired matron with giant arms wrapped in the gray cloth of her blouse, with the headline "The Nobel Laureate Visits Lagerlöf's Home, Marbacka."

The next day we were all invited to a lunch in Ōe's honor hosted by the Swedish publishing house Bonnier Verlag. It was held at a house the family used for formal occasions in a residential park on one of Stockholm's islands. At the entrance, there was a line of guests moving toward the front door. Ōe was waiting just inside to greet us in an elegant foyer whose yellow walls were hung with photographs of the Bonnier family posing with authors. I was excited. This would be our first encounter face to face in many years. Barney and Astrid were just ahead of us in line; Ōe beamed at Barney and clasped his hand in both of his. I stepped forward expectantly; Ōe's eyes met mine and slid off—a beat too quickly—as he reached past to grip someone else's hand in greeting. The slight took my breath away. I felt ashamed, afraid someone might have noticed. I have no memory in that moment of Diane, although she must have been with me. I moved forward into a large living room as through a dark tunnel. What choice did I have? For a long time we had been as close as brothers; that's how I felt about him. And it was I, after all, whose translations had allowed the Swedish Academy to perceive the dimensions of his brilliance; everyone was saying I had had a hand in the prize, and Ōe knew it better than anyone else. What I had wanted and expected was an acknowledgment that I was as special to him as he had always been to me.

My only memory of that lunch was struggling to appear present despite the fact that I was consumed with feeling sorry for myself. I do remember Karl Otto Bonnier standing to welcome Ōe and inviting him to say a few words, and Ōe standing at his table behind me—I couldn't bring myself to turn and face him—to tell a story about his son addressing his father's foot tenderly when it was inflamed with gout.

Coffee was served in an adjoining sitting room with floor-to-ceiling windows that looked across the lawn to the water. I was standing with a cup of coffee in my hand, still in a daze but managing a conversation with someone, when two arms encircled me from behind and pulled me backward in a bear grip—Ōe of course, who then spoke into my ear in Japanese, "John! Do you know you're looking more and more like Lord Byron!" That was all; then he released me and moved away to other guests. I have no idea what this may have been about. But I was content again, able to feel that Ōe's craziness was a signal that he concurred in our specialness to each other. I was to that degree under the spell of his moods, if moods were what they were.

It was 3 p.m. when we left the luncheon and rode back to the Grand Hotel in a cab through the dusking light that had the city glowing. At 5:30 we went downstairs to a reception for Ōe hosted by the Japanese ambassador to Sweden. The ambassador and his wife were greeting guests with Ōe and his family from a dais at one end of the ballroom. Ōe's son, Hikari, in his tuxedo, stood stiffly as though propped up between his mother and his younger sister, Natsumiko, who were both in kimono.

Diane and I were still thirty feet from the dais when the ambassador's wife called out, "Nathan-*sensei!* At last!" Striding across the room to where we stood, an animated little woman in kimono brought us to the head of the line. "Do you recognize who I am?" she asked. I smiled and she rescued me; she was after all a diplomat's wife. "Reiko Ōoba; I was your student at Tsuda. You gave me a B- on my final essay!" Turning to her husband she said in Japanese, "This is Nathan-*sensei!*"

"I've been hearing about you for years," the ambassador said grimly. I was aware of Ōe observing impassively from the dais, and also aware that the long reception line was halted while our reunion was taking place. Reiko Matano née Ōoba now insisted on taking some photos to commemorate the moment; lifting both her arms above her head, she beckoned with her small hands, and a group of women emerged from the crowd and moved toward us with smiles and giggles, some young, some matronly, some in kimono and others in stylish

Living Carelessly in Tokyo and Elsewhere

Western dress. They were all, as it turned out, Tsuda alumnae (the school was well-known for preparing girls for international lives as diplomats' wives). We all posed, including Diane, for a series of photos, and while the photographer snapped pictures the reception waited.

The next morning Barney and I visited Ōe in his suite on the fourth floor of the hotel. The formal living room, bright with Christmas flowers, looked out on the harbor. When we arrived, a documentary film crew from Japanese National Television was standing by. Ōe's wife stayed only long enough to welcome us before disappearing into what appeared to be one of several large bedrooms. Barney and I had split the cost of a first edition of the first English translations of Spinoza published in London in 1871. I had read in the Japanese press that Ōe was studying Spinoza for several hours each morning, intending to make his way through the complete works. I hadn't known until I heard it from Sakai in Stockholm that he was reading the original Latin, three pages a day. We sat on a couch facing Ōe across a table heaped with copies of his books that he was inscribing to people on a long list—he complained that his right hand was swollen from signing so many—and I presented the book to him on camera. He examined it in silence, then solemnly announced in his pedantic way the seventeenth-century dates of composition of the *Ethics* and the *Treatise on Descartes*. I mentioned his Latin reading and suggested he might find the English translation useful as a pony. "Speaking of translation," he said to the camera with an impish smile that I recognized from the old days, "John Nathan is my greatest translator, but he has made one serious mistake in translating my work."

I knew the story Ōe was preparing to tell. Years after *A Personal Matter* had been published in my English translation, in the course of what must have been a drunken conversation at Ōe's house in Tokyo, I had accused him of sloppy imagery, citing a line in which the protagonist, Bird, watching television in the darkness with his lover, Himiko, "lifted his head only *like a baby sea urchin.*" Ōe nodded in agreement when I pointed out that a sea urchin has no head to lift, and then informed me that he had never written such a line. I insisted he had, and pulled the Japanese original from his bookshelf to prove it. Ōe glanced at the page and observed that I had confused two words differentiated in Japanese phonetic script by one short, vertical line no more substantial than an eyelash: *uni*, meaning "sea urchin," and *wani*, his actual choice, meaning "alligator." So the line should have read "lifting only his head like a baby alligator." "In doing so," Ōe now explained to the camera with relish, writing the words side by side on a pad of paper and pointing professorially to the difference, "John Nathan was distorting the writing of a Nobel laureate in literature!"

For an hour afterward, while others in the room looked on or scribbled notes or moved about in search of better camera angles, Barney and Ōe and I recalled stories from our past together and laughed aloud as we had laughed thirty years earlier: drinking in the Bar Gordon with our late friend, Kōbō Abe; the turkish bath incident; eggs Benedict every day for a solid month of lunches with book reviewers; a summer excursion to the writers colony in Karuizawa when I had chauffered Ōe's family and my own in a Cadillac borrowed from Teshigahara that was too large to negotiate Japanese roads. I had been warned by friends who had seen him more recently than I that his despair at the world around him had extinguished his humor. I was happy to discover that morning in Stockholm that Ōe had retained his gift for laughter. As Barney and I were leaving, he said wistfully that laughing out loud was something he no longer did in Japan.

Saturday, December 10, was the day of the awards. That morning, tuxedos that had been ordered were wheeled into the hotel lobby on clothing racks for guests to pick up. Buses pulled away from the curb at 3:30. We were about to leave when Tatemi Sakai made a last-minute dash for the bus, a dandy in a long vermillion scarf trailing down his back that was the only colorful marking on the distinguished penguin herd loaded into the buses.

At the Concert Hall, standing in a semicircle on the stage, the laureates were introduced by their designated sponsors from the academy and then stepped forward one by one to receive their gold medals from the hands of H.M. the King of Sweden. John Nash was one of three who received the prize in economic sciences. Ōe was suffering an attack of gout and had to limp forward to receive his medal. The awards were interspersed with performances of Grieg, Sibelius, and Nielsen by the Royal Stockholm Philharmonic conducted by Herbert Blomstedt.

The buses were waiting outside to transport us to City Hall, the Stadshuset, for the culminating event of the week, the Nobel Banquet. I had to go to the Nobel offices to pay for the dinners, 800 krona each, about $200. It was a very cold night; the walk past flickering lanterns to the building was chilling. The laureates and their families had arrived in limos and were being introduced to the royal family in the Gallery of the Prince. The rest of us were packed into another gallery where we waited in semidarkness for doors to swing open and admit us into the Blue Hall, where the feast was to be held. Among us were a large number of university students wearing the traditional costumes and elaborate caps of their medieval student associations. Alfred Nobel had left instructions in his will that students were to be included in the celebration to liven it up. Each year, 125 university students from across the country were chosen in a national lottery to attend the banquet and the ball; their charm and youthful excitement were indeed distinct ingredients in the atmosphere that evening.

Stockholm

The Blue Hall is actually a vast interior courtyard with brick walls that rise 150 feet to a vaulted ceiling. Though it was completed in 1923, the space felt medieval. At 7 p.m., the king and queen and their guests of honor entered in procession and took their places at the Royal Table, which extended the length of the hall with seats for eighty-eight. Ōe was sitting a few places down from the king and directly opposite the prime minister; the king's sister, Princess Cristina, who customarily reserved for herself the company of the laureate in literature, was on his right. John Nash was opposite him two seats away. Mrs. Ōe, opposite Mrs. Nash, was next to the Japanese ambassador.

Twenty-four tables seating thirty guests each were at right angles to the table of honor, twelve on each side; the students were seated at thirty-five additional tables along the walls. Our table, number 4, was for Ōe's people: Diane and I, Barney and Astrid, Morgan Entrekin and Joan Bingham, the new owners of Grove Press, and a number of Ōe's European publishers—Marion Boyars from London, the Herraldes from Spain, Karl Otto Bonnier and his wife, and Tomas Fischer, head of Germany's Fischer Verlag, with a longer list of Ōe's works in translation than anywhere else in the world (Gallimard of France was second). Vilgot Sjoman was seated next to Diane; he was shooting a feature film about Alfred Nobel and had just been informed that his cameraman would be permitted to film the king's toast to Nobel that opens the banquet.

At 7:08, on schedule, the chairman of the board of the Nobel Foundation proposed His Majesty's toast and the king rose to offer the traditional toast to Nobel's memory. Vilgot glanced upward at one of the alcoves in the massive brick wall, as if to reassure himself that his cameraman, alone behind his tripod and in his tuxedo, was filming the toast. As the king resumed his seat, musicians positioned in alcoves high above the floor began to play, horns resounding off the vaulted ceiling, and a corps of 150 male and female servers in white suits and gold epaulets descended the stairs from the gallery that overlooked the Hall and moved among the tables with plates of smoked breast of duck. Following the clatter of fourteen hundred sets of silverware being cleared and changed, the main course was served: filets of veal with mushrooms and tomatoes stuffed with spinach. There was a chorus of twenty-five singers, "figurants" from the Royal Dramatic Theater, a green-clad girl who spoke in tongues, and a whirling dervish all in white. I noticed that Ōe sat through much of this with his head lowered or rubbed his eyes with fatigue. Barney Rosset appeared to be similarly discomfited. The final flourish, preceded by a brass fanfare, was the traditional dessert borne down to us from the gallery on silver platters held aloft, *Parfait Nobel en Voile*, ice cream shaped like watermelon halves with a sorbet center and a garnish of green cotton candy. It tasted like ice cream cake from Baskin-Robbins. In general the food was nothing special.

As coffee was being served, another fanfare signaled the commencement of the three-minute after-dinner speeches by laureates. On the elevated marble landing at the far end of the hall, a Stockholm University student who appeared to be the mistress of ceremonies moved to the podium. She wore a formal white gown, white gloves, a white student cap with a glossy black peak, and, diagonally across her chest, a silk sash of Swedish blue and gold. She began, in British English, "Your Majesties, Your Royal Highnesses, Ladies and Gentlemen," then switched to perfect Japanese to invite Ōe to deliver his remarks. A second fanfare, and Ōe rose and, limping painfully, followed his student escort down the long Table of Honor past the king and up the marble steps; students in the gallery above the hall dipped the banners of their unions in salute as he passed them.

No one was surprised that his subject was *Nils*. This time, his coup de théâtre, he outdid himself. The "ponderous weight" of importance he had attached to *Nils*, he began, had contributed to what he called his "literary pretentiousness," leading him to turn away in disdain from his own classical literature and to respect Selma Lagerlöf more than Lady Murasaki, author of *The Tale of Genji*. Recently, however, he had recalled that Prince Genji, in a poem written at the end of his life, had dispatched a flock of geese to search for his wife's departed soul. It was his hope and his intention to fly home to *Genji* and the world of his own classical tradition on the back of Nils's magical goose! For an instant, the glittering audience seemed uncertain how to take this sleight of hand. Then a groan of gratification escaped the Swedes in the room and Ōe limped back to his seat to applause.

After the banquet there was a ball upstairs in the Golden Hall. Music was provided by Lars Almgren and his Stockholm Light Orchestra, thirty-five players including strings. (Think Lawrence Welk and you'll get the picture.) It was amusing, briefly, to watch the students ballroom dancing alongside European heads of state, boys and girls alike wearing their caps with shiny back peaks. Diane and I left early and rode a cab back to the hotel through the pouring rain. We knew that the entire company was invited to join the students at their fraternities for parties from midnight to dawn, but we were too tired to go.

The next morning the Rossets left Sweden and we checked into the Esplanade to save some money for a few nights while we looked around Stockholm. We went to the Vasa Museum, built around a Swedish man-of-war that sank in the harbor on its maiden voyage in 1628, and spent a pleasant day at Skansen, an entire island of old farmsteads being worked by people in

Living Carelessly in Tokyo and Elsewhere

authentic dress and an early village filled with real bakers and glassblowers, an outdoor museum very like Weald and Downland in England. With its zoos and miniature cars, this living recreation of Sweden's past was a children's paradise; we resolved to return with the children in the summer when we could wander the island in the light of the midnight sun. We never got around to it.

13

Familiar Roads

Within months of our return from Stockholm my professional life was in orbit around Japan again, a reentry so effortless and inevitable it felt as though I had never left.

In April 1995, the semiconductor giant NEC employed me to design a presentation about long-distance learning on the Internet and then to perform it, playing myself, at a trade show in Geneva in October. My collaborator was Howard Rheingold, Internet guru extraordinaire. A fluent, irresistible speaker with a keen mind, Howard was an unrepentant hippie out of the sixties with his eyes on the future; this singular merger of antiqueness and hip prescience was at the heart of his carefully calculated panache. He spoke of "Rheingoldian writing" and "Rheingoldian art," by which he meant the many-colored beatific visions he created not unskillfully in watercolors, and his hand-painted shoes, but even when he was self-promoting he managed to do it charmingly.

Three times that summer Howard and I traveled to Tokyo for brainstorming sessions with the NEC creative team; Howard insisted on showing up at the company's starkly unadorned $800 million Super Tower dressed in lilac or fire-engine-red suits and sporting a white fedora and painted shoes, which he invariably put forward proudly for inspection. I sensed that the gray suits in the conference rooms we lived in during those weeks were dismayed, but no one ever blinked an eye.

During our ten-day stay in Geneva, Rheingold and I put on our fifteen-minute dog and pony show seven times each day. This made for a tiring, and tiresome, day, but we were being paid so richly for the work that we scarcely griped about it to each other and stayed mainly serious during our presentations, clowning only occasionally. (There was small pleasure to be had in indulging in tongue-and-cheek since our employers wouldn't have recognized what we were up to.)

When we weren't onstage we wandered the vast hall watching the elaborate shows produced by other electronics companies and chatting up the young women from around the world who were employed at the fair as guides. Late one afternoon I accompanied Howard to the opening of what may have been, judging from the fanfare that accompanied it, Geneva's first Internet café. In his capacity as international Internet visionary he had been invited to cut the ribbon and preside at the ceremony; as we stepped from the cab he was surrounded by cyberspace fans whom he seemed to know only by their user names who were eager to meet and shake hands with their idol. I remember a portly gentleman in particular who rushed from the café to embrace Howard wearing rubber pig ears. Later I learned he was an early dot.com entrepreneur from London who logged on as "Oink."

Howard turned his purse of gold into a study annexed to his modest house in Mill Valley, with doors that opened on his scaled-down model of Monet's garden in Giverny. I pictured him sitting in his walled garden, barefoot in the sun and stoned, painting his watercolor miniatures, and felt envious, wondering if I would ever sail in to the extraordinary mildness I continued to long for.

Familiar Roads

What tranquility I have experienced has always been inside my family, and Thanksgiving that year is a luminous example. We had just purchased our first home in Santa Barbara, a large, gracious house on a street actually called Penny Lane that included a library with floor-to-ceiling bookshelves and a real sliding ladder. For some reason we decided to prepare a proper Thanksgiving dinner just for ourselves. We laid out the dishes on an antique sideboard in the formal dining room. Toby and I dressed up in ties and jackets and Diane and Emily wore dresses and we sat down to dinner at five. As we ate, we pretended to be actors having a meal on camera, cutting and forking up tiny portions of food and savoring it theatrically, smacking our lips as we exchanged self-conscious dialogue, and took turns video-taping the performance. I think we all felt the pleasure, and the comfort, of entertaining one another, self-sufficiently a family. I have never been happier.

The project for NEC wasn't my only corporate job that year; I was working for Sony at the same time, worrying that one company might find out about the other. Sony had commissioned me to produce a film commemorating its famous founders, Akio Morita and Masaru Ibuka, in time for the company's fiftieth anniversary in November 1996. It was a big project, a forty-minute film in English and Japanese versions, and two versions of a seven-minute condensation. My theme had been nebulously defined as "the Founders' spirit." Ibuka and Morita had both been left aphasic by recent strokes, so I decided to reflect them in a montage of on-camera reminiscences from everyone still alive who had known them when they ran the company as a team. I asked Maureen Ryan, formerly my producer at Nathan/Tyler, to manage the project from New York, and hired a Hollywood cameraman, Ralph Bode. In March 1996, I traveled to Tokyo with Ralph and my friend and longtime lighting man, Jon Fontana, to begin filming interviews with Sony old-timers, including Ibuka's favorite engineer, Nobutoshi Kihara, and the developers of Walkman, Trinitron, Betamax, and the compact disc. The filming took us back to Tokyo several times, to New York to interview Morita's American friends, and later to Holland and Germany.

The work went well, uneventfully, until the time came to sit down with Maestro Norio Ohga, the musician-merchant who maintained foppish dominion over Sony from the chairman's office. I had saved Ohga for last, partly because of his impossible schedule—he had honored a promise to himself to return to music when he turned sixty and was conducting orchestras all over the world—and because he knew more about Sony than anyone and I was hoping he would fill in blanks left by others. We interviewed him in the chairman's office on the penthouse (thirty-fourth) floor of the Sony Building in New York on Madison Avenue between Fifty-fifth and Fifty-sixth Streets. It was the northwest corner office, originally designed by Philip Johnson for AT&T chairman Robert Allen, with windows fifteen feet high that overlooked the Hudson River to the West and Central Park to the north. Though Ohga was rarely in New York in those final days before his retirement, the office was reserved for his occasional use. We arrived hours early, took our time lighting the room, and waited nervously for Ohga to show up, which he did promptly at 3 p.m. Settling himself in the chair we had positioned for him, he folded his hands prissily in his lap and delivered in response to my questions a cornucopia of colorful material for close to two hours. We were on our seventh or eighth ten-minute magazine of film when he told a story about Kazuo Iwama, Morita's brother-in-law and briefly president of the company. During his six years as president, Iwama, a beloved figure in the Sony legend, had devoted himself to developing the CCD, a tiny electric eye that could "see" color and convert it to electrical impulses. Iwama died of colon cancer in August 1982, just before his CCD chip went into mass production. The following month, Ohga was appointed president of the company. When the first chips came off the production line in November, he took one to the burial plot adjoining his own in a Buddhist temple in Kamakura and affixed it to Iwama's gravestone with Crazy Glue. "I said to him, 'Iwama-*san*!'" Ohga recalled for me on camera, "'Here's the CCD you made for us. Look through it and see how beautiful the world appears in Sony color!'"

I returned to the hotel exhausted from the effort of guiding Ohga where I wanted him to go. I was in the shower when the phone rang, someone from Sony urging me to return at once: Ohga was "furious and considering canceling the project." I was dumbfounded. He had been more than usually responsive and apparently relaxed, joking with Ralph Bode in German and telling me more than once as though fondly that I was a "disarming rogue." I took a cab back uptown and was shown to a reception area outside the chairman's conference room. Several of Ohga's aides-de-camp nodded to me grimly; it felt like waiting in front of the princpal's office. Sony's newly appointed president, Nobuyuki Idei, hurried by and said to me with a knowing smile, "Ganbatte, Nathan-*san*!"—Hang in there!

Ohga made his usual entrance, through the door that opened directly into his office, and launched right in as he took his seat, not bothering with a greeting. "Mr. Nathan, I have a pain here, in my heart, when I imagine what Morita-*san* must be thinking right now!" I listened to the lament that followed in amazement, thinking as my heart sank a thought that has occurred to me countless times over the years: that Japan is an imponderable place. The gist of the maestro's distress, which had him highly agitated, was that we were using a film camera to make a documentary about the company founders despite the fact that Sony had devoted the past thirty years to replacing film around the world with its Betacam video cameras and videotape. It was bad enough that we had already brought a film camera into the organization; now we were preparing to embarrass Sony by taking film with us to Philips in Holland, Sony's dear friends and collaborators on the CD. This was more than Ohga could bear, particularly when he considered the pain it would cause Messrs. Morita and Ibuka should they learn of it.

Ohga's sentimentality might have seemed comical if I hadn't been so certain that he was capable in the emotion of the moment of scuttling the project. His objection to using film, coming now as it did months into the process, was outrageous: I had had long discussions in Tokyo about whether to use film or tape before we began. The original idea had been to use Sony's high-definition video format, but it was relatively early days for high-def and the available cameras, designed for studio use, were still too bulky to take on location. If high-definition was out of the question, I had argued, we should forget about video altogether and shoot film, Super-16mm, which would give us a gorgeously saturated negative we could transfer to tape at the end with no loss of resolution. The client in Tokyo had agreed and I had hired Bode, a feature film director of photography. Ohga inquired angrily who had approved the film decision, causing his aides to pale and shake their heads and draw their breath in sharply with a hiss.

But clearly none of this was relevant: Ohga was in the grip of emotions I knew were real, though I was having difficulty fathoming them. All of a sudden, in the strained moment of silence after he had concluded and was staring at the carpet with a flush on his pale cheeks, I conceived perhaps the only clever business idea I have ever had and blurted, "*Kaichō* [Mr. Chairman], let me do it all over again in videotape. I promise it will be a beautiful tribute to the founders!" The hangdog retainers in the room looked at me as though I were mad and turned toward their master, who said, after a pause, "How many people have you interviewed so far?" An assistant produced from his suit jacket pocket a list, a long list, of completed interviews. Ohga ran his finger down it and stopped at Henry Kissinger (a close friend of Morita's). "I don't want to bother Dr. Kissinger again. And if you use any of this I want a subtitle saying 'Due to circumstances beyond our control this footage was recorded on film'—is that clear?" Ohga rose and headed toward his office. "*Kaichō*," I asked, "may we have you again tomorrow for a reshoot on tape?" Ohga looked at me and shook his head with just the hint of a smile on his lips. "Arrange it with my secretary." He went through the door and left us sitting there. The others appeared to be in shock, but I could scarcely contain the rush of victory I felt. All over again! Everyone in the room knew what that meant: a new budget on my terms. On my way out, I tried to prepare the Sony team by mentioning that extending the length of this job would require me to cancel other work. Moreover, since time was of the essence, I hoped that the budget I would be submitting in the morning would be approved at once without the usual negotiations. No one said a word.

The crew exulted as they listened to my story. Maureen was most excited of all because she now had an assignment that came to producers only in their dreams, to deploy her skill to the opposite effect of her normal challenge: the creation of a budget in which every line item was estimated as expensively as she could conceive it. When we added a hefty production markup of 35 percent to the subtotal we had a number substantially larger than the original. By noon the next day the new budget had been approved.

We set up once again in Ohga's office, but this time every piece of equipment we used bore the Sony logo: cameras, monitors, boom microphones—the room looked like a display at a Sony product fair. Ohga showed up just on time, as before. On his way to his chair he paused in front of the monitor, studied the screen, and exclaimed with a broad smile, "That's a picture worth looking at!" Then he settled himself and gave us an excellent interview. I had been worried that the Iwama story might feel canned the second time around. When Ohga delivered a version identical to the first down to gestures, sighs, and pauses I realized that it was canned and that he was a masterly performer.

From New York we traveled with our cases of video gear to Holland, and from there to Cologne, where we interviewed former and current heads of Sony Europe and an intense Morita protégé named Ron Sommer, who had served briefly as the head of Sony USA and was now the chairman of Deutsche Telekom. Next, my crew and I flew directly from Frankfurt to Tokyo to begin taping interviews with Sony's Japanese family all over again. I had returned the hours of film we had shot, developed, and transferred to tape for editing to Sony; now, on three successive trips, I put similar questions to the same subjects in the same locations. As enough time had elapsed to allow a sense of spontaneity, this worked better than I had imagined it would. I edited the film on an Avid I installed in an upstairs bedroom in our house, designating edits to a befuddled editor from Los Angeles who spoke no Japanese.

Choosing music for a film sponsored by Sony turned out to be an intensely pleasurable experience. Someone in Tokyo wanted to use classical selections from the Sony label, and when I objected that we hadn't budgeted the expense of securing permissions, the company agreed to pay extra to clear recordings by major orchestras. In New York I dropped in on Thomas "Tommy" Mottola, then president of Sony Music Entertainment, and when I explained that I was working for Ohga and told him what I needed he led me to a wall of CDs and invited me to help myself. I pulled dozens off the shelves. I asked Andy

Kulberg to help me select and time what I needed. Andy had written every bar of music I had used since *In Search of Excellence*. This was the last time we worked together; he died of a rare blood cancer in 2002. I miss him.

I wound up using Aaron Copland, a plaintive piece for solo piano called "In Evening Air," and "The Red Pony," and an excerpt from Nielson's Flute Concerto, but the complete Sony recordings of Copland, Shostakovich, Stravinsky, Gershwin, Horowitz, and many others are now part of my own library, and I continue to experience an added measure of satisfaction when I am listening to them. I'll mention in passing that the only other premium I ever extracted from Sony or any other Japanese corporation was a PlayStation that I gave my son Toby just before it went on the market in the United States, making him the first kid on his block, or on any block in America, to have one.

The finished video—it still rankles me to call it that—had its premiere at a banquet in Tokyo in November 1996, which began a month of events celebrating the company's fiftieth anniversary. As no one ever mentioned it to me again, I assume it was poorly received, but my association with Sony was far from over. Collecting the upbeat anecdotes for the anniversary video confection, I had sensed that the deeper Sony story was a saga of difficulty and conflict that mirrored Japan's struggle for postwar viability. In September 1996 I went to see Mitsuru Ohki, an Ohga vassal who was the head of corporate communications, and told him I wished to write a serious book about the company. His first question was how much I would expect to be paid; I explained that the history I had in mind would have to be written independently of the company to be taken seriously. In fact, to interest a reputable publisher I would need a letter from Sony guaranteeing me access to whomever I wished to interview and relinquishing the customary right to review and approve my manuscript.

Living Carelessly in Tokyo and Elsewhere

Ohki didn't say much at the time, but within a month I had a letter in English signed by him which closely followed a draft I had proposed:

November 14, 1996

Dear Professor Nathan:

We are pleased to learn that you will be writing a book about Sony Corporation, its history and operations in the United States, including Hollywood. With the depth of your understanding of Sony, we feel that you are in a favorable position to write such a book. We are prepared to cooperate with your efforts to research this book by arranging all requested interviews and providing relevant documents and photographs from our archives.

We understand that your book is a project entirely independent of Sony and that we have no editorial control whatsoever.

We look forward to a book that we hope will contribute to improved understanding of not only Sony but of Japanese society in general.

Mitsuru Ohki
Senior General Manager,
    Corporate Communications
Sony Corporation

As anyone who has attempted to move backstage in a major corporation will understand, the letter granted me remarkable freedom as an author. I was surprised when I received it, delighted but puzzled, it was so against the grain of the company's reflexive defensiveness. I have no idea how it happened, though I am certain Ohki would never have issued me blanket permission on his own authority and must have run it by Ohga first. Perhaps he had broached the subject to his boss when the maestro was distracted. During the two years I researched the book on frequent trips to Tokyo the company kept its word, arranging interviews, often more than once, with everyone I asked to meet. As I probed more deeply beneath the public surface of the organization I worried that I was about to receive an ultimatum to submit my unfinished manuscript before I was allowed to complete my research, but none ever came.

When *Sony: The Private Life* was published in 1999, it was soon clear that the company regretted the degree to which it had cooperated with me. A year passed before anyone—Ohga himself!—said anything to me directly, but I became aware of Sony's position on the book quickly enough: an acquaintance at the business desk at *Newsweek* informed me that the chief of corporate communications at Sony's New York headquarters was insisting in daily phone calls that the book was full of "groundless fabrication" and pressuring him not to review it. *Newsweek* was dismayed by Sony's lobbying and published a favorable review notwithstanding. At the Japan Society of New York I fared less well. For twenty-five years, beginning with the publication of my biography of Yukio Mishima in 1974, the society had offered me a lecture and a reception on the occasion of a new book or film, and I had also participated in many of their other cultural events. Based on our long, congenial history, I called with some confidence to inquire about arranging a similar evening and was surprised by the pointed chilliness I encountered. I pursued this, and was finally told point blank by then-president William Clark, a former ambassador to India, that he was not about to incur Sony's displeasure by inviting me to speak about a book he "had heard" they objected to. I protested that the Japan Society was foreclosing an opportunity for a provocative dialogue in order to curry favor with a corporate donor; our conversation terminated abruptly and heatedly, and I have not felt welcome since at the Japan Society. I should add that the Japan Society of San Francisco's executive director at the time, Christopher Segur, admitted sheepishly to me that his board had declined to invite me to speak for the same reason.

I was angry about this but also confused: I had undertaken to write an affirmative book about Sony, and in light of the responses it was invoking from critics and readers I was confident that my portrait conveyed the heroic energy that had animated the company under Ibuka and Morita. In time I learned that Ohga especially was furious. In Tokyo a year later I requested a meeting and he granted me a brief audience. He informed me unceremoniously that my book was riddled with what he chose to call lies and betrayals. With a straight face he declared, perhaps forgetting that I had taped all of my many interviews with him, that he had never said many of the things I had quoted him as saying, particularly the disparaging remarks about Nobuyuki Idei, the man he himself had elevated to company president. "And what you wrote about Mr. Morita being a cruel father is completely untrue!" he continued. I pointed out that my portrait of Morita the father had come directly from testimony by both his sons, whom I had quoted at length. "They were lying of course!" Ohga bellowed—it was my first encounter with his famously intimidating operatic baritone in anger—and, before I had a chance to wonder aloud why his children would have been moved to calumniate their deceased father, he rose and strode out of the room without a bow or good-bye.

In the course of other conversations I came to understand that the organization felt that I had elicited candor in interviews by intentionally misleading people into believing that Sony would review the manuscript. This was an unreasonable accusation. When I began the first round of interviews in the spring

of 1997, I had been unpleasantly surprised by the memo that
Ohki was circulating to everyone scheduled to meet with me.
For reasons of his own, in direct contradiction of the letter he
had written to me, Ohki had chosen to frame the book as a
project sponsored by Sony:

> Re: Research for a new "Sony Hardcover" to be writ-
> ten by John Nathan
>
> . . . It is our view at Corporate Communications that
> a new book in English is needed to promote under-
> standing of the new Sony in countries around the
> world. . . . Accordingly, we have asked University
> of California Professor of Japanese Cultural Studies
> John Nathan to write such a book, and are proceed-
> ing with plans for publication by Houghton Mifflin
> Company in the fall of 1999. . . . Your cooperation
> will be appreciated.

Anyone reading this would naturally have assumed that Sony
would review and appropriately edit the manuscript. At every
interview I had emphasized that I had not been employed by
Sony and was researching a book on my own. But possibly
nothing I said or might have said could have overridden an
impression created by an official Sony document. If members
of the Sony family had been lulled into a false security, it was
Ohki's memo that was responsible.

In the spring of 1997 I flew to New York for an onstage
dialogue with Kenzaburō Ōe on translation at Columbia University's Miller Theater. We had put on a similar show two
years before at the Japan Society in New York and at the Folger
Library in Washington, DC. This time the event, part of the *Theater of Ideas* series, was sponsored by the Donald Keene Center

of Japanese Culture. Diane accompanied me to New York; our talk was on April 8, her birthday and our wedding anniversary. Ōe came in from Princeton, where he was in residence that year. Professor Carol Gluck began by promising the audience an evening of delight featuring "the Japanese luminary of literature and his old sidekick, luminary of Japanese translation," and then passed to "local luminary" Donald Keene, who reminisced about his long friendship with Ōe and ended cleverly by suggesting that Ōe was still, forty years later, Japan's "youngest important writer." In passing, Keene said generously that I had produced a "superb translation" of *A Personal Matter*, which, he added, "was responsible immediately for Ōe's fame throughout the world." Ōe and I then took the stage, sitting at a table we had heaped with books, and engaged for two hours in the affectionate badinage that came naturally to us after so much time in each other's company. The audience was attentive throughout, laughed often, and had many questions for Ōe at the end. Afterward Carol hosted a party at her large apartment down the street near Riverside Drive; the room was filled with considerable figures from the literary community, book and magazine publishers, critics, and familiar authors, and I received my share of compliments for an evening that seemed to have blended intensity and humor in an entertaining way. I was proud of myself, proud to be someone capable of eliciting from Ōe his most appealing self, and happy that Diane had been present to bask in our success.

That August I was in Tokyo again with the family, the first time they had accompanied me in ten years. NHK was producing a series of documentaries about foreigners with deep connections to Japan and had proposed to follow me on a visit to the caterers I had filmed in *Full Moon Lunch*. I agreed on the condition that Emily could come along; the slightly different premise would be that I was taking my daughter with me to allow her a better understanding of the roads her father had traveled. NHK agreed; for ten days in the suffocating August heat, with Diane and Toby tagging along behind the cameras, Emily and I paid repeated visits to the Sugiura family, drove in their truck at dawn to the Tsukiji fish market, and strolled the twisting streets of the neighborhood, window shopping or stopping to refresh ourselves with shaved ice and green tea–flavored syrup. It was rough going for Emily, twelve at the time, but she was game, struggling not to appear squeamish as she bit into sashimi on camera, exclaiming in wonder when she was pleasantly surprised at the real flowers the Sugiuras used as garnish in their box lunches or some brightly colored baby crabs fashioned entirely from bamboo, wincing or grimacing at unfamiliar sights and sounds, and delivering to the camera, one hand on my shoulder, California-girl commentary on her experiences: "They make everything look pretty. In America the food doesn't look pretty. But here they make everything decorative, it has to look pretty and it makes you want to eat it."

At my suggestion, we also took a side trip to the home of my Noh actor friend, Otoshige Sakai. Sitting at the foot of the Noh stage in Sakai's house, Emily tried on sixteenth-century Noh costumes that were national treasures and was shown the range of emotion a Noh mask can convey as it is tilted forward and backwards. Then Sakai's three sons, now full-fledged performers, took her up onto the stage and coached her through a mini-lesson in Noh movements and gestures. To Emily, this exposure so close at hand to the endlessly ramifying richness of the Noh tradition must have been overwhelming, more trying perhaps than pleasurable, but it was thrilling for me, and for Diane, to watch her as she stood on Sakai's Noh stage and lifted her hand slowly to her brow in the stylized representation of grief that she was imitating. When the day was over, Sakai invited us to join his wife and three sons for dinner at the Kobe beef and sea-

Living Carelessly in Tokyo and Elsewhere

food grill Sazanka in the Hotel Okura. At the end of the meal the chef behind the *teppan* grill prepared one of the specialties of the house, fried rice with Kobe beefsteak fat. Ten years later my son Toby, nine years old at the time, still smacks his lips at the memory of what he calls the "most delicious food" he has ever tasted.

Happily, there came a moment during that family trip to Tokyo when it was Toby's turn to step into the spotlight. I had written Ōe that I would be in Tokyo in August with the family and he had responded with a note inviting us all to dinner at his house:

July 29, 1997

Dear John:

Thanks for your letter. I am overjoyed that I will be able to meet you and your family in August. I am leaving for Hungary on the 26, but am expecting you at my home on the 23, 24, or 25, whichever suits you.

I hope to introduce your wife's serene dignity and the materializations in your daughter of your literary talent that has been (Oh, thank God!) wasted for the work of translation.

Sincerely yours, Kenzaburō Ōe

Diane understood how important this first meeting of our two families was to me and insisted that the children dress up that night, Emily in a party dress and Toby in slacks and a sport shirt. We rode the train to Seijo and from the station walked the fifteen minutes it took down side streets to reach Ōe's house, taking the same wrong turns along the way that I had been repeating for forty years. Ōe greeted us warmly at the door and took us into the living room, where Hikari was waiting, stiff as a board, his eyes rolled up at the ceiling. (We still called him Pooh though by this time he was a recorded composer, the only savant in medical history able to compose original music.) From the moment he saw him, Toby seemed determined to establish contact. He achieved his breakthrough at dinner. When Pooh's mother served him his plate of steak, potato salad, and spaghetti, he cut the steak into bite-size pieces with surgical precision, then loaded the steak into his mouth piece by piece until his cheeks were bulging with the entire portion of meat, packed in the potato salad and spaghetti, clearing his plate, and began slowly to work his jaws like a python engorging a rabbit. Toby watched this performance from across the table with eyes wide and then resolutely followed suit, cutting his own steak and forking the entire portion into his mouth so that his own cheeks bulged and he was red in the face. As he began to chew, he choked and sputtered, coughing bits of meat onto the table. Pooh sprang up nimbly, stepped into the kitchen and emerged a minute later with a large green bowl he had filled with water to the brim. Toby, lowering his mouth to the bowl as though bobbing for apples, washed the food down with a long drink while Pooh stood over him solicitously. Ōe observed this interaction with unconcealed pleasure on his face and complimented Toby in English for being a "fine and sensitive young boy." I was very proud of him. After dinner we returned to the living room for cake and coffee and Pooh beckoned Toby to sit with him on the floor in front of the CD player. While Toby sat on the floor listening to music with Hikari, Kenzaburō engaged Emily in a serious conversation about her poetry. Listening to my dear friend the Nobel laureate discussing imagery and rhyme with my twelve-year-old daughter, I thought myself a fortunate man.

14

Detachment

I didn't sit down to translate another Ōe novel until 1999, five years after Stockholm. *Rouse Up, O Young Men of the New Age!*, written in 1985, is a chronicle of a family's life in the shadow of a retarded twenty-year-old child; the narrator, an author who is Ōe's alter ego, looks to William Blake for wisdom and inspiration as he struggles to transfigure his son's bleak reality with the power of his imagination. Ōe himself translated the verses of Blake that fill the book. I worked with a two-volume Blake compendium to locate the English; fitting the original English into my translated text as seamlessly as Ōe had made his translations work in his Japanese original was difficult. The entire undertaking was vexing; Ōe's style during his middle years was dense, serpentine, and driven by energy the language could scarcely contain. But *Rouse Up* was worth the effort; it is a brilliant and deeply moving book and stands easily alongside the singular early novels, from *A Personal Matter* to *The Silent Cry*.

In the twelve years since I committed in Stockholm to making Ōe's writing more available to English readers I have translated only *Rouse Up*, an important work to be sure but far less than I agreed to do. There are translators who have devoted their lives to rendering the work of a great writer—Constance Garnett, H. T. Lowe-Porter, C. K. Scott-Moncrieff—and who have thereby earned themselves a permanent seat at the table of literary history. I might have served Ōe in that way, toiling away at my craft. Certainly the scale and depth of his oeuvre would have more than requited my efforts and my own modest gift. In the process I might have acquired a sustainable reputation and even tasted the tranquility I continue to believe is what I have always wanted. But my unceasing efforts to undermine myself allowed me to invalidate even translation as a genuine measure of creative gift. In the early days, translating Mishima and then Ōe, I had succeeded in feeling that I was an artist in my own right. Even if James Joyce had known Japanese as well as I did, I told myself, he wouldn't have been able to render Ōe in the fullness of my translations unless he possessed, as I did, the translator's art. Somewhere along the way that incantation lost its power. Eventually I became grimly certain that Joyce, reading Japanese, would have been a far greater translator of Ōe than I because he was a better writer. And how much of a writer was I? If I hoped to find out I couldn't afford to devote time to translation. I had already come to that conclusion in 1979 when I left Princeton. It was foolish of me to have believed in 1994 that I was now ready to be content with life as a dedicated translator.

In fairness to myself I should add that there were financial considerations. In some countries readers have an appetite for foreign books that allows translators to thrive in the marketplace. Until recently, Japan was among the most dramatic examples: the Japanese hunger for Western knowledge and culture sat the translators of Dostoevsky and even Pascal in Rolls Royces. In the Soviet Union in the 1960s and 1970s, Kōbō Abe was a best-selling author whose Russian translator prospered. Ōe himself, difficult as he is, has a large readership in Europe, particularly in Germany and France. In Stockholm, Tatemi Sakai negotiated deals with Fischer Verlag and Gallimard in the six figures, far more than Grove Press was willing to put up for options on Ōe.

Americans have never had much interest in reading translations, certainly not Asian fiction in translation. (Two Japanese exceptions have been, briefly in the 1980s, Banana Yoshimoto, and, more continuously, Haruki Murakami, whose agile, postmodern cool has endeared him to *The New Yorker*.) The royalties I earned over the years for Mishima and Ōe translations were proof of this; my family made a joke of the checks I received from Knopf and Grove biannually: "Royalties are here—new shoelaces, anyone?" Not even the splendor of the Nobel Prize made a lasting difference. My royalty checks fattened surprisingly for one payment period following the prize and then returned to the under-$10 payments they had always been. In Stockholm, I had asked Karl Otto Bonnier about the next Ōe book he was planning to publish and was surprised when he told me his company had no further plans for Ōe. "This Nobel excitement is just a blip, it won't last long," he explained, and he was right.

My progress on *Rouse Up* was halting, and I see by the faxes I received from Ōe that he was eager to have it in English:

The greatest joy of mine is the possibility of your version of "Rouse Up" (Dec. 29, 1999)

I am happy to welcome you on December 13. [Morgan] Entrekin came to my house and said that it is the best news to hear your translation is nearly completed! (Nov. 27, 2000)

Detachment

> I am tremendously happy to know that your elab-
> orated work on "Rouse Up" ... has been accom-
> plished. ... I hope the beautiful [Blake painting of]
> Los will be printed on the cover of our long expected
> book! ... I hope to see you soon. I thank you for your
> splendid afterword. I am especially impressed by your
> fervent and deep style. Yes! You also lived so much
> time with W. Blake. (July 17, 2001)

The book took some time to produce and wasn't published until
April 2002. On April 15 I received a letter from Ōe in Japanese
that made me feel that my labors had been worthwhile.

> *Le 15 Avril, 2002*
>
> I received the Grove edition of Rouse Up. My wife
> and daughter agreed with me that the edition is beau-
> tiful and they were both pleased. I read it through at a
> single sitting, staying up all night. Your translation is
> miraculous—I felt as if I were discovering my book all
> over again. There is *candor* in your English. I know
> the word comes from the root "white" but I think of
> white radiance, in other words, "Hikari" [Ōe's son's
> name]. There were new joys of that kind throughout
> the book for me. I thank you from the bottom of my
> heart. Please thank your wife as well.
>
> Kenzaburō

Although this was my first full-length translation in twenty-
five years, I know it was the most faithful I have ever done—I
mean the closest to capturing in English the rhythms, the pitch,
and the timbre of Ōe's unmistakable voice in Japanese. Inci-
dentally, no one other than Ōe himself—and to be sure that

295

is what mattered most to me—seemed to notice. The reviews were favorable, and I understood that when a critic effused "an unparalleled writer at his sparkling best," he was responding in part to my translation. Nonetheless, I was disappointed, and further disappointed when the book was not awarded a translation prize here or in Japan.

By the time *Rouse Up* was published I was halfway through a new book of my own, *Japan Unbound,* a portrait of contemporary Japan in the grip of what I described as a national identity crisis. My research was largely interviews, this time with prominent figures and ordinary people across the landscape of Japanese society. I began shuttling to Tokyo at the end of May 2001, and made eight trips between then and September 2002.

I began the writing of the book with a *New Yorker* profile of Shintarō Ishihara, formerly a best-selling novelist and pop idol and now the governor of Tokyo, among the most inflammatory and influential ultranationalists in the country. I was hoping to write a series of profiles for the magazine that would become chapters in the book; my agent, Andrew Wylie, had approached editor David Remnick with my proposal and arranged a meeting with him so I could pitch my idea. Remnick commissioned me to do a piece on Ishihara. I worked hard on the profile and submitted a ten-thousand-word story early in January 2001. After a harrowing and protracted editing experience at the hands of a remorseless senior editor named Sharon DeLano, it appeared in the April 8, 2001, issue of the magazine. It was Passover week; we went to a faculty friend's house for seder, and there on the coffee table in the living room the magazine was opened to the story. I was pleased to observe the other guests making assumptions that suited me nicely. But I was less impressed than they were: my wavering confidence in myself as a writer was, if anything, more battered than buoyed by *The New Yorker* experience.

Detachment

The chapter on Ishihara I wrote for *Japan Unbound*, "The Sun King," was twice the length of the *New Yorker* piece and, I'm certain of it, a much livelier and more revealing portrait. Though I had no memory of having met the governor when I was living in Japan, I learned indirectly as I was preparing to request a series of interviews with him that he was nursing a grudge about an unfortunate encounter with me; apparently, forty years ago, I had crashed a party he was hosting with his superstar brother, Yūjirō, and he had thrown me off the yacht he had chartered for the occasion. Ishihara got over his lingering resentment, and as I worked on the book I saw him often in Tokyo and we shared some interesting moments.

Late in December 2000 he invited me to a geisha party he and some of his wealthy friends were hosting for Alberto Fujimori, the Peruvian president who had fled his country following a corruption scandal and was living in Japan in exile. (Peru wanted him back to face charges, but Japan was refusing to extradite him.) Fujimori's solution to a hostage crisis involving Japanese residents in Peru had made him a hero in the eyes of Japanese ultranationalists like Ishihara. In December 1996 fourteen Tupac Ameru rebels had occupied the Japanese ambassador's residence in Lima during a party celebrating the emperor's birthday and had taken 452 guests hostage. For four months, Fujimori refused to negotiate; in fact, he was buying time while a tunnel under the residence was being dug. On April 22, 1997, Peruvian commandos entered the building through the basement, killed all fourteen guerrillas, and rescued all but one of the hostages.

Ishihara and his gang saw Fujimori's action as a manifestation of the "warrior spirit" they wanted their compromised country to reclaim; when he used his dual citizenship to gain entrance to Japan, they became his patrons. The geisha party was a response to the fugitive's complaint that he was lonely and would be glad of an attentive young woman to keep him company.

The party was held at a traditional restaurant on a side street in Akasaka, one of a few very private establishments that cater to politicians and business moguls. The other guests, half a dozen of them, included a surgeon with his own medical clinic, the chairman of a television network, and an investment banker. Not surprisingly, all were members of the affluent, conservative Hitotsubashi University alumni fraternity that had been funding Ishihara's campaigns since he became a politician in 1968. Fujimori made a late entrance, arriving in the chauffeured Jaguar that had been provided for his use while he remained in Japan. His Japanese was halting and rural, farmer's language from the area in southern Kyushu, where his father had grown up. What intrigued me most about him was the air of presidential authority he managed to convey. This was a man who had left behind him a ruined economy (that he was accused of having plundered) and who was now living in hiding from his countrymen, yet there was nothing in the least apologetic, not to mention cowed, about him: he seemed at ease with the deference he was being shown, as though he were fraternizing with subordinates in his inner circle. A bevy of carefully selected and well-briefed geisha showed up and the party commenced; Ishihara produced a packet of lyrics, traditional love ballads of his own composition, and performed them in an appealing voice (his brother Yūjirō had also been a recording star). At first, Fujimori was sociable, laughing amiably and clapping hands in time to the singing; later in the evening he focused his attention on a young geisha in kimono he seemed to fancy, dancing closely with her in a corner of the room and ignoring the rest of the party. Perhaps he had arranged to meet the young woman later; he left early and alone. We hadn't spoken a word all evening, though Ishihara had introduced us when he arrived. On his way out he turned to me and said, in perfect English (I learned later that he had an MA in math from the University of Wisconsin), "Mr. Nathan, don't believe everything you read in the press." It felt more like a command than a suggestion.

The Fujimori episode was a curiosity. A conversation with Ishihara during that same trip led to the creation of the Japanese Literature Publishing Project. We were having dinner at Figaro, a French restaurant that has been around for so long that its eccentric chef-owner scarcely remembers his sojourn in Paris. Ishihara was complaining about his country's ineptitude at representing itself appealingly to the outside world; I took the opportunity to suggest that the government should subsidize translations of Japanese literature worthy of the original, including, needless to say, his own largely untranslated work. I described the discouraging economics of translation and the consequence: that many important Japanese writers either were unavailable in Western languages or were represented by execrable translations that were likely to be out of print. Why not pay gifted translators appropriately for their work and provide an incentive to publishers with a subvention of publishing costs? Ishihara listened carefully, and when I had finished he asked whether $10 million would suffice to get us started. I allowed that $10 million would be ample, not taking him seriously.

Six weeks later, I received a call in Santa Barbara from Ishihara's special assistant, Hideki Takai: the governor had raised the money and wanted me in Tokyo at once. I didn't know what to think, but I could hardly ignore the invitation. On February 5, I met with Ishihara in his private office on the seventh floor of City Hall. He barely mentioned the business at hand except to say that there was still some "footwork" to do (he used the English word, as in a boxer's footwork). I had no idea what he meant by this; his cryptic explanation was that we had an important meeting with Shizuka Kamei, a powerful politician

Living Carelessly in Tokyo and Elsewhere

who was at the time chairman of the ruling Liberal Democratic Party's Policy Research Council. In the meantime, I was to write up an abstract of my plan in Japanese and create a budget that accounted for as close to $10 million as I could manage. We agreed to call the organization the Japanese Literature Translation Institute. Ishihara would serve as regent and I would be the executive director. Our purpose: "To deepen understanding of Japan and the Japanese by publishing in the U.S. and Europe large numbers of Japan's literary masterpieces in superior translations."

I spent all day Tuesday preparing the documents in my room at the Hotel Okura. For each title I allowed $40,000 for purchasing rights, a buyout, from the author or the author's estate; a translation fee of $35,000 each for English, French, and German versions; and $35,000 to subsidize publication in the United States, England, France, and Germany. Assuming twenty titles, this brought translation and publication costs to a total of $5.7 million.

Under "Administrative Expenses," I put myself down for an annual salary of $250,000 and budgeted travel expenses of $91,000 for six round trips to New York and four round trips to Tokyo and Europe. Including an office and secretary in Santa Barbara at $71,000, the administrative total was $409,009. The grand total for twenty-five titles was $7.53 million. I was in earnest about this; I saw myself chairing the selection committee, monitoring for quality each translation into English, and negotiating deals with American publishers. I had no idea how the European operation would actually work, but given the value I knew I could provide, my portion of the budget struck me as reasonable. In light of what evolved—I should say "devolved"—my expectations were laughable.

Our meeting with Mr. Kamei confirmed my feeling that Japanese politics is an impenetrable enigma to outsiders. Ishihara picked me up in his official car and we drove together to the ugly concrete blockhouse that was Liberal Democratic Party headquarters. Reporters assigned to the building surrounded us as Ishihara stepped from the car. There were rumors that he was contemplating a run for prime minister, and this was his first public visit in over a year to his old friend, Kamei, the Party's chief strategist. (In 2003 it was Kamei who ran for prime minister and lost to the incumbent, Junichi Koizumi.) The first Chinese character in Kamei's name, *kame*, means "turtle"; there were turtles everywhere you looked in his office, large and small turtles in many colors made of glass, wood, and origami. Sitting in an easy chair in front of his desk, Kamei absently stroked a turtle figurine on a table beside him, making its porcelain head bob.

Ishihara explained "his" idea for promoting Japan by enabling translations of Japanese literature, and briefly introduced me as the man for the job. Kamei looked at me incuriously for an instant and then ignored me as if I were absent from the room. He also ignored the commissioner for cultural affairs, a former Education Ministry bureaucrat named Sasaki, who had been waiting in a holding pen until he was summoned to the office. He reminded me of Emmett Kelly, the sad-sack clown who opened the Ringling Bros. Circus by trying to sweep away the pool of light cast by an arc lamp. While the two politicians discussed siphoning funds from his budget at the Agency for Cultural Affairs to a translation project—Kamei reckoned that $8 million to $10 million could be diverted from the agency's $750 million budget for fiscal 2001—Sasaki drooped silently in his chair in an attitude of abject bewilderment. Presently Kamei addressed him directly, as though he were speaking to a dog—"Commissioner, go ahead and make that happen"—and dismissed him from the meeting. A few minutes later Ishihara asked for a minute alone with Kamei; as I waited outside I wondered whether he had used the translation project as a pretext for a private strategy meeting. On our way to the car fifteen minutes later, reporters surrounded us again and Ishihara gave them a short statement and left me behind to answer questions. The following day, February 8, the story was in all the morning papers: "Governor Ishihara puts the squeeze on Kamei for federal funding of translations." Every article quoted the governor's most provocative remark: "This project will benefit our country much more than throwing money away on a stupid bullet train in Kyushu!" Only one, the *Tokyo Shimbun*, mentioned me as "leader of the team" that would also include Kazuya Fukuda, the young Keio University professor and prolific author who was Ishihara's intellectual sidekick. The *Asahi Shimbun* article conjectured that both politicians might be attempting to soften their images as hard-liners with sharp tongues by reminding the public that they were also artists (Kamei was an amateur painter).

The next day, Fukuda accompanied me to the agency for a meeting with Commissioner Sasaki and his deputy. On home ground, the commissioner was overbearing and brusque. Ignoring me, he left the talking to his deputy and Fukuda, interrupting to point out sourly that what we were proposing was unlikely to happen. At the end of thirty disheartening minutes, he promised only to "look into the matter." I knew that the phrase he used—*kentō shimasu*—was a marker signaling that an issue was in danger of being dropped into an oubliette.

A year passed before funds were finally earmarked for the project from the federal budget: $2.5 million beginning in fiscal 2002. By that time, despite assurances from Ishihara, who seemed to have receded from the picture, the agency had taken ownership of the money and total control of the project. I was one of five jurors at the first meeting of the title selection committee sponsored by the agency on April 25, 2002. The others were Ishihara's man, Fukuda; a writer best known for his librettos, Masahiko Shimada; and two women authors of popular fiction, Yumie Hiraiwa, the seventy-year-old daughter of the head priest of the Yoyogi Hachiman Shrine, a somber, deliberate person who was impressively well read, and an eccentrically high-spirited seventy-four-year-old dame in a garish red dress and red shoes and purse to match and a red panache in her elaborate hat, Seiko Tanabe. All day, while the bureaucrats looked on in deferential silence, we debated and voted in successive ballots on a list of eighty works of fiction; I hadn't read half of them, and there were a number of authors in the "popular" group whose names I didn't know. Eventually, we chose thirty titles, including three I had been advocating: novellas by the late nineteenth-century writer who always reminded me of Emily Dickinson, Ichiyō Higuchi; a new translation of Sōseki Natsume's comic novel, *Botchan*, unreadable in the version in print; and improved translations of short stories by Ryūnosuke Akutagawa.

My most vivid memory of the day is lunch. I was seated next to Ms. Tanabe, as witty and exuberantly lewd an old woman as I have ever met, and was looking forward to chatting with her. But the minute we were served our lunches in lacquer boxes she turned her back on me. I wondered if I had offended her in some way, or was she simply uncomfortable in the presence of a foreigner? I began to eat glumly, disappointed; presently she turned and pushed across the table a perfect origami chopstick holder she had been folding for me. I was delighted, wondering where she had found the patterned paper. "I keep what I need in my purse," she replied.

It became clear soon enough that the blueprint I had created was a pipe dream. It wasn't simply that there would be no foundation or institute in the United States run by me or anyone else; all spending of federal funds had to conform to a list of preestablished rates that were deemed acceptable. This applied to translation fees and to my services as overseer of the project. There would be no office in Santa Barbara, no secretary, no travel expenses.

I was angry and deeply disappointed. But I had already committed to checking several translations of titles that had been selected and to recommending translators for others. I realized I had no heart for this kind of work, particularly not for the pennies that were allowed. I should have begged off the project at once; instead, I fumed about it and ignored the deadlines Tokyo was expecting me to meet. The next thing I knew I was informed that someone else had been appointed chair of the project's English Language Advisory Committee, Paul Anderer, a former student of Donald Keene's who was now a professor of Japanese literature at Columbia University. In the same letter I was invited to join the committee and advised that the first meeting would take place at Columbia in New York on June 10, 2002. I declined the invitation. I had been behaving truculently but I felt humiliated nonetheless, as though I had been cashiered from my own project.

At that point something fascinating happened: I received a call from Ishihara's assistant, Takai, the first time I had heard from City Hall in many months. The governor had been disappointed to learn that I would not be joining the committee and hoped I would reconsider my decision: the project was, after all, my brainchild, and we were its cofounders. I realized I was being pressured in an indirect, Japanese way to stay in the game. Since Ishihara and Kamei were both on record supporting the project and recommending me, it would be awkward if I dropped out.

Allowing the Japanese part of myself to feel constrained, I attended the meeting in New York. The other members of the committee were young scholars and translators in the generation after mine, and several publishers, including the head of the Asian Division of Columbia University Press. I brought Andrew Wylie along. Anderer asked me for a summary of the project's history and I obliged, trying to keep the resentment I was feeling out of my account. Asked for his views, Wylie declared that the only way to ensure wide distribution of the new books would be to place them with a premier publisher who would commit to promoting them and keeping them in print. In fact, he had already interested the publisher of the New American Library in a Library of Modern Japanese Literature. Anderer let him finish before announcing the most recent bad news from Tokyo: a project funded with federal money could not favor a single publisher; in principle, no publisher should be given more than one title, possibly two. The subvention I had planned was also out of the question (federal funds again); as an incentive, the project could agree to purchase at a discount a certain number of copies for free distribution to embassies and consulates around the world. Wylie was appalled: his only comment was, "Like magazines at a dentist's office."

That was my final day on the project. I stayed on the committee but did not attend the annual meetings.

The project has continued to grow. According to an expensively produced booklet, sixteen translations have been published as of August 2005; six in English, including Sōseki's *Botchan*, five in French, and, in Russian, a volume of Higuchi novellas and five others. Of twenty-six other volumes in progress, twelve are listed as "available to publishers." This is probably the first time translations of Japanese literature have been commissioned with no publisher in sight.

Overall, the list is heavier in minor works, mysteries and historical novels, than I would have preferred. As I haven't read the translations I cannot assess their quality, but I imagine, based on the names of the translators I recognize, that they are above average, which means that the project has accomplished something important given the constraints imposed by the bureaucracy. And yet the glossy pamphlets issued by the Japanese Literature Publishing and Promotion Center have no emotional effect on me, as though I had nothing to do with them. Perhaps the disconnection is an echo of the remoteness I am feeling from Japan in general.

In Tokyo a year ago, I spent the day before my departure hiking on Takao Mountain. For the first time in decades I rode a Chuo Line express west from Shinjuku across the Musashino plain, the same route I had traveled on my weekly trips to Tsuda College. Though it was 6:40 on a Sunday morning, the train was already crowded with passengers equipped for a day on the mountain with identical gear, as if they had shopped at the same outfitter. Clearly they, too, were headed for Takao at the end of the line fifty minutes away.

At the terminal station, Takao Trailhead, I bought two bottles of water and a backpack for $8 and followed the flow of foot traffic to a map the size of a billboard with a legend indicating trails, difficulty, and times to destination. I chose the main trail to the peak 2,000 feet up, a "moderately strenuous hike" of ninety minutes. It was a perfect November day at the height of maple-viewing season: the trail was jammed with hikers, backpack to identical backpack. Climbers of all ages passed me as I toiled up the hill, the only hiker in street clothes.

The grassy meadow at the peak had the festival air of a community picnic. There were couples and families everywhere, sitting on blankets they had spread on the grass, elaborate lunches arrayed in lacquer boxes they had packed at home. I bought a paper plate of o-*den* from one of the stands that lined the meadow and sat down on a bench to observe the lively scene.

Detachment

As I sat there, charmed as always by what I saw, time collapsed: I was watching other families on other Sundays long ago at the amusement park on the banks of the Tama River near my first Tokyo apartment. And I was feeling what I had felt then: the loneliness of the outsider. It was as if I were once again the stranger I had been when I began my Japan adventure, an alien looking through a window at a life that wasn't mine. As if to confirm the separateness I was feeling, an old man in a Mr. Magoo hat approached and explained affably in English, "This is, you know, top peak of Takao Mountain!" I nodded appreciatively and smiled; in the old days, infuriated at being treated like a tourist, I would have responded with something venomous in Japanese. The passion to belong to Japan that had driven me for so long had dimmed.

I hadn't planned to go hiking on Mount Takao. The truth is, I had made the effort because I was unprepared to acknowledge to myself that after forty-five years of engagement with Japan I found myself with time on my hands on the last day of a trip to Tokyo. It was as if I were in a foreign city, burned out on Buddhist temples and museums, anxious to be home and content to waste the last day staring out the window of my hotel room (just what I would have done, I feared, had I not taken myself off to the mountain). But this was hardly a foreign city; this was my Tokyo, a palimpsest of memories I carried around in amber, home to friends with whom I had lived the best times of my youth. I felt ashamed of the empty day ahead of me, as if it were evidence of my tenuous connection to a place in which I had invested so much of myself. Japan, it seemed, had come to mean less to me. Small wonder. I had never practiced a Japanese instrument, or *aikidō*, or any of the performing arts I had admired. Unlike other Japan hands, I had never studied with a Japanese mentor or collaborated with Japanese colleagues. And as for friendships, I had done little to sustain them, dropping people like stitches over the years, until now it seemed that my bond to a country I had never truly adopted had come undone. Except for my teaching, about which I was still capable of feeling passionate, there was nothing of Japan in the life I lived. I still spoke the language better than most, but sometimes it seemed that the edge was coming off my fluency.

I shall of course return; the remoteness I am feeling doesn't mean that I am finished with a culture that still fills me with wonder. If I have lost anything it is the hopeless desire to discover my fugitive identity in a society where I will never belong. I know that I'll be moved again to translate a uniquely Japanese moment so that others may share in the pleasure it affords me—sooner or later, something will rekindle the excitement I have felt so often in the past. Meanwhile, I long to travel other roads that will lead me to a place I can finally call home.

Index

Index

Brandauer, Klaus Maria, 218
Brando, Marlon, 4, 64
Brower, Ruben, 124
Brown, Jerry, 194
Brown, Kay, 131, 139
Buddhism, 48, 192, 193, 196
bundan (community of Japanese
    writers), 72, 74, 87
Bunraku puppeteers, 97–99, 241
Burke, Alan, 113–14

Cable, Stuart, 256
California, University of (Santa
    Barbara), 258–62
calligraphy, 237–38
Cambridge, Mass., 66–67, 123–31,
    139, 252
    see also Harvard University
Casey's, 109–10
Castille, Rand, 171–72
CBS, 202
China, Red Guard in, 122
Clark, William, 285–86
Cohan, Abraham, 1
Cohen, Joel, 125
Colgate College, 126
Colloredo-Mansfield, Ferdinand
    "Moose," 248, 256
Colonel Goes to Japan, The (TV
    program), 212–13, 214
Columbia University, 103, 106–7, 118,
    304
    translation dialogue at, 287–88
comic monologues (*rakugo*), 99–102
commercials, 231–36, 242
Competitive Advantage of Nations, The
    (video), 252–53
Conroy, Frank, 107
Coppola, Francis, 206–8, 211, 214
Coyote, Marilyn, 209
Coyote, Peter, 197, 209–10, 211
Cristina, Princess, 271

Daiei Studios, 182, 184, 186
Dazai, Osamu, 28, 97
Dean, James, 182
de Bary, Theodore, 103
de Kooning, Willem, 111, 112
DeLano, Sharon, 296
Des Pres, Terrence, 125–26, 129–30
Diamond Game, The (film), 215,
    220–22
Doig, John, 231–32, 234
Donald Keene Center of Japanese
    Culture, 287–88
Donne, John, 76
Dor-Ner, Zvi, 212, 214

Doty, Paul, 124
Dubrovnik, 104–5
Duvall, Robert, 217, 218
Dylan, Bob, 107, 155

East Hampton, 110–13, 121
Edo, 99, 100
ELEC (the English-Language
    Exploratory Council), 5, 17, 19,
    29, 36, 37, 38, 213
Eliot, George, 127
Eliot, T. S., 2, 45
Eliseef, Serge, 3
Ellman, Richard, 157
Emmy Awards, 214, 218
Endō, Shūsaku, 87
Enright, D. J., 119–20
Enterprise (documentary series),
    212–15, 218, 220
Entrekin, Morgan, 271, 294
Entrepreneurs (documentary), 227–28
Essex, Mass., author's house in,
    245–50
Evergreen Review, 79, 108
    author's column for, 113, 114

Face of Another, The (Abe), 88, 115
Face of Another, The (film), 88–89
Farm Song (film), 173–81, 237
Farrar, Straus, 156
Farrell, Barry, 114
Faulkner, William, 150
Fiedler, Kurt, 6
Field, Norma, 258
film festivals, 142, 151, 169
Fischer Verlag, 271, 294
Fitts, Dudley, 2
Flaming Green Tree, The (Ōe), 261–62,
    263
Fontana, Jon, 236, 277–78
Forbidden Colors (Mishima), 120
Ford Foundation, 5
foreigners, in Japan, 53, 72, 95
    anxiety about, 28, 32, 33, 36, 37, 68,
        93, 175
    disrespect of, 46
    Japanese sponsors of, 8–9
    NHK videos about, 288–89
    rumors about, 24
Fortune, 254–55
Fremont-Smith, Eliot, 120
French Impressionists, 41
Freund, Paul, 124
Frost, Robert, 77, 124
Frye, Northrup, 53
Fūgetsudō, 28
Fujimori, Alberto, 297–99

Index

Index

Index

Index

Nathan, Jeremiah Jirō, 129–30, 139,
  152, 167, 196
  birth of, 129, 136
  in California, 192, 196, 201, 211
  in Japan, 143, 159–61, 173, 176,
    178–79
  in Princeton, 153–54, 168
Nathan, John (author):
  acting of, 4–5, 88–95, 101–2
  appearance of, 1, 5, 35, 49, 61, 89,
    95, 134
  carelessness of, 45–47, 130, 196–97,
    223, 238, 253, 257–58
  at Columbia, 103, 106–7, 118
  dream of, 116–17
  English teaching of, 5, 10, 17, 28, 29,
    36, 37, 38, 213
  European travels of, 104–5
  family background of, 1
  as father, 115–18, 130, 159–61, 168,
    192, 196, 226, 234, 236
  as film director, 147, 152, 158–59,
    161–95
  fund-raising of, 161, 170–73
  group identification of, 57–58
  at Harvard, 1–6, 123–27, 208
  hypochondria of, 49
  income of, 37, 65, 105, 113, 139,
    158, 202, 232, 234, 258, 294
  insecurity of, 65, 66, 73, 111, 146,
    156, 209, 296
  as Jew, 1, 34, 35, 70, 84, 85, 209,
    221–24
  journals of, 147–49, 176–79,
    187–91, 244, 246
  loneliness of, 7, 13, 17, 34–35, 168,
    192, 218, 257, 307
  manipulativeness of, 176–77
  marriages of, see Nathan, Diane
    Siegelman; Oda, Mayumi
  as play director, 10, 13, 17
  as professor, 51, 118, 151–52,
    258–61, 308
  romantic longings of, 12–13, 14,
    17, 20
  screenplays of, 130–32, 135,
    143–46, 201–2, 208, 214–18,
    228
  self-importance of, 65, 71
  in Stockholm, 264–74, 292, 294
Nathan, Jules (author's father), 2, 35,
  49, 134–37, 221, 223, 226
Nathan, Nancy, 2, 65, 132–35
Nathan, Natasha (author's niece),
  133–37

Nathan, Tobias, 244, 258, 274
  birth of, 234
  in Japan, 236, 289–91
  at Rocky Hill, 246, 247, 250
Nathan, Zachary Tarō, 128, 136, 139,
  152, 167, 227
  in California, 192, 196, 201, 211
  in Japan, 123, 143, 173, 176, 178–79
  nanny of, 117–18
  in New York, 115–18, 196
  in Princeton, 153–54, 168
Nathan/Tyler, 226, 228–31, 235, 243,
  247, 249, 251–58, 277
National Broadcasting Company
  (NHK), 99, 262, 275–77, 288–89
National Gallery of Art, 235–36
National University of Fine Arts and
  Music (Geidai), 27, 142
Natsume, Sōseki, 52, 303, 305
NBC, 198, 202, 205
Needham, John, 254–55
Nemeth, Lane, 227
New Adventures of Zatō Ichi (TV
  series), 186
New American Library, 305
New Japan Hotel, 143–46
Newsweek, 91, 285
New Year's, 20–22, 52, 69, 129–30
  at Katō farm, 175, 178, 179
New York, N.Y., 2, 70, 155, 277
  author in, 2, 5, 6, 66, 105–10,
    114–20, 137–38, 151, 215, 218,
    220–24, 231–33, 235, 242,
    278–83, 287–88
  Japan Society in, 169, 171, 194,
    285–86, 287
  Lower East Side in, 1
  restaurants in, 109–10, 119, 138,
    171–72
  Teshigahara in, 142, 145
New Yorker, 77, 294, 296–97
New York Review of Books, 119–20
New York Times, 120, 169
NHK, see National Broadcasting
  Company
Nicholson, Jack, 245
Nishimachi International School, 173
Nobel, Alfred, 270, 271
Nobel Prize, 63, 69, 70, 77, 78, 261–73,
  294
Noguchi, Isamu, 112
Noguchi, Takehiko, 52–54
Noguchi, Yoshiko, 54
Noh theater, 238–40, 289
No Longer Human (Dazai), 28

314

Index

Index

Index

317

About the Author

In June 1961, **John Nathan** graduated from Harvard magna cum laude with a degree in Far Eastern Languages and went to Japan to pursue his study of Japanese literature. In the winter of 1963, he passed the entrance examinations to Tokyo University and became the first American to be admitted as a regularly enrolled student. In 1964, he published the first of many translations, Yukio Mishima's *The Sailor Who Fell from Grace with the Sea*. In 1967, he introduced Kenzaburō Ōe to Western readers with his translation of *A Personal Matter*.

Nathan returned to America to continue his academic career, then wrote and codirected, with Hiroshi Teshigahara, a feature film about American deserters from Viet Nam in the Japanese peace underground: *Summer Soldiers* opened the Lincoln Center Film Festival in 1972 and was hailed by Jean-Paul Sartre as "the best anti-war film ever made." In 1974, Nathan received his PhD from Harvard and published his biography of Yukio Mishima: *Mishima: A Biography*.

On leave from Princeton University in 1977, Nathan produced, wrote, and directed a trilogy of hour-long documentary portraits of life in Japan. Televised nationally on PBS, *The Japanese* won major documentary awards. Nathan has since written and produced forty documentaries.

In 1994, Nathan became the first Takashima Professor of Japanese Cultural Studies at the University of California, Santa Barbara. In 1999, he published *Sony: The Private Life*. In 2002, his translation of Ōe's *Rouse Up, O Young Men of the New Age!* was published. His most recent book, *Japan Unbound*, was published by Houghton Mifflin in February 2004.

Nathan teaches courses on Japanese film and literature, consults for Japanese and Asian corporations, and continues to translate Kenzaburō Ōe, the 1994 Nobel Laureate in Literature. He lives with his family in Santa Barbara, California.

Printed in the United States
By Bookmasters